CONDUCTION APHASIA

CONDUCTION APHASIA

Edited by

Susan E. Kohn
Braintree Hospital
Boston University School of Medicine

LEA LAWRENCE ERLBAUM ASSOCIATES, PUBLISHERS
1992   Hillsdale, New Jersey   Hove and London

Lawrence Erlbaum Associates, Inc., Publishers
365 Broadway
Hillsdale, New Jersey 07642

Library of Congress Cataloging-in-Publication Data

Conduction aphasia / edited by Susan E. Kohn.
    p.   cm.
    Includes bibliographical references and index.
    ISBN 0-8058-0681-4
    1. Conduction aphasia. I. Kohn, Susan E.
    [DNLM: 1. Aphasia—diagnosis. WL 340.5 C746]
    RC425.3.C66 1992
    616.85'52—dc20
    DNLM/DLC
    for Library of Congress   91-18219
                                                    CIP

Printed in the United States of America
10 9 8 7 6 5 4 3 2 1

Contents

Preface

Over the past decade, questions about the clinical classification and experimental examination of aphasic patients have been raised (e.g., Caramazza, 1984; Caramazza & Badecker, 1989). Growing doubts about the validity and reliability of standard clinical diagnoses have been responsible, in part, for the explosion of case studies in the neurolinguistic literature. In turn, rejection of classical aphasia diagnoses has made it difficult to synthesize much of this literature. No alternative method for selecting and comparing aphasic patients has emerged.

While there has been a consistent decrease in the use of standard diagnoses in contemporary neurolinguistic studies of language production and comprehension, contemporary studies of acquired alexia have inspired the development of new syndromes. However, these new syndromes are flawed in ways that seriously undermine their utility as theoretical constructs. These syndromes have been developed without a clear understanding of what symptoms are and how they co-occur to form a symptom-complex, or syndrome (see Friedman, 1991, for an attempt to clarify the relationship between deep and phonological dyslexia).

This volume was motivated by a desire to take a fresh look at the benefits that aphasia diagnosis has for both clinical and experimental work. This is accomplished by exploring one classical aphasia syndrome from a multidisciplinary perspective; that is, by presenting information from the disciplines of neurology, speech-language pathology, and experimental neurolinguistics. Given the range of perspectives represented, it is hoped that this work will appeal to an equally broad range of readers.

As the title indicates, conduction aphasia has been chosen for this exercise. This syndrome was chosen for two reasons. Unlike the other classical syndromes, its recognition and development as a clinical entity was heavily influenced by the neurobehavioral models of the late 1800s (see chapter 2, this volume). Also, recent research has identified distinctive phonological characteristics in the speech of conduction aphasics that are important for determining the functional deficit(s) responsible for this syndrome (e.g., Kohn, 1984, in press; Nespoulous, Joanette, Ska, Caplan, & Lecours, 1987).

Given the importance of one's definition of syndrome to the evaluation of a particular syndrome, this volume lays the groundwork for developing a definition of conduction aphasia by first exploring the definition of syndrome (see chapter 1). There is little positive discussion in the recent aphasia literature about the decisions that could or should be made in defining a syndrome and applying it to a particular population (but see Zurif, Gardner, & Brownell, 1989; Zurif, Swinney, & Fodor, 1991). The issues raised in the introductory chapter should, at the very least, demonstrate that more thinking has to be done about how to best set up a classification system before deciding to reject any notion of aphasia syndrome. Moreover, we hope that this chapter will inspire further constructive discussion about aphasia diagnosis. With an understanding of the issues involved in defining a syndrome, current information about the language assessment (chapter 3), neuroanatomy (chapter 4), and experimental findings (chapters 5 and 6) of conduction aphasia are then presented, preceded by an examination of the history of this syndrome (chapter 2). The concluding chapter (7) attempts to combine the information presented in these chapters to develop a definition of conduction aphasia that can be applied broadly.

This volume should serve as a multidisciplinary study of a class of aphasic patients that can be divided into clear subtypes, depending on how, for example, impaired auditory-verbal short-term memory and auditory comprehension are handled in rendering a diagnosis (see chapter 6). The consensus of most chapters is that, despite some degree of heterogeneity, conduction aphasia can be reliably diagnosed in patients with a phonological deficit restricted to output. This deficit appears to involve a stage of phonological production that occurs after the most abstract phonological form has been accessed, although questions have been raised about the disruption of earlier lexical-phonological processing as well (see chapters 5 and 6).

There is no reason to doubt that a similar level of clarity can be brought to other syndromes with perhaps even more diversity in expression, such as Broca's and Wernicke's aphasia, in order to reach a viable level of agreement in diagnosis and to determine directions for future work. The broader goal of this volume is to demonstrate that, by combining information from all disciplines that work with neurobehavioral patients, a system of patient classification can be developed that relates to the same cognitive models that are used in studies that reject standard diagnosis.

I would like to thank Katherine Smith for contributing to all phases in the preparation of this volume.

REFERENCES

Caramazza, A. (1984). The logic of neuropsychological research and the problem of patient classification in aphasia. *Brain and Language, 21,* 9–20.

Caramazza, A., & Badecker, W. (1989). Patient classification in neuropsychological research. *Brain and Cognition, 10,* 256–295.

Friedman, R. B. (1991). *Is there a continuum of phonological/deep dyslexia?* Paper presented at the Deep Dyslexia 12 meeting, London, England.

Kohn, S. E. (1984). The nature of the phonological disorder in conduction aphasia. *Brain and Language, 23,* 97–115.

Kohn, S. E. (in press). Segmental disorders in aphasia. In G. Blanken, J. Dittmann, H. Grimm, & J. C. Marshall (Eds.), *Linguistic disorders and pathologies. An international handbook.* Berlin: Walter de Gruyter.

Nespoulous, J.-L., Joanette, Y., Ska, B., Caplan, D., & Lecours, A. R. (1987). Production deficits in Broca's and conduction aphasia: Repetition vs. reading. In E. Keller & M. Gopnik (Eds.), *Motor and sensory processes of language* (pp. 53–79). Hillsdale, NJ: Lawrence Erlbaum Associates.

Zurif, E. B., Gardner, H., & Brownell, H. H. (1989). The case against the cast against group studies. *Brain and Cognition, 10,* 237–255.

Zurif, E. B., Swinney, D., & Fodor, J. A. (1991). An evaluation of assumptions underlying the single-patient-only position in neuropsychological research: A reply. *Brain and Cognition, 16,* 198–210.

Chapter 1

Introduction: On the Notion of "Aphasia Syndrome"

Susan E. Kohn
Katherine L. Smith
Braintree Hospital
Boston University School of Medicine

In the late 1800s, theoretical discussion of the neurological localization of language functions found support in case descriptions of individuals with focal lesions and concomitant language difficulty (Lee, 1981). A diagnostic system for classifying aphasic patients emerged from this work, including such syndromes as Broca's, Wernicke's, conduction, and the transcortical aphasias (cf. Lichtheim, 1985; Wernicke, 1874/1977). Whereas the reliability and validity of this classical system is currently under debate, it still influences clinical and experimental work in cognitive neuropsychology.

During the 1940s, the methodology of experimental psychology was adopted, so that group studies were undertaken that averaged performance of aphasics with similar difficulties (Shallice, 1988). Although case studies began to reappear in the late 1960s, the group study approach dominated the literature until the early 1980s, when researchers became disillusioned with this methodology because of the heterogeneity typically present in experimental groups of aphasics (Marshall, 1986). As a result, the case study has once again gained popularity for neuropsychological research. Contemporary case studies are much more detailed and systematic than those undertaken by the early diagram makers, with greater emphasis placed on relating impaired performance to normal functioning (cf. Shallice, 1988).

The recent revival of the case study has prompted much discussion about the proper methodology for studying the cognitive and linguistic deficits of neurologically impaired adults. In addition to questioning the merit of the group study, the validity of the classical aphasia syndromes has come under attack.

1

Both have been criticized for poor reliability (Badecker & Caramazza, 1985; Caramazza & McCloskey, 1988). Syndromes have also been criticized for not being able to classify enough aphasic patients (Lecours, Basso, Moraschini, & Nespoulous, 1984; Marshall, 1986).

Although there is continued support for group studies in cognitive neuropsychology (Caplan, 1988; Newcombe & Marshall, 1988; Poeck, 1983; Zurif, Gardner, & Brownell, 1989), there is growing discontent with the use of syndromes, especially the classical ones, for research purposes (and even for clinical purposes; Caplan, 1992). The rejection of the classical aphasia syndromes in the current literature is rather ironic, given the return to case studies (i.e., the methodology of the early diagram makers) and the fact that the cognitive models used to explain these modern cases reflect the spirit of the early diagram makers (Shallice, 1988). Both approaches consider language processing to be composed of separate abilities that can be independently impaired by neurological damage. There has been virtually no recent detailed discussion of the definition of aphasia syndrome by those who still appeal at some level to the classical framework.

Perhaps the "antisyndrome" literature paints too bleak a picture, because it fails to consider all the issues needed to properly define an aphasia syndrome. For example, a nonoptimal definition of "syndrome" is sometimes adopted (cf. Schwartz, 1984), and a questionable syndrome is often used to argue against the notion of "syndrome" (e.g., agrammatism; Badecker & Caramazza, 1985—see following).

Moreover, few alternatives to the use of syndromes in the clinical and research domain have been suggested. Both Ellis (1987) and Caramazza (Caramazza, 1986; Caramazza & McCloskey, 1988; McCloskey & Caramazza, 1988) proposed that intensive experimental study of individual aphasic patients provides sufficient information for relating deficits to impairment within a model of normal cognitive functioning. Shallice (1988) followed basically the same plan, adding that the experimental study of aphasic patients should include baseline testing to identify similar patients for replicating findings and should include attempts to recognize task-specific strategies. In the clinical domain, Caplan (1992) described a similar approach to patient assessment for treatment purposes.

Whereas cognitive models are important to the process of explaining neurolinguistic deficits, model-based evaluations of aphasia involve many of the same issues as evaluations that are guided by a classification system (e.g., identifying adaptive strategies to deficits; distinguishing deficits with similar behavioral manifestations; see later). We argue that the notion of syndrome is a useful construct for furthering both clinical and experimental work in cognitive neuropsychology. The field of aphasia is inherently eclectic, attracting researchers and clinicians from such fields as linguistics, neuropsychology, cognitive psychology, neurology, and speech pathology. With these different disciplines come differences in terminology and methods for characterizing aphasic behavior. Work in these domains will be more fruitful if there is a common system of aphasia classification. This framework will promote better understanding of work outside one's specialty and facilitate communication across the different domains. Because the focus of an aphasia evaluation will differ according to one's discipline, such a classification system cannot be all inclusive but can provide guidance for furthering work in one's discipline (cf. Poeck, 1983; see later).

This chapter begins by considering the nature of the syndrome at a level that is appropriate for assessing neuropsychological deficits. To facilitate an understanding of our proposals with respect to aphasia classification, illustrative examples involve language breakdown. Once a definition of syndrome is developed, several issues that are important for creating an aphasia classification system are examined. The chapter ends with a topic that can be considered properly once the definition of aphasia syndrome has been discussed—the applications of an aphasia classification system.

The opinions that follow are not necessarily held by the other authors in this volume. However, the issues raised are critical for the general purpose of this book—developing an optimal definition of conduction aphasia that is relevant for both clinical and experimental work.

DEFINING "SYMPTOM"

All definitions of *syndrome* involve the identification of behavioral features, or symptoms, that in some way cluster to form a "symptom-complex." The standard medical definition of a symptom involves a patient's subjective report of behavioral changes. However, such a definition is not appropriate in neuropsychology, because patients can be unaware of their deficits (e.g., anosognosia). With aphasia, there is another common complication in that patients' language difficulties can interfere with their ability to articulate their problems. Identification of symptoms due to neuropsychological deficits will always have to be determined, or at least verified, by behavioral testing.

Brown (1988) offered a conception of symptom that is more relevant for the current context. He referred to "an error or positive symptom" as "a moment in flow prematurely displayed." He believes that symptoms are "submerged levels *processed normally* distal to the point of damage," and that "pathology disrupts the subsurface stage and exposes the normal processing at the disrupted segment" (pp. 10–11). For example, the phonemic paraphasias of conduction aphasics reflect breakdown at a phonemic level of planning that is part of the normal speech production system (see Buckingham, this volume, for details).

Kolk and Heeschen (1990) made an important distinction with respect to neuropsychological symptoms. In addition to the type of behavior described by Brown, which they referred to as "impairment symptoms," they recognized the existence of "behavioral abnormalities that are the result of a patient adapting to impairment" (p. 221). They referred to these behaviors as "adaptation symptoms." We discuss later the distinctions between behaviors that are direct reflections of a functional deficit versus adaptive strategies to this deficit that is critical for developing a valid understanding of aphasia syndromes.

A distinction must also be made between behaviors that exist acutely and those that emerge during recovery (Kertesz, 1983; Marshall, 1986). Errors in aphasia diagnosis are made because syndrome definitions rarely include information about the evolution of symptoms (Schwartz, 1984). When attempts are made to recognize changes over time, a change in aphasia diagnosis is usually made. For example, when the comprehension difficulties of a Wernicke's aphasic diminish, but repetition difficulties remain severe, the diagnosis is often changed to conduction aphasia (e.g., Basso, Capitani, & Zanobio, 1982; Naeser & Hayward, 1978). However, this change in diagnosis does not clarify the nature of the aphasia. If syndromes differ with respect to their associated underlying deficits (see later), then a change in diagnosis implies that the deficit has changed. It is unlikely that the so-called Wernicke's-to-conduction aphasic has actually suffered one deficit acutely and another one after the aphasia begins to resolve. (This situation should be distinguished from one in which a deficit is masked acutely yet becomes evident later on; e.g., dysarthria obscuring phonemic paraphasias.) It would be less confusing to call such a patient, for example, a resolving Wernicke's aphasic, given that the source of impaired repetition differs between Wernicke's and conduction aphasia (see chapters 3 and 7, this volume, for further discussion).

The effects of symptom evolution are also usually ignored in experimental investigations of aphasia (but see Crary & Kertesz, 1988; Green, 1969; Kohn & Smith, 1991; Panzeri, Semenza, & Butterworth, 1987). As Caramazza and Badecker (1989) pointed out, we are not certain of the impact of this issue on our understanding of neuropsychological phenomena; it could be considerable.

A symptom is often described at a level where more than one underlying functional deficit could be responsible, and, consequently, it could be associated with more than one syndrome (Kertesz, 1990). For example, Broca's, Wernicke's, and conduction aphasics produce phonemic paraphasias. Only statistical analysis can identify variables that distinguish among these syndromes, such as the effects of target length and the phonemic accuracy of paraphasias (Kohn, 1985, 1988).

The fact that a given symptom can result from different underlying deficits is one motivation behind Shallice's (1988) "critical-variable approach" for investigating neuropsychological deficits. He argued that different sources of a particular symptom can be distinguished by comparing patients who perform at a similar level on a task and yet are affected by different task variables. For example, two patients might score similarly on a test of oral reading; yet one patient produces more errors as words decrease in frequency, whereas the other patient produces more errors as words increase in length.

One possible response to such symptom-deficit ambiguity is to describe symptoms at a detailed enough level that such ambiguities are avoided. In the preceding example, then, the symptom would not be "impaired oral reading," but, rather, "reading difficulty that is affected by word length." However, increasing the specificity of symptoms creates other problems. The number of symptoms would likely escalate to an unwieldy number for a viable classification system. In addition, the identification of highly specific symptoms requires a level of analysis that could not always be accomplished by a simple bedside exam, rendering the classification system less desirable for neurological assessment. For these reasons, symptoms should be described at a more general level, using patterns of symptom co-occurrence to distinguish deficits (see following).

In addition to the qualitative issues surrounding the definition of symptom, there are quantitative issues concerning the methodology for determining when an individual is displaying a particular symptom. We cannot expect symptoms to occur during all relevant contexts, given that performance disrupted by a neuropsychological deficit can vary from one moment to the next. As Brown (1979/1988) observed, syndromes "are not stable entities but rather refer to the qualitative mean of performance" (p. 43).

Typically, problems frequently displayed by an individual are the ones that are given the status of a symptom. For example, verbal paraphasias are often numerous in Wernicke's aphasics, but not in conduction aphasics. As a result, this error type is identified as a symptom in Wernicke's, but not conduction, aphasia (Goodglass & Kaplan, 1983).

It is difficult to specify how frequently a behavior must be displayed by an individual in order to constitute a symptom. In the case of an aphasic, every observed abnormality cannot be considered to be symptomatic of a syndrome. There are distal effects of language deficits on other components of the language system that surface only on occasion (e.g., semantic paraphasias in the conversation of conduction aphasics). Only if an infrequent behavior is consistently associated with one deficit should it be considered a symptom; its occurrence would then always have a clear relationship to a syndrome.

Summary

Although the methods needed for the precise identification of a symptom require further study, the concept of a symptom is clear enough to proceed in the next section with a discussion of the role it plays in defining a syndrome. In the present context, we consider a symptom to involve a frequently occurring impaired behavior, distinguishing between behaviors that directly reflect deficits versus those that involve adaptive strategies to deficits, and between behaviors that appear acutely versus those that emerge later postonset.

DEFINING "SYNDROME"

Critiquing Past Definitions

Usually, a syndrome label in neuropsychology is used clinically and experimentally without a precise definition of the syndrome with respect to the distribution of its symptoms. There are two basic approaches to symptom distribution: Either the members of a symptom-complex represent a statistical phenomenon or they represent a fixed set (see later).

The definition of syndrome that appears to be used most frequently is the weaker of the two basic approaches identified previously. This definition equates a syndrome with a set of symptoms that reliably, or statistically, co-occur (e.g., Benson, 1979; Marshall, 1982, 1986; Poeck, 1983). In this way, all symptoms are treated equally, so that no single symptom need be present to render a diagnosis. Caramazza (1984) referred to this approach as the *psychologically weak sense* of syndrome, Newcombe and Marshall (1988) referred to it as a *"variable" definition* of syndrome, and Schwartz (1984) referred to it as a *polytypic syndrome* based on "family resemblance."

The polytypic syndrome has a fundamental weakness. The fact that any one of the diagnostic features may or may not be present implies that there may not be a unitary reason for the co-occurrence of the corresponding symptoms. How can a particular language deficit(s) exist for an aphasia syndrome, if any symptom need not occur for diagnosis (Caramazza, 1984)?

This problem with a polytypic syndrome has contributed to the view that the classical aphasia syndromes are atheoretical and necessarily heterogeneous (cf. Caramazza, 1984). However, the classical syndromes as originally conceived were not of this psychologically weak sense. Only through recent usage has the sense of the syndrome been so weakened and made less precise (Schwartz, 1984). For example, Wernicke initially conceived of conduction aphasia as a disconnection between Wernicke's and Broca's area (i.e., between acoustic and motor word forms) and considered the route between these two areas to play an indirect regulatory role in speech production (Wernicke, 1874/1977). Consequently, his initial description of the syndrome emphasized the hesitant paraphasic speech of these aphasics. Given the reliance of repetition on this temporofrontal route, it is not surprising that Lichtheim (1885), and later Wernicke (1906/1977), added impaired repetition to the list of expected symptoms. Over the years, the status of repetition has become central to the diagnosis of conduction aphasia, presumably because it is easy to assess.

This change in orientation has distorted the understanding of this syndrome (see following, and chapter 7, this volume).

The polytypic syndrome also presents problems in reliability with respect to providing a patient with a diagnosis that different clinicians and researchers agree on. Difficulties in determining the proper diagnosis are created because the symptoms of this type of syndrome are unweighted and potentially not present, yet, as argued before, symptoms can occur in multiple syndromes (i.e., are not mutually exclusive; Caramazza, 1984). For example, impaired word finding is widespread in aphasia; the severity/prominence of this symptom in relationship to other symptoms must be established in order to determine the proper diagnosis. At the experimental level, one of the consequences of a poly-typic syndrome is that findings are hard to generalize across studies, because aphasics with the same diagnosis can vary in their symptomatology (cf. Schwartz, 1984).

Despite the shortcomings of a polytypic syndrome, it can play an early role in the development of a particular syndrome. An observed set of behaviors can be given a tentative label. Further study can then determine whether the co-occurrence of the symptoms is systematic enough to reflect a syndrome (cf. Zurif et al., 1989; see following). In this way, syndromes can evolve from clinical observation.

As the preceding discussion implies, a definition of syndrome must specify a set of symptoms that are necessary and sufficient for its identification. This approach corresponds to the other basic type of syndrome and has been labeled by Strub and Geschwind (1974, 1983) as a *medical syndrome,* by Caramazza (1984) as the *psychologically strong sense* of syndrome, and by Newcombe and Marshall (1988) as a *fixed syndrome.*

Although we believe that the notion of a fixed syndrome should form the basis of the definition of syndrome, it must be expanded in order to accept systematically a degree of variability in the observed symptomatology. That is, in addition to symptoms that are necessary and sufficient for diagnosis, allowances must be made for symptoms that are not necessary for diagnosis but are frequently associated. This modification does not necessarily diminish the diagnostic power of the necessary co-occurring symptoms. Geschwind and Strub (1975) argued: ''The concept of a syndrome is in no way invalidated by the finding of other defects'' (p. 297).

A syndrome can systematically accommodate some variability by including two levels of symptoms: (a) ''defining'' symptoms, which must be present and are sufficient for rendering a diagnosis (e.g., word fragments are frequent only in conduction aphasia; Kohn, 1984, 1988); and (b) ''characteristic'' symptoms, which are often, but not necessarily, present (e.g., features of deep dyslexia in Broca's aphasia; cf. work in semantic memory; Smith, Rips, & Shoben, 1974; Smith, Shoben, & Rips, 1974). Recall that because symptoms are not necessarily mutually exclusive among syndromes, a behavior may occur as a defining symptom in more than one syndrome as well as occur as a characteristic symptom in other syndromes. Consequently, diagnosis must be based on the entire set of defining symptoms. Recognition of the characteristic symptoms will reduce the impression that the variability in symptomatology is too great to build a viable system of classification. Characteristic symptoms can also be used to develop clear subtypes of syndromes.

Although the distinction between defining and characteristic symptoms does not seem to be made explicitly in discussions of syndrome definition, it is used in practice. For example, the definition of conduction aphasia by Benson et al. (1973) entailed features that must all be present to render a diagnosis, as well as additional features that may also be present. Their defining features are: (a) fluent paraphasic speech, mostly of the phonemic variety; (b) normal comprehension for conversation; and (c) a repetition disturbance that is most severe for multisyllabic words and multiword phrases. Their characteristic symptoms include disturbances in naming and oral reading, and ideomotor apraxia. The behavioral markers of conduction aphasia and their relative prominence for rendering a diagnosis are examined by Goodglass (chapter 3, this volume).

Note that Benson et al.'s list of defining features includes one aspect of preserved language processing—comprehension for conversation. Technically, this feature does not meet our definition of symptom and can be inferred from the list of impaired behaviors. This example reveals that when describing aphasic syndromes mention is often made of preserved abilities that help distinguish that syndrome from another. In this case, the level of auditory comprehension is important for distinguishing conduction from Wernicke's aphasia.

Relating Symptom-Complexes to Functional Deficits

With a precise system for identifying specific symptom-complexes, the functional deficit(s) responsible for the co-occurring symptoms can be more accurately determined. Associating a symptom-complex with its underlying deficit is critical for explaining the relationship between co-occurring symptoms (Caplan, 1985). A classification system of deficit-based syndromes provides an independent framework for guiding more detailed theoretical work, both in terms of constructing the appropriate experimental tests and selecting the appropriate patients for studies. An understanding of the deficits responsible for an aphasic's symptoms is critical for guiding rehabilitation (see following).

It follows that deficit-based syndromes depend on the behavioral model used to generate and characterize states of disruption. Problems can arise if there is disagreement about the structure of certain components of a model or if certain components are underspecified. An example of the issues involved in delineating a functional deficit within a processing model is agrammatism. The considerable variation in production errors displayed by agrammatic patients has encouraged some researchers to reject the notion that at some cognitive level these disorders can be related (Miceli, Silveri, Romani, & Caramazza, 1989). On the other hand, Caplan (1991) argued that we are not yet able to make such a determination. For example, it is not clear at which stage(s) of sentence processing impairment arises in agrammatism, and how compensatory mechanisms may obscure underlying deficit(s). Consequently, Caplan (1991) asserted that "It may be that the diversity of patterns of speech [Miceli et al., 1989] have described reflect selective impairments to operations affecting the production of specific items at a single stage of the sentence production process, rather than disturbances affecting different items at different stages of the process" (p. 279).

The preceding discussion of agrammatism indicates that research is needed to develop certain syndromes so that impaired behaviors, or symptoms, are accurately related to functional deficits. Functional deficits can be aligned with symptom-complexes in two basic ways. One can start from an observed symptom-complex and deduce the deficit(s) responsible with reference to the model. In this way, the relationship between apparently disparate types of impaired behaviors that co-occur may be clarified. Consider, for example, three common symptoms of conduction aphasia: impaired picture naming, oral reading, and repetition. As stated earlier, clinicians often focus on difficulties in one of these modalities—hence, the popular association of conduction aphasia with impaired repetition (Goodglass & Kaplan, 1983). However, examination of these three symptoms with reference to a cognitive model indicates that all three difficulties are due to a general phonological output deficit (Caplan, 1985; Kohn, 1989, in press; see Buckingham, chapter 5, this volume, for details).

Another way of aligning symptoms and deficits is to start from a hypothesized breakdown in the model and make predictions about expected symptoms. Expected manifestations of particular functional deficits include predictions about which behaviors should always be present (i.e., defining symptoms) and those that should be common, but not always present (i.e., characteristic symptoms). For example, it can be argued that a phonemic output deficit always causes the phonemic distortion of recognizable words; only with severe impairment should the distortion be so great as to sometimes obscure target words. Thus, phonemic paraphasias can be viewed as a defining symptom of a phonemic output deficit and neologisms as a characteristic symptom of this deficit.

Just as with the identification of particular symptoms, there is a potential range of specificity involved in defining particular functional deficits. Once again, a balance must be found between a level that is too general to be informative versus one so narrow that too many deficits must be accounted for by the classification system.

The Number of Deficits Potentially Associated
With a Syndrome

There is one final issue to be addressed before we relate the proposed classification system to aphasic phenomena—the number of deficits that can be associated with a syndrome. The simplest solution would be to restrict syndromes to a single causal deficit. In this way, an understanding of how single deficits are manifested is developed before examining multideficit cases where it is more difficult to determine which deficits are responsible for which symptoms.

There is a long tradition of viewing aphasia syndromes as reflecting single deficits. As originally conceived, Wernicke's aphasia was said to represent impairment to the acoustic storehouse for words, Broca's aphasia was said to represent impairment to the motor storehouse for words, and conduction aphasia was said to represent a disconnection between the two storehouses (Lichtheim, 1885; Wernicke, 1874/1977, 1906/1977). (See Henderson, chapter 2, this volume, for details about the history of conduction aphasia.)

A major criterion for determining whether to restrict syndromes to single functional deficits is how often one sees such a simple presentation of symptoms. Ellis (1987) is skeptical about aphasia, believing that only rarely will focal neurological damage impair a single language module. Certainly, multideficit cases of aphasia exist because of the way that the cognitive system is neurologically instantiated. But, given the current difficulties characterizing deficits responsible for symptoms, the frequency of single-deficit cases is yet to be determined. As indicated by the aforementioned discussion of agrammatism, the deficit responsible for a symptom could be misidentified because the model is unclear/incorrect or adaptation mechanisms are misunderstood.

Although the frequency of truly multideficit cases of aphasia (and other neuropsychological deficits) is unclear, they are certainly common enough that a classification system should provide a systematic way of handling symptom combinations that involve more than one functional deficit. The most straightforward solution is to restrict syndromes to a single deficit and identify combinations of deficits with a hybrid diagnosis (see later for a possible exception). Frequent deficit combinations should be noted (e.g., speech impaired by both phonetic and agrammatic errors). This will facilitate the assessment of certain cases and encourage investigations into the causes of frequently co-occurring deficits.

Because the process of developing valid and reliable syndromes is complex, involving series of approximations as theoretical predictions are empirically tested, there may be an intermediary stage of development for some syndromes where certain behaviors are regularly associated with that syndrome but are not predicted by its functional deficit. Further research would then be needed to determine whether such unexpected behaviors involve an initially misunderstood manifestation of the syndrome's deficit. Those symptoms that turn out to be truly unrelated to the recognized deficit of the syndrome signal the presence of a common hybrid aphasia.

One could wait to include unexpected symptoms in a syndrome definition until the deficit(s) responsible are identified. However, even if poorly understood, a symptom can affect research and rehabilitation. Such symptoms could help determine which test paradigms are appropriate for patients and help structure a clinical evaluation. For example, conduction aphasia is sometimes associated with impaired auditory-verbal short-term memory, although the relationship between this problem and the phonemic output deficit seen in this syndrome is unclear. Consequently, experimental and clinical investigation of the output problems of these aphasics should not routinely employ methods that stress the short-term memory system. In addition, short-term memory, which is not always assessed by speech–language pathologists, should be evaluated in these cases (see Caplan & Waters, chapter 6, this volume, for further discussion on this topic).

Summary

Our current working definition of a syndrome involves an extension of the fixed syndrome in that two levels of symptoms are recognized: those that are necessary and sufficient for diagnosis (defining) and those that are common but not necessary for diagnosis (characteristic). Syndromes are explained by their associated functional deficit(s), which are characterized with reference to a behavioral model. With this notion of syndrome, we can now consider issues that are important, but not necessarily unique, to aphasia.

ISSUES IMPORTANT
FOR AN APHASIA CLASSIFICATION SYSTEM

The Role of a Cognitive Model
in an Aphasia Classification System

As stressed earlier, the identification and explanation of the functional deficit(s) associated with a symptom-complex is best accomplished with reference to a behavioral model. Neuropsychological deficits are usually explained with reference to breakdown in a model of normal cognitive processing. This approach began with the early diagram makers and continues today (Marshall, 1986). In Caramazza and Badecker's (1989) terms, we are attempting to develop patient classifications that correspond to "natural categories" of impairment to the normal processing system.

Although relating aphasic deficits to breakdown in normal processing has increased our understanding of both aphasic and normal processing, the assumptions and difficulties involved in using current models must be recognized. At the heart of the process of identifying deficits is the common assumption that aphasic behavior can directly reflect selective impairment of components of normal cognitive functions, what Caramazza (1986) referred to as the "transparency assumption." At a theoretical level, this assumption relies on the notion that the normal cognitive system is composed of subsystems that have some degree of functional independence and that can be selectively impaired by neurological damage (cf. Shallice, 1988).

Most investigations of aphasia follow the transparency assumption, with little acknowledgment of a major constraint on its application. That is, the transparency assumption relies on the ability to distinguish aphasic behaviors that directly reflect disrupted normal processing from those that involve an "idiosyncratic coping strategy" (Shallice, 1988, p. 31) or a reorganization of preserved language capacities (Marshall, 1986). These distinctions have obvious implications for conducting research, as well as classifying aphasic patients. As indicated earlier, more studies about the role of compensatory mechanisms in aphasic behavior are critically needed (Caplan, 1991).

Finally, in identifying the functional deficit(s) of an aphasic, one must always remember that there is no agreed on stable model of normal cognitive processing (cf. Ellis, 1987). Most models offer only crude and tentative hypotheses about normal cognitive systems (Shallice, 1988). Because of these shortcomings, there must be room for work that is not explicitly guided by a cognitive model. One must be open to pretheoretical generalizations based on empirical observation that can help to inform our models (Shallice, 1988), and that permit the development of syndromes that are initially based on family resemblance (Zurif et al., 1989).

The Role of Neurological Information in an Aphasia Classification System

Misconceptions about the nature of neurolinguistic deficits can be created by relating them to a cognitive model, while ignoring neurological information. Extreme examples involve cases with purportedly similar functional deficits, yet lesions in opposite hemispheres. For example, Patterson's (1982) case of phonological alexia following a right hemisphere lesion has been related to cases of phonological alexia that follow left hemisphere damage without considering possible effects of lesion differences (e.g., Denes, Cipolotti, & Semenza, 1987). However, the cognitive system of her patient may not be typical. The inclusion of such patients in discussions of phonological alexia is one possible source of confusion about the defining features of this alexia (cf. Ellis, 1987).

As just implied, one major way to constrain the application of a normal cognitive model in the process of aphasia diagnosis is to incorporate some information about lesion locus into the syndrome definition. At the very least, one must recognize signs of unusual neurological organization (e.g., anomalous dominance, crossed aphasia) that may, in turn, entail an atypical cognitive system. Atypical lesion distributions should encourage a closer evaluation of the patient than is normally done and may indicate different expectations about prognosis.

However, the question remains as to how circumscribed a lesion distribution should be in order to be associated reliably with an aphasia syndrome. Given the assumption that cognitive functions have some degree of neurological localization, the real issue, then, is to determine the level of cognitive description at which such localization exists (e.g., subcomponents of modules vs. systems of modules). Damasio and Damasio (1988) believe that one should not expect localization to be in terms of a fixed brain area, but in terms of associating neural systems with certain types of cognitive operations (cf. Mesulam, 1981).

In establishing what neurological damage is expected with particular syndromes, factors responsible for variation must be considered, such as etiology, age of onset, handedness, and gender (Kertesz, 1983). Such potential for variability may account for the fact that both Benson (1979) and Albert, Goodglass, Helm, Rubens, and Alexander (1981) believe that a symptom-complex is associated with a lesion locus, but not invariably. Nonetheless, this variability is small enough for Marshall (1982) to assert that the lesions associated with the classical syndromes have stood the test of time extremely well. Caplan (1992) proposed that the localizing value of the classical syndromes may be due to the invariant localization of the motor system. It would follow from this latter viewpoint that there may be substantial variability among individuals with respect to the localization of components of the language system.

Clearly, there is much to learn about how cognitive operations are neurologically distributed. With a more precise system for defining the symptoms associated with an aphasia syndrome, such as being suggested here, as well as improved technology for determining lesion distributions, the reliability of lesion localization may improve. This issue is explored by Palumbo, Alexander, and Naeser (chapter 4, this volume) as it relates to conduction aphasia.

Constraining the Number of Aphasia Syndromes

Once there is agreement about how to define broadly a system of aphasia classification, the next task is to determine the actual syndromes that should be identified. This process should include determining which of the known symptom-complexes would now qualify for syndrome status (cf. Marshall, 1982, 1986). For example, as discussed earlier, one could question whether agrammatism reflects a single syndrome, given the variety of independent ways that the speech of aphasics can become agrammatic (e.g., omission/substitution of functors vs. reduced phrase length; Caramazza & Badecker, 1989; Miceli et al., 1989). Some of the recently proposed varieties of alexia may also reflect variable deficits (e.g., surface dyslexia; Ellis, 1987).

There is also room for new diagnostic categories. New syndromes can be developed by either clinical observation (i.e., via family resemblance) or experimental analysis of single cases (i.e., via reference to a language model). However, the recognition of new syndromes raises questions about whether there should be limits placed on the size of the classification system (Ellis, 1987).

If one decides to constrain the classification system, one way to proceed is to give prominence to a major aspect of language processing that is disrupted in most aphasics. By focusing on one aspect of language processing, there is a single orientation for investigating the relationship between different behaviors. This orientation also provides a method for reducing the number of recognized syndromes by specifying certain conditions for accepting syndromes with multiple deficits (see following).

Word production is a good candidate for constructing an aphasia taxonomy. From a clinical perspective, speech disturbances are usually more readily discernible than comprehension disturbances. Aphasics with severely impaired auditory comprehension may still evince an understanding of personally relevant topics, so that an initial meeting may not uncover an input problem without specific testing. By contrast, even a casual conversation will reveal an output disturbance. The widespread nature of word production disturbances is indicated by the fact that virtually all aphasics have some degree of word-finding difficulty (Kohn & Goodglass, 1985), and a specific aspect of phonological processing appears to impair the word production of the three major classical aphasia syndromes (Kohn, 1985, 1988, in press).

Support for focusing on word production to construct a classification system can be found in the literature. Brown (1979/1988) proposed that predominant error patterns in naming can determine a patient's syndrome. Poeck (1983) asserted that it is possible to make a diagnosis solely on the basis of production, given that aphasic syndromes are "expressive syndromes" (p. 85). Despite his belief that comprehension is compromised in all aphasics, he does not think that syndromes have a clearly defined "receptive" aspect. According to Poeck, this distinction arises from "the fact that the neural substrate underlying comprehension has diffuse and bilateral organization, as opposed to the unilateral and more focal organization of the neural substrate for language production" (p. 84).

There is also some agreement among researchers about stages of normal word production, even though this information may be presented in a modularized form (cf. Caramazza, Miceli, & Villa, 1986; Patterson & Shewell, 1987) or a distributed form (cf. Dell, 1986). For example, most models of word production contain the storage of phonological characteristics of words, such as number of syllables, syllabic stress, and features of component segments, and contain a means for accounting for dissociations between semantic and phonological information.

Within a classification system based on word production disturbances, comprehension disturbances are explained in two basic ways. Some comprehension disturbances will be related to the production deficit of a syndrome. For example, disruption within the phonological lexicon, viewed as a major source of impaired speech production in Wernicke's aphasics (Kohn, 1985, 1988; Miller & Ellis, 1987), may be a source of some instances of word-meaning deafness (Kohn & Smith, 1991). Other comprehension disturbances will involve an additional deficit. If such independent comprehension deficits are commonly associated with a particular production deficit, they should be included in the definition of the syndrome associated with the production deficit. This would create the only context where a single aphasia syndrome is associated with multiple independent language deficits (see earlier). The alternative solution, that of identifying each comprehension disturbance as a separate syndrome, is undesirable because it would greatly escalate the number of syndromes. The only case that the plan to base syndromes on production disturbances would not cover is an isolated comprehension deficit. Aside from pure word deafness, isolated comprehension disturbances (i.e., those with no associated production problem) appear to be relatively rare (Kimura & Watson, 1989) and should be recognized as separate syndromes.

By focusing on word production, the major classical syndromes could still be recognized after some modifications. For example, instead of characterizing conduction aphasia as a functional disconnection between input and output word forms, it can be recast as a disturbance to a postlexical stage of phonemic string construction. This deficit would account for the hesitant speech, *conduites d'approche,* phonemic paraphasias, and word fragments associated with this syndrome (Kohn, 1989, in press). Chapter 5 explores the phonological disturbance in conduction aphasia, and the final chapter by Kohn considers in more detail how this updated characterization of conduction aphasia relates to its original conceptualization by Wernicke and Lichtheim.

Empirical work is needed to determine the viability of an aphasia classification system that focuses on deficits that impair word production. For example, it is necessary to determine how much of the language system would be implicated by these output deficits. Are they restricted to the phonological system, or will semantic processing be included? The latter would seem to be particularly relevant for an evaluation of the fluent aphasias, which includes patients whose speech can contain semantic, as well as phonological, errors.

THE PURPOSE OF A SYSTEM
OF APHASIA CLASSIFICATION

We have argued throughout this chapter that a common aphasia classification system be employed by all disciplines that study aphasia. This topic is now reviewed and expanded on.

To be useful for clinicians, a classification system should provide the following (cf. Sokal, 1977): (a) economy of memory, (b) ease of information retrieval and manipulation, (c) comparison of similar cases, and (d) generation of testable hypotheses. Moreover, the classification system should be simple enough to render a diagnosis at bedside, which can be more fully documented with a standardized language assessment. A possible bedside diagnosis would make the classification system more appropriate for the patient's neurologist.

By making explicit the symptoms that must co-occur for a syndrome, the proposed classification system should render more reliable diagnoses than exist presently. By making explicit the deficit(s) involved in each syndrome, treatment programs can be tailored to the particular strengths and weaknesses of a patient (cf. Caplan, 1992; Kohn, Smith, & Arsenault, 1990). Finally, by including information on the evolution of symptoms, better predictions about recovery can be developed. This approach resembles the "psycholinguistic approach to aphasia" described by Caplan (1992), in that this system also involves determining the components of the language processing system that are disturbed and bases diagnosis and treatment on this information (see also Byng, Kay, Edmundson, & Scott, 1990).

As stated in the introduction to this chapter, the current classification system should also be extended to the experimental domain. In this domain, a reliable system for aphasia classification can provide a means for (a) helping to communicate experimental findings, (b) helping different researchers examine similar phenomena, (c) facilitating the replication of findings from case studies, and (d) conducting group studies. These benefits are derived from the notion that a system of aphasia classification provides criteria for subject selection and comparison. As argued before, even case studies need some independent means for determining which aphasics are appropriate for studying particular deficits.

At a more general level, working within the context of a classification system encourages the researcher to consider how various disorders are distributed across the aphasic population. This is important for determining which patients are appropriate for particular studies and reduces the temptation to focus exclusively on an aspect of language breakdown without considering critically related behaviors. As Brown (1989) recognized, any aspect of practiced behavior, if studied closely enough, can appear to be modularized (e.g., playing the piano).

Whereas much of the current work being conducted in aphasiology would benefit from appealing to a patient classification system, it is not necessary in all contexts. In particular, an a priori diagnosis is not needed for a research plan that, instead of focusing on particular functional deficits, involves detailed examination of an area of language processing in order to identify potential dissociations between abilities following brain damage (e.g., Caplan & Hildebrandt, 1988).

Some researchers believe that a patient classification system is irrelevant for all research in cognitive neuropsychology. For example, Caramazza (1984) argued that individual aphasics can be studied exhaustively without appealing to an aphasia classification (part of his "sufficiency condition"), because "a discrepant result will tend to diverge from other results and thereby diminish its 'evidential weight'" (Caramazza & Badecker, 1989, p. 264). He went a step further by positing that this research plan is actually hindered by an a priori attempt to classify a patient (cf. Caramazza & Badecker, 1989).

The success of such a research plan depends first on the ability to perform an exhaustive evaluation of an aphasic and then to determine the relevant body of past data for evaluating findings. Neither criterion can be met totally. The examination of an aphasic subject can never be truly exhaustive, because the cognitive models that determine which variables are examined and how performance is interpreted are always changing (see earlier), and a patient's difficulties may seriously limit the ability to assess key variables (e.g., word deafness can preclude a complete examination of the status of a patient's phonological lexicon). The difficulties of performing an exhaustive evaluation of a patient make it critical that patients with similar problems be compared, so that behaviors associated with deficits can be clarified (e.g., whether phonological alexia involves a part of speech effect). However, if there is no guidance with respect to subject selection, what are the criteria for determining which subjects to compare? This is another way of stating our second concern—determining how to relate disparate pieces of data. In fact, we seem to be suffering from the consequences of this second difficulty, given that we are currently beginning to drown in the data from case studies that are difficult to compare to one another (cf. Shallice, 1988).

It follows from this discussion that, in many cases, the study of individuals and groups of aphasics will benefit from an a priori means for subject identification. Patient identification is circular if the experimental findings are the only means for subject identification. In addition, there must be guidance for replicating findings, which is important for determining those behaviors that reflect reduced normal processing, as opposed to abnormal processing (cf. Newcombe & Marshall, 1988). The use of syndromes (and subtypes of syndromes, depending on the context) provides guidance for both selecting and comparing subjects for experimental studies.

CONCLUSIONS

This chapter has sketched a plan for developing a system for diagnosing aphasics that can benefit both clinical and experimental work. It is important to realize that no system can classify every aphasic within a single diagnostic category. Because of individual differences in, for example, the neurological organization of language functions and lesion distribution, there will inevitably be aphasics who represent an atypical aphasia. However, even these atypical cases benefit by having clear conceptions of how deficits are typically manifested. There must be some standard for evaluating how these cases do not fit neatly into a single or hybrid aphasia diagnosis.

Another goal of this chapter was to set the general context for the chapters that follow. This book represents an example of the methodological riches that emerge from a strong system of aphasia classification. Conduction aphasia has been chosen for detailed study, because this syndrome followed directly from Wernicke's model. A separate chapter is devoted to each of the following aspects of this syndrome: history, clinical diagnosis, neuroanatomy, primary linguistic deficit(s), and related deficits. The contemporary work on conduction aphasia contains two basic approaches to this syndrome—viewing conduction aphasia as due to either (a) a primary deficit that affects speech production only during repetition (Shallice & Warrington, 1977; Strub & Gardner, 1974), or (b) a primary deficit that affects speech production in all modalities (Brown, 1975; Dubois, Hécaen, Angelergues, Maufras de Chatelier, & Marcie, 1964; Kohn, 1984, 1985, 1988; Nespoulous, Joanette, Ska, Caplan, & Lecours, 1987). In the final chapter, we use all the information presented in chapters 2 through 6 to evaluate these two views. The ultimate goal is to develop a definition of conduction aphasia that can further both clinical and experimental work.

ACKNOWLEDGMENT

This work was supported, in part, by NIH Grant DC00447.

REFERENCES

Albert, M. L., Goodglass, H., Helm, N. A., Rubens, A. B., & Alexander, M. P. (1981). *Clinical aspects of dysphasia. Disorders of human communications* (Vol. 2). New York: Springer.

Badecker, W., & Caramazza, A. (1985). On considerations of method and theory governing the use of clinical categories in neurolinguistics and cognitive neuropsychology: The case against agrammatism. *Cognition, 20,* 97–125.

Basso, A., Capitani, E., & Zanobio, M. E. (1982). Pattern of recovery of oral and written expression and comprehension in aphasic patients. *Behavioral Brain Research, 6,* 115–128.

Benson, D. F. (1979). *Aphasia, alexia, and agraphia.* New York: Churchill Livingstone.

Benson, D. F., Sheremata, W. A., Bouchard, R., Segarra, J. M., Price, D., & Geschwind, N. (1973). Conduction aphasia: A clinicopathological study. *Archives of Neurology, 28,* 339–346.

Brown, J. W. (1975). The problem of repetition: A study of "conduction" aphasia and the "isolation" syndrome. *Cortex, 11,* 37–52.

Brown, J. W. (1979). Language representation in the brain. In H. Steklis & M. Raleigh (Eds.), *Neurobiology of social communication in primates.* New York: Academic Press. Reprinted in J. W. Brown (Ed.). (1988). *The life of the mind* (pp. 29–68). Hillsdale, NJ: Lawrence Erlbaum Associates.

Brown, J. W. (Ed.). (1988). *The life of the mind.* Hillsdale, NJ: Lawrence Erlbaum Associates.

Brown, J. W. (1989). Preliminaries for a theory of mind. In E. Goldberg (Ed.), *Contemporary neuropsychology and the legacy of Luria* (pp. 195–210). Hillsdale, NJ: Lawrence Erlbaum Associates.

Byng, S., Kay, J., Edmundson, A., & Scott, C. (1990). Aphasia tests reconsidered. *Aphasiology, 4,* 67–91.

Caplan, D. (1985). Syntactic and semantic structures in agrammatism. In M.-L. Kean (Ed.), *Agrammatism* (pp. 125–152). New York: Academic Press.

Caplan, D. (1988). On the role of group studies in neuropsychological and pathopsychological research. *Cognitive Neuropsychology, 5,* 535–548.

Caplan, D. (1991). Agrammatism is a theoretically coherent aphasic category. *Brain and Language, 40,* 274–281.

Caplan, D. (1992). *Language: Structure, processing, and disorders.* Cambridge: MIT Press.

Caplan, D., & Hildebrandt, N. (1988). *Disorders of syntactic comprehension.* Cambridge: MIT Press.

Caramazza, A. (1984). The logic of neuropsychological research and the problem of patient classification in aphasia. *Brain and Language, 21,* 9–20.

Caramazza, A. (1986). On drawing inferences about the structure of normal cognitive systems from the analysis of patterns of impaired performance: The case for single-patient studies. *Brain and Cognition, 5,* 41–66.

Caramazza, A., & Badecker, W. (1989). Patient classification in neuropsychological research. *Brain and Cognition, 10,* 256–295.

Caramazza, A., & McCloskey, M. (1988). The case for single-patient studies. *Cognitive Neuropsychology, 5,* 517–528.

Caramazza, A., Miceli, G., & Villa, G. (1986). The role of the (output) phonological buffer in reading, writing, and repetition. *Cognitive Neuropsychology, 31,* 37–76.

Crary, M. A., & Kertesz, A. (1988). Evolving error profiles during aphasia syndrome remission. *Aphasiology, 2,* 67–78.

Damasio, A., & Damasio, H. (1988). Cognitive neuroscience and the status of aphasiology. *Aphasiology, 2,* 271–278.

Dell, G. S. (1986). A spreading-activation theory of retrieval in sentence production. *Psychological Review, 93,* 283–321.

Denes, G., Cipolotti, L., & Semenza, C. (1987). How does a phonological dyslexic read words she has never seen? *Cognitive Neuropsychology, 4,* 11–31.

Dubois, J., Hécaen, H., Angelergues, R., Maufras de Chatelier, A., & Marcie, P. (1964). Etude neurolinguistique de l'aphasie de conduction [Neurolinguistic study of conduction aphasia]. *Neuropsychologia, 2,* 9–44.

Ellis, A. W. (1987). Intimations of modularity, or, the modularity of the mind: Doing cognitive neuropsychology without syndromes. In M. Coltheart, G. Sartori, & R. Job (Eds.), *The cognitive neuropsychology of language* (pp. 388–408). London: Lawrence Erlbaum Associates.

Geschwind, N., & Strub, R. (1975). Gerstmann syndrome without aphasia: A reply to Poeck and Orgass. *Cortex, 11,* 296–298.

Goodglass, H., & Kaplan, E. (1983). *The assessment of aphasia and related disorders* (2nd ed.). Philadelphia: Lea & Febiger.

Green, E. (1969). Phonological and grammatical aspects of jargon in an aphasic patient. A case study. *Language and Speech, 12,* 103–118.

Kertesz, A. (1983). Issues in localization. In A. Kertesz (Ed.), *Localization in neuropsychology* (pp. 1–20). New York: Academic Press.

Kertesz, A. (1990). What should be the core of aphasia tests? (The authors promise but fail to deliver). *Aphasiology, 4,* 97–101.

Kimura, D., & Watson, N. (1989). The relation between oral movement control and speech. *Brain and Language, 37,* 565–590.

Kohn, S. E. (1984). The nature of the phonological disorder in conduction aphasia. *Brain and Language, 23,* 97–115.

Kohn, S. E. (1985). *Phonological breakdown in aphasia.* Doctoral dissertation, Tufts University, Boston, MA.

Kohn, S. E. (1988). Phonological production deficits in aphasia. In H. A. Whitaker (Ed.), *Phonological processes and brain mechanisms* (pp. 91–117). New York: Springer-Verlag.

Kohn, S. E. (1989). The nature of the phonemic string deficit in conduction aphasia. *Aphasiology, 3,* 209–239.

Kohn, S. E. (in press). Segmental disorders in aphasia. In G. Blanken, J. Dittmann, H. Grimm, & J. C. Marshall (Eds.), *Linguistic disorders and pathologies. An international handbook.* Berlin: Walter de Gruyter.

Kohn, S. E., & Goodglass, H. (1985). Picture naming in aphasia. *Brain and Language, 24,* 266–283.

Kohn, S. E., & Smith, K. L. (1991). *Evolution of impaired access to the phonological lexicon.* Unpublished manuscript, Braintree Hospital, Braintree, MA.

Kohn, S. E., Smith, K. L., & Arsenault, J. K. (1990). The remediation of conduction aphasia via sentence repetition: A case study. *The British Journal of Disorders of Communication, 25,* 45–60.

Kolk, H., & Heeschen, C. (1990). Adaptation symptoms and impairment symptoms in Broca's aphasia. *Aphasiology, 4,* 221–231.

Lecours, A. R., Basso, A., Moraschini, S., & Nespoulous, J. L. (1984). Where is the speech area, and who has seen it? In D. Caplan, A. R. Lecours, & A. Smith (Eds.), *Biological perspectives on language* (pp. 220–246). Cambridge: MIT Press.

Lee, D. A. (1981). Paul Broca and the history of aphasia: Roland P. Mackay Award Essay, 1980. *Neurology, 31,* 600–602.

Lichtheim, L. (1985). On aphasia. *Brain, 7,* 433–484.

Marshall, J. C. (1982). What is a symptom-complex? In M. A. Arbib, D. Caplan, & J. C. Marshall (Eds.), *Neural models of language processes* (pp. 389–409). New York: Academic Press.

Marshall, J. C. (1986). The description and interpretation of aphasic language disorder. *Neuropsychologia, 24,* 5–24.

McCloskey, M., & Caramazza, A. (1988). Theory and methodology in cognitive neuropsychology: A response to our critics. *Cognitive Neuropsychology, 5,* 583–623.

Mesulam, M. M. (1981). A cortical network for directed attention and unilateral neglect. *Annals of Neurology, 10,* 309–325.

Miceli, G., Silveri, M. C., Romani, C., & Caramazza, A. (1989). Variation in the pattern of omissions and substitutions of grammatical morphemes in the spontaneous speech of so-called agrammatic patients. *Brain and Language, 36,* 447–492.

Miller, D., & Ellis, A. W. (1987). Speech and writing errors in "neologistic jargonaphasia": A lexical activation hypothesis. In M. Coltheart, G. Sartori, & R. Job (Eds.), *The cognitive neuropsychology of language* (pp. 253–271). London: Lawrence Erlbaum Associates.

Naeser, M. A., & Hayward, R. W. (1978). Resolving stroke and aphasia: A case study with computerized tomography. *Archives of Neurology, 36,* 233–235.

Nespoulous, J-L., Joanette, Y., Ska, B., Caplan, D., & Lecours, A. R. (1987). Production deficits in Broca's and conduction aphasia: Repetition vs. reading. In E. Keller & M. Gopnik (Eds.), *Motor and sensory processes in language* (pp. 53–79). Hillsdale, NJ: Lawrence Erlbaum Associates.

Newcombe, F., & Marshall, J. C. (1988). Idealization meets psychometrics: The case for the right groups and the right individuals. *Cognitive Neuropsychology, 5,* 549–564.

Panzeri, M., Semenza, C., & Butterworth, B. (1987). Compensatory processes in the evolution of severe jargon aphasia. *Neuropsychologia, 25,* 919–933.

Patterson, K. E. (1982). The relation between reading and phonological coding: Further neuro-psychological observations. In A. W. Ellis (Ed.), *Normality and pathology in cognitive functions* (pp. 77–111). London: Academic Press.

Patterson, K. E., & Shewell, C. (1987). Speak and spell: Dissociations and word-class effects. In M. Coltheart, G. Sartori, & R. Job (Eds.), *The cognitive neuropsychology of language* (pp. 273–294). London: Lawrence Erlbaum Associates.

Poeck, K. (1983). What do we mean by aphasia syndromes? A neurologist's view. *Brain and Language, 20,* 79–89.

Schwartz, M. (1984). What the classical aphasia categories can't do for us, and why. *Brain and Language, 21,* 3–8.

Shallice, T. (1988). *From neuropsychology to mental structures.* Cambridge: Cambridge University Press.

Shallice, T., & Warrington, E. K. (1977). Auditory-verbal short-term memory impairment and conduction aphasia. *Brain and Language, 4,* 479–491.

Smith, E. E., Rips, L. J., & Shoben, E. J. (1974). Semantic memory and psychological semantics. In G. H. Bower (Ed.), *The psychology of learning and motivation* (Vol. 8, pp. 1–45). New York: Academic Press.

Smith, E. E., Shoben, E. J., & Rips, L. J. (1974). Structure and process in semantic memory: A featural model for semantic decisions. *Psychological Review, 81,* 214–241.

Sokal, R. R. (1977). Classification: Purposes, principals, progress, prospects. In P. N. Johnson-Laird & P. C. Wason (Eds.), *Thinking: Readings in cognitive science* (pp. 185–198). Cambridge University Press.

Strub, R. L., & Gardner, H. (1974). The repetition deficit in conduction aphasia: Mnestic or linguistic? *Brain and Language, 1,* 241–255.

Strub, R. L., & Geschwind, N. (1974). Gerstmann syndrome without aphasia. *Cortex, 10,* 378–387.

Strub, R. L., & Geschwind, N. (1983). Localization in Gerstmann syndrome. In A. Kertesz (Ed.), *Localization in neuropsychology* (pp. 295–321). New York: Academic Press.

Wernicke, C. (1977). Der aphasische symptomenkomplex: Eine psychologische studie auf anatomischer basis [The aphasia symptom complex: A psychological study on an anatomic basis]. In G. H. Eggert (Ed. and Trans.), *Wernicke's works on aphasia* (pp. 91–145). New York: Mouton. (Original work published in 1874)

Wernicke, C. (1977). Der aphasie symptomenkomplex [The aphasia symptom complex]. In G. H. Eggert (Ed. and Trans.), *Wernicke's works on aphasia* (pp. 219–287). New York: Mouton. (Original work published in 1906)

Zurif, E. B., Gardner, H., & Brownell, H. H. (1989). The case against the case against group studies. *Brain and Cognition, 10,* 237–255.

Chapter 2

Early Concepts of Conduction Aphasia

Victor W. Henderson
University of Southern California, Los Angeles

In his influential book, *Aphasia and Kindred Disorders of Speech*, Henry Head (1926) castigated those who would relegate brain and language to the level of Euclidian diagrams. He was especially critical of Carl Wernicke, a man whose "clinical obtuseness and want of scientific insight" had led him to "deduce clinical manifestations from hypothetical lesions" (p. 63). Most esteem Wernicke's contributions more highly, but if Wernicke was Head's archtypical diagram maker, then conduction aphasia, was—and is—the quintessential aphasic syndrome derived from diagrammatic schemes. As originally formulated by Wernicke in 1874, conduction aphasia resulted from the interruption of a white matter pathway linking two postulated speech centers.

In the following overview of the early history of conduction aphasia, the focus is on defects in the production and comprehension of oral language, although reading and writing disturbances also occur in conduction aphasia and were often considered by early writers. Some views in this chapter have been previously discussed (Henderson, 1992).

APHASIOLOGY BEFORE WERNICKE

Wernicke's famous monograph *Der Aphasische Symptomencomplex: Eine Psychologische Studie auf Anatomischer Basis* appeared in 1874, but modern aphasiology had begun a decade before with the revolutionary observations of Paul Broca. Prior to Broca, it was assumed that the two cerebral hemispheres were somehow concerned with intellectual activity but that there was no regional differentiation with regard to discrete motor, sensory, or cognitive functions. This strong antilocalizationist view, buttressed especially by the physiological experiments of Pierre Flourens (1842), was a reaction against the radical phrenology of Franz Gall [1758–1828] and his followers. Gall (1825), an accomplished neuroanatomist, had argued that complex psychological, emotional and moral propensities were discrete functions of sharply delineated regions of the cerebral cortex. Its tenets were that (a) the brain was the organ of the mind; (b) the mind encompassed a collection of discrete mental faculties, each linked to specific cortical centers; (c) the size of each center reflected the development of the corresponding mental faculty; and (d) the form of these cortical centers was reflected in the size and shape of the overlying skull (Critchley, 1965). Until discredited, phrenology had been enormously influential as a popular science, or pseudoscience, of the brain (Cooter, 1976).

Broca's speculations on a special role for the frontal lobe in speech were tentative (Broca, 1861, 1863; Henderson, 1990) until the accumulation of additional clinical observations and postmortem anatomical correlations allowed him to proclaim that a specialized region of the *left* frontal lobe was critical to speech and language (Broca, 1865). Broca's (1865) contention was that damage to the region of the posterior inferior frontal gyrus now known as Broca's area would lead to a particular speech defect that he termed *aphemia*. Aphemics, according to Broca (1861), had lost the ability to produce articulate speech. This loss of speech was not due to a loss of muscle strength, for aphemics usually retained the ability to move their tongue and other speech organs with normal facility. Nor could aphemia be attributed to a more global cognitive deficit, for these patients, Broca (1861) asserted, "hear and understand all that one tells them [and] they possess all of their intelligence" (p. 332).

Broca's well-documented reports created an immediate stir. His was the first convincing suggestion that certain aspects of cortical function might be linked anatomically to discrete loci and, more startlingly, that one cerebral hemisphere might subserve functions quite distinct from those of its seemingly mirror-image counterpart. Broca initially depicted aphemia as a disorder whose deficits were strictly limited to articulate speech. *Language* functions per se, including the understanding of speech, were entirely spared. Later, however, in response to challenges by other investigators, Broca acknowledged that some, if not most, aphemics were impaired on various language tasks when carefully assessed. Indeed, by 1869 Broca had described clinical features of several aphasic syndromes (Broca, 1869; Henderson, 1986), but he failed to recognize that injury of more posterior regions of the left hemisphere would also disturb language.

WERNICKE'S FORMULATION
OF CONDUCTION APHASIA

Wernicke's 1874 monograph on the symptom-complex of aphasia was a major landmark in modern aphasiology. Others had appreciated the existence of "sensory" forms of aphasia distinct from the "motor" aphasia of Broca (e.g., Bastian, 1869; Broca, 1869; Sanders, 1866; Wyllie, 1866 [cited in Nielsen,

1936]). Wernicke [1848–1904], however, who was only 26 years old at the time, was the first to distinguish clinical varieties of aphasia within a plausible anatomical framework. He was profoundly influenced by the Viennese neuroanatomist and psychiatrist Theodor Meynert [1833–1892], in whose laboratory Wernicke had worked for some 6 months. In his monograph, Wernicke (1874/1977) pays homage to his mentor, stating,[1] "The work here submitted is an attempt to provide . . . a practical application of Meynert's teachings of brain anatomy to the study of normal speech processes and the disorders generally recognized as aphasia. Such a study should certainly be grounded in anatomical principles" (p. 92).

Wernicke (1874/1977) rejected "the Flourens concept of the intellect as a single unity, claiming equivalence of all brain areas" but cautioned that "primary functions alone can be referred to specific cortical areas" (p. 92). He adduced evidence from Meynert that the portion of the brain anterior to the Rolandic sulcus was motor in nature, and, conversely, that the temporal-occipital cortex was sensory. Wernicke held that complex functions depend upon nerve fiber pathways interconnecting different cerebral regions and that memory, including sensory and motor images, was meditated through decreased resistance along those pathways that were most often used (see Meynert, 1885). For Wernicke (1874/1977), then, the *"underlying basis of [aphasia lay] . . . in a disruption of the psychic reflex-arc necessary for the normal speech process"* (p. 143).

In proposing a language role for a portion of the left temporal lobe, Wernicke relied on several observations. He accepted Broca's formulations on the clinical symptomatology of Broca's aphasia (or aphemia) and it pathoanatomical substrate within the left interior frontal gyrus. Drawing from the work of Meynert, Wernicke also postulated that auditory functions were represented within cortex of the temporal lobe adjacent to the Sylvian fissure. In addition, Wernicke assumed that cortical areas abutting the Sylvian fissure were functionally related, a possibility previously considered by Broca [Broca, 1864; Henderson, 1986]. On the basis of comparative and developmental anatomy, several authorities had described cortical gyri surrounding the Sylvian fissure as components of a single primordial gyrus that encircled the insula (Foville, 1844). The superior temporal gyrus, which subserved a sensory function, could thus be viewed as in direct continuity with the inferior frontal region, which subserved motor functions and which included Broca's area. Fiber tracing experiments in postmortem brain suggested to Wernicke that major fiber tracts were located subcortically in this region, presumably linking the inferior frontal lobe, superior temporal lobe containing "acoustic imagery" (hereafter referred to as Wernicke's area[2]), and the underlying insula; these three regions together

---

[1]All English-language quotations from Wernicke (1874) are from Eggert's (1977) translation.

[2]Wernicke (1874/1977) indicated that his acoustic imagery center was located within the cortex of the superior temporal gyrus. Later, he provisionally placed his sensory speech area in the left superior temporal gyrus and conjoined portions of the middle temporal gyrus (Wernicke, 1910).

functioned as a "speech center." Finally, from these assumptions and from the recognized variability of aphasic symptomatology, Wernicke posited that aphasia would result from damage at any point within this broad speech region and that clinical features would depend on which specific centers or pathways were involved (Fig. 2.1). It was from these anatomical and psychological cornerstones, in conjunction with Meynert's reflexology, that Wernicke's aphasiological edifice was constructed.

Wernicke (1874/1977) postulated that loss of Wernicke's sensory speech area (*a1*, Fig. 2.1) would result in the "obliteration of the names of all objects from memory . . . [although] the concept itself . . . would remain fully clear" (p. 106) if tactile and visual associations remained. Words would be heard as "meaningless noise" and comprehension would be impossible. The ability to generate names for objects would be retained because of spared connections from cortical sensory regions concerned with tactile and visual imagery to Broca's area. Speech in this case, however, would be paraphasic[3], with "frequent word-confusion" and "no consistency of correct use of the word" (Wernicke, 1874/1977, p. 107).

Conduction aphasia, or *Leitungsaphasie,* was viewed as the consequence of interruption of the pathway *a1–b* between Wernicke's and Broca's areas, a tract that Wernicke believed lay within the insula.[4] Unlike Wernicke's aphasia, comprehension would be normal. However, as with Wernicke's aphasics, most conduction aphasics would be expected to speak copiously and show word confusion with a disturbance of word choice (Wernicke, 1874/1977):

> He speaks a great deal but shows a disturbance in his choice of words very much like the other type [i.e., like Wernicke's aphasia]. The auditory image is intact. It is activated by the residual sensory imagery [from other cortical regions] forming the concept. However, since pathway *a1–b* is disrupted, it cannot make its own unique contribution to the appropriate selection of the motor images [in Broca's area]. (p. 109)

Conduction aphasics differed in another way from those with Wernicke's aphasia. Because they could hear and understand their own incorrect speech, these patients might show great frustration (Wernicke 1874/1977): "The acoustic nerve is intact and permits transfer of the sound of the spoken word to the undamaged area containing acoustic imagery. The spoken word can therefore be heard and its accuracy assessed. The patient has definite awareness of his error and therefore often becomes emotionally upset" (p. 109).

---

[3]The term *paraphasia,* soon to be introduced by Kussmaul (1877), did not appear in Wernicke's original monograph.

[4]According to Bastian (1887), the idea that damage to commissural fibers traversing the insula might lead to aphasia originated with Meynert in 1868. Wernicke (1910) later renounced this localization, stating that autopsy findings did not support his earlier contention.

FIG. 2.1. Wernicke's (1874) scheme for speech producation. C = central fissure; F = frontal lobe; O = occipital lobe; S = Sylvian Fissure; a = acoustic nerve in the medulla; a_1 = center for acoustic imagery, or the central termination of the acoustic nerve in the cortex of the superior temporal lobe; b = motor images concerns with speech production in the frontal lobe; b_1 = efferent pathways concerned with speech. Association pathway a_1–b lies within the insula. Interestingly, Wernicke's diagram depicts the *right* cerebral hemisphere, although he clearly recognized the leading role of the left hemisphere in language functions.

In milder cases, according to Wernicke, word confusion would be less evident, and speech would be hesitant and laborious with long word-finding pauses. Wernicke (1874/1977) did not discuss speech repetition in the context of conduction aphasia, but in describing Wernicke's aphasia, he had explicitly noted that interruption of the pathway a–$a1$–b–$b1$ (Fig. 2.1) would lead to impaired repetition. Implicitly then, even in 1874, Wernicke might have realized that repetition should be disturbed in his formulation of conduction aphasia, a point that was later emphasized by Lichtheim (1885) and by Wernicke (1910) himself.

In his 1874 monograph, Wernicke reported clinical symptoms of 10 aphasics; postmortem findings were available in only two of these. Two cases (Cases 3 and 4)—neither of whom were autopsied—were adduced as examples of conduction aphasia. Wernicke's (1874/1977) first conduction aphasic was described as follows:

Beckman, a 64 year old pharmacist . . . comprehended adequately, and response to suggestion-questions was consistently accurate. His use and recognition of objects was appropriate. There was no trace of motor aphasia and no reduction in fund of words. Nevertheless, he had difficulty in finding the names of many objects. He would struggle to find the appropriate words, and in the process became irritated . . . He might speak fluently in conversation for some time, then suddenly come upon a word and hesitate, remain hanging for a time, struggle to find the word, but each attempt was inappropriate. He repeatedly corrected himself, but the harder he tried, the more frustrating the situation became. . . .

Further observation indicated a wide variation in the severity and consistency of the aphasia symptoms. At times it was essentially non-existent, and at other times it was severe. Moreover, only substantives, and among these particularly the names of places and people, were occasionally absent. (pp. 126–127)

Clinical details of Wernicke's (1874/1977) second conduction aphasic were obscured by a number of nonaphasic symptoms:

> Kunschkel, a 50 year old goldsmith, suffered from urinary and fecal incontinence for a two-year period . . . [On the mental ward, he] was surly and morose, demonstrating marked agitation and irritability . . . He seemed to be completely disoriented as to place. . . .
>
> On March 26, he was involved in a quarrel . . . [and] received a blow to the right ear . . . On the next morning, a hematoma of the right ear, a marked aphasia, and paralysis of the right leg were found. . . .
>
> The aphasia revealed itself in the following way. The patient spoke for long periods without hesitation, but frequently a wrong word, apparently added unconsciously, would slip out at the end of a sentence. If one questioned him about the word just spoken, he would attempt to correct it, and in the process produced meaningless combinations of words and syllables, a jargon which was difficult to record. In response to some interjected questions, however, he answered in complete and accurate sentences. His answers in so far as speech was possible were essentially correct and appropriate in meaning. Furthermore, his answers to suggestion-questions indicated a ready and intact comprehension. (p. 128)

Summarizing essential features of these two cases of conduction aphasia, Wernicke (1874/1977) stated, "Both have intact comprehension of the spoken word and a large fund of words available. But the availability of this word-store is inconsistent" (p. 130). He added, "During speech, Beckman frequently became blocked in the middle of a sentence and struggled for expression. Kunschkel, on the contrary, compensated for his errors by the use of meaningless words or new combinations or syllables" (p. 130).

COMMISSURAL DEFECTS
AND COMMISSURAL PARAPHASIA

Ludwig Lichtheim, firmly in the diagram-maker camp, extended Wernicke's concept of conduction aphasia. According to Lichtheim in an influential paper later belittled by Head (1926) as "a parody of the tendencies of the time" (p. 65), the aphasiologist's task (Lichtheim, 1885) was:

> . . . to determine the connections and localisation of the paths of innervation subservient to language and its correlated functions. On the supposition of our having reached this end, we should then be able to determine the exact place of any solution of continuity in these paths and account for its symptomatic manifestations with the same precision as we do for those of a motor or sensory paralysis depending on a lesion of the peripheral nerves. (p. 434)

The first, and simplest, of Lichtheim's diagrams postulated centers for "auditory images," "motor images," and "concepts." Seven different forms of aphasia were predicted, including that of conduction aphasia, which Lichtheim termed *commissural paraphasia* (Fig. 2.2). Based on Fig. 2.2, interruption of commissural pathway *A–M* (lesion 3) between Broca's area ("centre of motor images"—*M*) and Wernicke's area ("centre of auditory images"—*A*) would not affect understanding of spoken language (because *A* is intact) but would lead to paraphasic errors during spontaneous speech. Lichtheim explicitly stated that similar errors would occur during speech repetition. Complete abolition of speech does not occur because the tract *A–B–M* partially substitutes for tract *A–M*, where *B* represents cortical regions in which concepts *(Begriffe)* are elaborated.

Lichtheim (1885) reported the case of a 46-year-old laborer with conduction aphasia:

> *Speech* much altered . . . He strings together in a fluent manner numerous words, of which scarcely one now and then can be made out. The following were noted: "Evening, five and twenty, and." Patient is aware of the incorrectness of his diction . . . His own name he mutilates.
>
> *Repeating.* When he repeats connected sentences he manifests the same defects as in volitional speech; single short words are pretty correctly rendered. . . .
>
> *Understanding of Speech* entire. (p. 445)

Lichtheim tentatively agreed with Wernicke's anatomical formulation that conduction aphasia was due to damage in the region of the insula. Postmortem findings in Lichtheim's case (1885) supported this contention, although neighboring frontal, parietal, and temporal convolutions were affected in addition to the left insular region. He proposed that the term *insular aphasia* could be appropriately applied if this pathological substrate could be convincingly confirmed.

Most other late-19th-century workers (with the notable exceptions of Hughlings Jackson in London and Adolph Kussmaul in Strassburg) accepted the Wernicke-Lichtheim scheme of a pathway linking Broca's frontal center with that of Wernicke's temporal center, and most descriptions of conduction aphasia symptoms resembled those described by these two diagram makers. The Scottish physician John Wyllie (1894), for example, stated that a lesion cutting across these "conducting fibers" (p. 329) would cause symptoms that could be distinguished from Wernicke's aphasia only by the absence of "word deafness" (p. 331) (i.e., by the absence of impaired comprehension) at the onset of aphasic symptoms.

An interesting and somewhat different interpretation of conduction aphasia was offered by Charlton Bastian [1837–1915]. Bastian proposed four "word-centres" (Bastian 1880, 1887): an auditory word center in the neighborhood of the left posterior, superior temporal gyrus, a glossokinaesthetic center

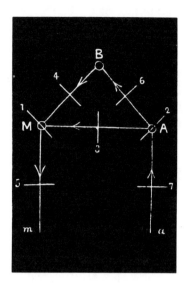

FIG. 2.2. Lichtheim's (1885, p. 436) diagram of language centers, commissural pathways, and postulated sites of lesions that would cause aphasia. A = the "centre of auditory images" (Wernicke's area), M = the "centre of motor images" (Broca's area), and B = cortical regions in which "concepts" *(Begriffe)* are elaborated. Center lesions 1 and 2 and commissural lesion 3 would cause Broca's, Wernicke's, and conduction aphasia, respectively.

(viewed by Bastian as a kinesthetic sensory center and localized in the region of Broca's area or the adjacent portion of the ascending frontal gyrus), an occipital visual word center important for reading and visual confrontation naming, and a frontal cheiro-kinaesthetic center involved in writing (Fig. 2.3). He specifically rejected a separate "concept" center, such as had been postulated by Wernicke and Lichtheim, but like these workers Bastian (1887) also distinguished "centric defects" from "commissural defects." Each might be associated with faulty recollection of words, but only a center lesion could cause the actual loss of stored memories. Practically speaking, however, Bastian believed that clinical differentiation of a centric defect from a commissural defect would be extremely difficult. Bastian (1887) proposed that "lesion of any part of the audio-kinaesthetic commissure should produce an aphasia indistinguishable from that which would be produced by damage to the glosso-kinaesthetic centre itself . . . [and] ought also to give rise to a typical aphasia similar to that resulting from a lesion in Broca's region" (p. 986). Thus, Bastian's conduction aphasia would assume the characteristics of a Broca's aphasia. This alternative formulation underscores the difficulty in deducing aphasic symptoms from diagrammatic considerations.

A CRITICAL STUDY: SIGMUND FREUD

Before achieving fame as the founder of psychoanalysis, Freud [1856–1939] undertook research in histology and comparative neurophysiology with Ernst von Brücke and in human neuroanatomy with Meynert (Jelliffe, 1937; Jones,

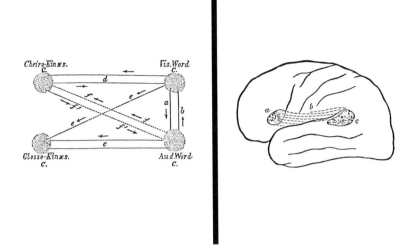

FIG. 2.3. Left side: Bastian's (1887, p. 933) diagram of left hemisphere language centers. *Aud Word C* = "auditory word centre," *Glosso-Kinaes C* = "glosso-kinaesthetic word centre," *Vis Word C* = "visual word centre" concerned with reading, *Cheiro-kinaes C* = "cheiro-kinaesthetic commissure." Lesions of *Aud Word C, Glosso-Kinaes C,* and pathway *c* would cause Wernicke's, Broca's, and conduction aphasia, respectively. These three areas are also depicted in Fig. 2.3, right side (Bastian, 1887, p. 986), where *a* indicates the glosso-kinaesthetic center, *c* the auditory word centre, and *b* the linking commissural pathway implicated in conduction aphasia.

1953). He visited Jean-Martin Charcot at the Salpêtrière and published a German translation of Charcot's lectures on his return to Vienna (*Neue Vorlesungen über die Krankheiten des Nervensystems inbesondere über Hysterie*—Charcot, 1886). Freud's interests in aphasia were variously determined (Henderson, 1992) but were likely kindled by his sojourn in Paris. Five years after leaving Charcot's service, Freud (1891) published his *Zur Auffassung der Aphasien, Eine kritische Studie.* Freud's antilocalizationist views bore an intellectual debt to Hughlings Jackson, but he rejected Meynert's formulation of cortical centers and took strong issue with Wernicke and Lichtheim's concept of aphasia. Little noticed by most of Freud's contemporaries, this carefully crafted work later influenced Goldstein's concepts of conduction aphasia.

Freud (1891/1953)[5] began by decrying notions of functional localization ("the restriction of nervous functions to anatomically definable areas"):

The theory of aphasia . . . contains two assumptions which might profitably be revised. The first refers to the differentiation between aphasias caused by de-

---

[5]All Freud (1891) quotations and page number references are from Stengel's (1953) translation.

struction of centres and aphasias caused by destruction of pathways . . . The
second assumption is concerned with the topographical relationship between the
individual speech centres. It was adopted mainly by Wernicke and those workers who have accepted, and enlarged upon, his views. (p. 1)

Freud argued that the entire perisylvian cortex of the left hemisphere functioned more or less equivalently in speech. This continuous cortical region en-
tered into various associations (e.g., visual, auditory, and kinesthetic
associations) with other cortical areas, and lesions near the periphery of this
speech region (e.g., in Wernicke's area posteriorly or Broca's area anteriorly)
might interrupt one class of association fibers and thereby cause distinct aphasic
symptoms. More centrally located lesions could not have such discrete consequences. Freud (1891/1953) rejected "the differentiation between the so-called
centre or cortical aphasias and the conduction (association) aphasias, and [he
maintained] that all aphasias originate[d] in interruption of associations" (p.
67). Thus, "aphasia, through destruction or lesion of a centre is to us no more
and no less than aphasia through lesion of those association fibers which meet
in that nodal point called a centre" (pp. 67–68). The seeming significance of
Broca's area or Wernicke's area held "only for the pathology, and not for the
physiology of the speech apparatus" (p. 64).

Freud was particularly critical of conduction aphasia (Henderson, 1992),
and he challenged Wernicke and Lichtheim on the similarity of the postulated
speech disorder of conduction aphasia and Wernicke's aphasia. Wernicke
(1874/1977) had explained paraphasic speech in conduction aphasia on the basis
of the loss of innervation of Broca's area by the tract $a1–b$ (Fig. 2.1), although
speech could still be generated directly from the memory of concepts (B, in
Lichtheim's scheme of Fig. 2.2). Freud (1891/1874) stated, "according to Wernicke and Lichtheim, spontaneous speech in sensory aphasia (destruction of
A [Wernicke's area—see Fig. 2.2]) becomes paraphasic because the sound images in A which normally have a controlling function have been destroyed"
(p. 16). He argued that one would expect a different clinical picture if Wernicke's area remained intact but only a connecting pathway had been destroyed.
However, "the interruption of $A–M$ [Fig. 2.2] has the same effect as the destruction of A itself, i.e., paraphasia in spontaneous speech. This is another proof
that Wernicke's conduction aphasia is untenable" (Freud 1891/1953, p. 16).

Freud (1891/1953) went on to discuss speech repetition, noting that impaired
repetition never occurs unless spontaneous speech or speech comprehension
was also affected:

> There is something peculiar about Wernicke's conduction aphasia. The distur-
> bance of function attributed to it cannot be deduced from Wernicke's schema.
> Wernicke states that interpretation of $a1–b$ [Fig. 2.1] causes paraphasia; but if
> we ask what ought to be the result of this interruption the answer would have
> to be as follows: via the tract $a1–b$ the ability of reproducing perceived word sounds

has been learned; its function is that of repetition of words heard; its interruption ought to result in a loss of that ability while spontaneous speech and understanding ought to remain intact. Yet everybody will admit that such a dissociation of speech function has never been observed nor is it ever likely to be observed. The faculty of repeating is never lost as long as speaking and understanding are intact. (p. 11)

Freud's (1891/1953) conclusion was "that one and the same tract serves speaking and the repetition of spoken words" (p. 12). Freud anticipated a possible rebuttal and offered an alternative scenario of conduction aphasia. Perhaps speech repetition would actually be spared in conduction aphasia because of a "detour via 'understanding,' the connection A–B–M [Fig. 2.2] taking the place of the interrupted tract A–M which normally serves repetition" (Freud, 1891/1953, p. 14). In this case, however, conduction aphasia would have to be characterized by normal (i.e., non-paraphasic) speech and intact comprehension, as well as by the normal repetition of understood words. Only the repetition of nonsense words (e.g., unfamiliar words in a foreign language) would be impaired. Not surprisingly, Freud was skeptical of the existence of any such syndrome.

CENTRAL APHASIA

Kurt Goldstein [1878–1965] recalled (in Goldstein, 1948), that "when I began to be interested in the problem of aphasia, I was influenced by my teacher, C. Wernicke" (p. 23). Goldstein was also well acquainted with Freud's monograph on aphasia (Jelliffe, 1937). Although his break with the diagram makers was not as radical as is commonly assumed (Geschwind, 1964), Goldstein was to become the best-known spokesman for the holistic, or organismic, approach to aphasia. According to Goldstein (1948), this theoretical orientation "deviates essentially from the so-called classic theory of aphasia which is based on an 'atomistic' concept of the organism" (p. 21). In the past, Goldstein (1936) stated, "one tended to refer the aphasic symptoms to an impairment of definite discrete linguistic faculties or, anatomically speaking, an impairment of definite cerebral centers" (p. 586). More appropriately, Goldstein (1948) believed, "every *individual speech-performance is understandable only from the aspect of its relation to the function of the total organism in its endeavor to realize itself as much as possible in the given situation*" (p. 21). Obtuse and awkward to modern readers, Goldstein's formulations were well within the mainstream of the respected school of Gestalt psychology.

According to Goldstein (1948), neurological symptoms were caused by a variety of factors. Language disturbances represented more than the loss of function (or the dedifferentiation of function) by a circumscribed area of damaged nervous tissue. Aphasic symptoms also reflected isolated functions of undamaged regions, secondary effects on undamaged regions by a damaged area, and protective mechanisms designed to avoid global "catastrophic reactions." Although not a radical antilocalizationist, Goldstein (1948) believed that *"to each performance corresponds an excitation of definite structure in the cortex, indeed, not in a circumscribed area but widespread over the whole cortex, differently in each performance. This is what we should term localization"* (p. 50).

Goldstein's views of conduction aphasia, influenced by Wernicke's co-worker Ernst Storch (Levine & Calvanio, 1982; Storch, 1903), were discussed in 1912 and summarized in his 1927 monograph, *Die Lokalisation in der Grosshirnrinde.* His later work, *Language and Language Disorders* (1948) is based largely on this work (Geschwind, 1964).

Goldstein (1948) took strong issue with the connectionists' conception of the pathoanatomical basis of conduction aphasia: "The name conduction aphasia did not appear correct to me, because we are not dealing with a defect of conduction, as Wernicke had assumed as cause particularly of the disturbance of repetition and of the paraphasia, but with dedifferentiation of a complex apparatus which I believe to be justified to 'localize' in the center of the speech area" (pp. 229–230). He distinguished between language and "non-language" mental processes, and he stated that damage to central regions of the left hemisphere involved with language functions was especially apt to affect the basic, most concrete, aspects of language, the *speech instrumentalities,* as Goldstein termed them. Goldstein (1948) held conduction aphasia to be central to his scheme, for in this syndrome the speech instrumentalities were most affected: "We are dealing with an *impairment of the central part of language* (as far as instrumentalities are concerned), *all speech performances are more or less affected"* (p. 230).

In discussing conduction aphasia, Goldstein (1948) also referred to his concept of *inner speech,* which he described as belonging to "the experiences which precede speaking and [which can be] elicited by the hearing of speech" (p. 92). He distinguished between Wernicke's *Wortbegriffe,* or word concept, which represented an association between motor and sensory speech images, and his own view of *"inner speech [as] the totality of processes and experiences which occur when we are going to express our thought, etc., in external speech and when we perceive heard sounds as language"* (p. 94). Goldstein (1948) explained that conduction aphasia, which he termed *central aphasia,* represented the dedifferentiation of inner speech: "I call the symptom complex *central aphasia* because inner speech seems to me to be the *central phenomenon of instrumentalities of speech"* (p. 94). Inner speech includes the following characteristics (Goldstein, 1948):

> [I]nner speech consists . . . of *material fixed more or less by previous functioning of the "apparatus," by experience.* The concepts of letters, words, phrases, are more or less fixed wholes . . . and used as wholes to start the speaking activity. . . .

> The word is normally experienced as a phenomenon of a characteristic struc-
> ture in which the sounds follow in a definite sequence; it is not composed of parts,
> it is experienced as a simultaneous whole of a definite structure. (p. 99)

An impairment in inner speech leads to phonemic, or literal, paraphasic
errors so characteristic of conduction aphasia (Goldstein, 1948):

> The word may possess the previous length, rhythm, some characteristic outstand-
> ing sounds, but the inner structure is loosened or even broken up. The parts of
> which the word consists do not occur immediately in the right sequence. The
> first part of the word may be produced correctly but then disorder takes place.
> Some letters may fall out totally, others come to the fore abnormally and at the
> wrong place. This destruction of words produces certain characteristic phenomena
> of literal paraphasia: omission of letters, misplacing of correct letters, occurrence
> of incorrect letters due to increased "assimilation" as an expression of dedifferen-
> tiation, premature end of the word, etc. (p. 99)

Although "literal paraphasia is the most outstanding defect" (p. 231), conduction aphasics might also make semantic, or verbal, paraphasias when they
access undamaged nonlanguage areas of the cerebral hemispheres involved with
meaning: "The damage of the concepts of words will produce *verbal* paraphasia also . . . [T]he *inability to grasp the right word makes the patient enter the sphere
of non-speech mental processes* and summon up a word corresponding to the sphere
of the demanded word, if this new word is, for any reason, easier to produce"
(p. 101).

From his analyses of speech instrumentalities and inner speech, Goldstein
derived four salient features of oral language in central aphasia. First, there
was always some reluctance to engage in spontaneous speech: "They may,
as much as possible, avoid speaking at all because they have a great difficulty
to overcome and they will never be sure whether or not they are making mis-
takes" (p. 102). Second, comprehension, although often much better preserved,
was also disturbed, because word-concepts are affected in this form of aphasia. Third, there was word-finding difficulty of the type seen when speech instrumentalities are involved; phonemic paraphasias were common, but
circumlocutions were less often seen. Finally, there was a disturbance in speech
repetition, which Goldstein (1948) emphasized, was "not at all a simple
phenomenon as often has been assumed" (p. 70). Correct repetition is quite
distinct from parrot-like speech imitation and depends on integrity of word-
concepts that, when damaged, lead to phonemic and semantic paraphasic errors.

Anatomical Lesion of Central Aphasia

Goldstein accepted portions of Wernicke's anatomical formulations as to the
essential lesion of conduction aphasia. He cited Wernicke's supposition that
word concepts would be affected by lesions in the region of the insula that af-

fect association fibers connecting sensory and motor speech areas. Goldstein (1948) cautioned, "I considered the theory as, in principle, correct, but from my general point of view was not inclined to assume a disruption of a simple pathway as basis of a psychologic defect . . . [W]e cannot assume a defect of a simple fiber connection but dysfunction of a cortical apparatus" (pp. 239–240).

Like Wernicke, Goldstein suggested a significant role for left insular damage in central aphasia, but he also tentatively included adjacent areas of the temporal and parietal lobes. Goldstein cited the complicated case of a 54-year-old man that he had originally reported in 1911. During the middle part of the disease course, at a time when his symptoms were those of conduction aphasia, Goldstein (1948) noted

> . . . a *paraphasic destruction of the words, which became the outstanding symptom* in naming as well as in repetition and in spontaneous speech. It was *particularly severe in repetition. Repetition became increasingly more disturbed,* especially for words difficult to pronounce or those unknown to the patient . . . The first parts of the words were often well repeated, then paraphasia set in . . . *Understanding* of speech remained much better than the other speech performances till the latest period of the disease. (pp. 231–232)

At autopsy, Goldstein (1948) reported that there was an extensive neoplasm originating in the central part of the temporal lobe and infiltrating the insula and subthalamic region. Symptoms of central aphasia had occurred as the tumor "increasingly affected the central area in the Insula Reili and the temporal lobe" (pp. 232–233).

EPILOGUE

Conduction aphasia played a central role in the diagram-makers' view of how the brain functioned in language and proved a useful focus of attack for their detractors. However, the legacy of the aphasiological iconoclasts (e.g., Pierre Marie [Head, 1926]) and neurological holists was such that until recently many investigators doubted the very existence of conduction aphasia (e.g., Weisenburg & McBride, 1935). It is now evident that conduction aphasia (i.e., aphasia meeting general criteria of fluent, paraphasic speech, relatively preserved auditory comprehension on specified tasks, and impaired speech repetition) is far from uncommon (Benson et al., 1973) and that several syndromes of conduction aphasia can be distinguished by neuropsychological criteria. Wernicke's original pathoanatomical concept of a white matter disconnection between two speech centers is still accepted in portions of the modern literature (Geschwind, 1965), and indeed the arcuate fasciculus—the white matter bundle most often discussed in relation to the disconnection hypothesis of conduction aphasia—appears to be implicated in most conduction aphasics (Damasio

& Damasio, 1980). However, concomitant cortical damage is inevitably present as well (Damasio & Damasio, 1980), and a simple disconnection hypothesis no longer suffices to explain the rich variety of clinical and experimental observations in this important disorder. Furthermore, as the neuropsychological underpinnings of conduction aphasia are expanded and diluted—by the "neo-diagram-makers" (the "boxologists") under the banner of cognitive modularity—the usefulness of conduction aphasia as a nosological entity is again called into question. As in the 19th century, however, issues raised by this controversial disorder remain central to our understanding of language, of how language is represented within the brain, and of how language is altered by cerebral injury.

REFERENCES

Bastian, H. C. (1869). On the various forms of loss of speech in cerebral disease. *British and Foreign Medical-Chirurgical Review, 43,* 209–236, 470–492.

Bastian, H. C. (1880). *The brain as an organ of mind.* London: Kegan Paul.

Bastian, H. C. (1887). On different kinds of aphasia, with special reference to their classification and ultimate pathology. *British Medical Journal, 2,* 931–936, 985–990.

Benson, D. F., Sheremata, W. A., Bouchard, R., Segarra, J. M., Price, D., & Geschwind, N. (1973). Conduction aphasia: A clinicopathological study. *Archives of Neurology, 28,* 339–346.

Broca, P. (1861). Remarques sur le siége de la faculté du langage articulé, suivies d'une observation d'aphémie (perte de la parole) [Remarks on the seat of the faculty of articulate language, followed by an observation of aphemia (loss of speech)]. *Bulletins de la Société d'Anatomie, 36,* 330–357.

Broca, P. (1863). Localisation des fonctions cérébrales. Siége du langage articulé. [Localization of cerebral functions. Seat of articulate language]. *Bulletins de la Société d'Anthropologie de Paris, 4,* 200–204.

Broca, P. (1864). Deux cas d'aphémie traumatique produits par des lésions de la troisième circonvolution frontale gauche. Diagnostic chirurgical. [Two cases of traumatic aphemia caused by lesions of the left third frontal convolution. Surgical diagnosis.] *Gazette des Hôpitaux Civils et Militaires, 37,* 107.

Broca, P. (1865). Sur le siége de la faculté du langage articulé. [On the seat of the faculty of articulate language]. *Bulletins de la Société d'Anthropologie de Paris, 6,* 377–393.

Broca, P. (1869). Sur le siége de la faculté du langage articulé. [On the seat of the faculty of articulate language]. *La Tribune Médicale, 3,* 254–256, 265–269.

Charcot, J. M. (1886). *Neue Vorlesungen über die Krankheiten des Nervensystems inbesondere über Hysterie* (S. Freud, Trans.). Leipzig: Toeplitz & Deuticke.

Cooter, R. J. (1976). Phrenology and British alienists, *c.* 1825–1845. *Medical History, 20,* 1–21, 135–151.

Critchley, M. (1965). Neurology's debt to F. J. Gall (1758–1828). *British Medical Journal, 4,* 775–781.

Damasio, H., & Damasio, A. R. (1980). The anatomical basis of conduction aphasia. *Brain, 103,* 337–350.

Flourens, P. (1842). *Recherches expérimentales sur les propriétés et les fonctions du système nerveux dans les animaux.vertébrés* (2nd ed.) [Experimental research on the properties and functions of the vertebrate nervous system]. Paris: J.-B. Ballière.

Foville, A. L. (1844). *Traité complet de l'anatomie, de la physiologie et de la pathologie du système nerveux* [Treatise on the anatomy, physiology, and pathology of the nervous system]. Paris: Fortin. Cited in: F. Schiller (1979). *Paul Broca: Founder of French anthropology, explorer of the brain.* Berkeley: University of California Press.

Freud, S. (1953). *Zur Auffassung der Aphasien. Eine kritische Studie.* Leipzig: Deuticke. In E. Stengel (Trans.), *On aphasia: A critical study.* New York: International Universities Press. (Original work published in 1891)

Gall, F. J. (1825). *Sur les fonctions du cerveau.* [On functions of the brain]. Paris: J.-B. Ballière.

Geschwind, N. (1964). The paradoxical position of Kurt Goldstein in the history of aphasia. *Cortex, 1,* 214–224.

Geschwind, N. (1965). Disconnexion syndromes in animal and man (Part II). *Brain, 88,* 585–644.

Goldstein, K. (1912). Die zentral Aphasie [Central aphasia]. *Neurologisches Zentralblatt, 12,* 739–751.

Goldstein, K. (1927). *Die Lokalisation in der Grosshirnrinde nach den Erfahrungen am kranken Menschen. Handbuch der normalen und pathologischen Physiologie* (Vol. 10, pp. 600–842). [Localization in the cerebral cortex based on human disease. Handbook of normal and pathological physiology]. Berlin: Julius Springer.

Goldstein, K. (1936). The modifications of behavior consequent to cerebral lesions. *Psychiatric Quarterly, 10,* 586–610.

Goldstein, K. (1948). *Language and language disorders.* New York: Grune & Stratton.

Head, H. (1926). *Aphasia and kindred disorders of speech,* (vol. 1, pp. 54–66). London: Cambridge University Press.

Henderson, V. W. (1986). Paul Broca's less heralded contributions to aphasia research: Historical perspective and contemporary relevance. *Archives of Neurology, 43,* 609–612.

Henderson, V. W. (1990). Alalia, aphemia, and aphasia. *Archives of Neurology, 47,* 85–88.

Henderson, V. W. (1992). Sigmund Freud and the diagram-maker school of aphasiology. *Brain and Language, 43,* 19–41.

Jones, E. (1953). *The life and work of Sigmund Freud* (Vol. 1). *The formative years and the great discoveries 1856–1900.* New York: Basic Books.

Jelliffe, S. E. (1937). Sigmund Freud as a neurologist. *Journal of Nervous and Mental Disease, 85,* 696–711.

Kussmaul, A. (1877). *Die Störungen der Sprache. Versuch einer Pathologie der Sprache* [Disorders of speech. An attempt in the pathology of speech]. Leipzig: Verlag von F. C. W. Vogel.

Levine, D. N., & Calvanio, R. (1982). Conduction aphasia. In H. S. Kirshner & F. R. Freemon (Eds.), *The neurology of aphasia* (pp. 79–111). Lisse: Swets & Zeitlinger.

Lichtheim, L. (1885). On aphasia. *Brain, 7,* 433–484.

Meynert, T. (1885). *Psychiatry. A clinical treatise on diseases of the fore-brain based upon a study of its structure, functions, and nutrition* (B. Sachs, Trans.). New York: Putnam.

Neilsen, J. M. (1936). *Agnosia, apraxia, aphasia. Their value in cerebral localization* (p. 79). Los Angeles: Los Angeles Neurological Society.

Sanders, W. R. (1866). Lesion in the island of Reil extending into the external frontal convolution. *Lancet, 1,* 656.

Storch, E. (1903). Der aphasische Symptomenkomplex. [The symptom complex of aphasia]. *Monatsschrift für Psychiatrie und Neurologie, 13,* 321, 597.

Weisenburg, T., & McBride, K. E. (1935). *Aphasia. A clinical and psychological study.* New York: The Commonwealth Fund.

Wernicke, C. (1977). Der aphasische Symptomencomplex: Eine psychologische Studie auf anatomischer Basis [The aphasia symptom complex. A psychological study on an anatomic basis]. In G. H. Eggert (Trans.), *Wernicke's works on aphasia: A sourcebook and review* (pp. 91–145). New York: Mouton. (Original work published in 1874)

Wernicke, C. (1977). Einige neuere Arbeiten über Aphasie. [Recent works on aphasia]. *Fortschritte der Medizin, 3,* 824; *4,* 377; *4,* 463. In G. H. Eggert (Trans.), *Wernicke's works on aphasia: A sourcebook and review* (pp. 173–205). New York: Mouton. (Original work published in 1885–1886)

Wernicke, C. (1910). The symptom-complex of aphasia. In A. Church (Ed.), *Modern clinical medicine. Diseases of the nervous system* (pp. 265–324). New York: D. Appleton.

Wyllie, J. (1894). *The disorders of speech* (pp. 329–331). Edinburgh: Oliver & Boyd.

Chapter 3

Diagnosis of Conduction Aphasia

Harold Goodglass
Boston University

Like other syndromes of aphasia, conduction aphasia has a prototypical form that is easy to identify by standard examination procedures. It also appears in mixed and residual forms that expose the ambiguities in the definition of the disorder and in the concepts of its underlying cause. We treat the question of diagnosis and evaluation from the point of view that the "true nature" of conduction aphasia is not established, but that there is sufficient commonality among the instances of a recurring symptom configuration to justify a "working definition" for the disorder; further, that there is sufficient concurrence of lesion sites among these cases to justify the use of lesion data as confirmatory of behavioral data in making a diagnosis.

Conduction aphasia is the only one of the major syndromes of the classical writers whose existence was postulated on theoretical grounds before it had been observed clinically. Wernicke (1874), in the first version of his anatomo-associationistic model, proposed the possibility of a disconnection between an auditory language center and a motor speech center. Such a disconnection, he thought, would result in errors of word choice and difficulties in word finding, because the auditory representation of the word could not be conveyed to the motor speech center in the frontal language zone. Patients would perceive and recognize their errors perfectly well but would not be able to correct them. When Lichtheim (1885) published his elaboration of Wernicke's schema, he claimed, by sheer deduction, that the pathway between the auditory language center and the motor speech center was the pathway for repetition of auditorily perceived speech. Its interruption produced conduction aphasia, defined as a disorder of repetition. Wernicke himself subsequently endorsed this view.

The concept of conduction aphasia as a repetition disorder was soon strongly entrenched in the literature. Yet, in his monograph, Freud (1891) used this syndrome as an instance of a form that existed only in the Wernicke–Lichtheim model but had no clinical reality.

Clinical confirmation, however, was not long in coming. Stertz (1914) and Liepmann and Pappenheim (1914) reported cases of conduction aphasia. Goldstein (1911) equated conduction aphasia with what he preferred to call *central aphasia*. Numerous clinical descriptions appear in the subsequent literature both before and after World War II.

SYMPTOMATOLOGY OF CONDUCTION APHASIA

From the point of view of a bare profile of abilities and deficits, conduction aphasics show the following features:

1. Conversation includes runs of normally articulated words, with generally preserved use of grammatical inflections and syntactic structures. However, speech is marred by more or less frequent errors in the selection and sequencing of phonemes and syllables; these may be omitted, substituted, or transposed, creating "literal paraphasias."
2. Auditory comprehension is relatively well preserved and may even be completely normal.
3. The task of repeating words or sentences after the examiner may be particularly deficient, in comparison with the level of fluency observed in conversation.

Bedside Diagnosis

Because conduction aphasics are never so severely impaired as to preclude conversation, the free conversation provides the first opportunity to listen for features distinctive of this diagnosis. The speech pattern is one in which there are passages of well-articulated, grammatically correct phrases, or even sentences, punctuated by phonological paraphasias. These paraphasias consist of omissions, transpositions, or insertions of sounds or syllables. The patient's monitoring of these errors leads to self-corrective word repetition and to moments of stammering. Unlike Wernicke's aphasics, whose syntax is severely paragrammatic, conduction aphasics make few and relatively minor grammatical errors in free speech.

When an opening conversation reveals a speech output pattern that is suggestive of the foregoing, the bedside procedures that would most quickly "zero in" on establishing a diagnosis of conduction aphasia are picture naming and repetition of words and sentences. Because the phonological output difficulties of these patients are linked to the articulatory planning load, the objects or pictures to be named or repeated should include two-, three-, and four-syllable words. Words that involve the proper ordering of two or three consonants (e.g., baseball, elephant, pocketbook) may be insoluble tongue twisters to conduction aphasics, provoking repeated, often unsuccessful, attempts at self-correction (e.g., baselaw, lacelaw, basecall, casecall. . . .). This self-corrective pattern is labelled *conduite d'approche* in the French literature and is frequently cited as a prominent feature of conduction aphasia.

Testing of single-word repetition should be guided by the same criteria for item choice as picture naming. Because there is no need, in testing repetition, to restrict items to picturable objects, any type of words may be used, including compound words, like "baseball player." Sentence repetition, except for short overlearned phrases, is usually extremely difficult for conduction aphasics in the early phase of their illness.

Formal Test Profiles.   Conduction aphasia may be identified with a high degree of success on aphasia test batteries that explicitly test and score sentence repetition and the incidence of paraphasia of various types, among other variables. Such batteries are the Boston Diagnostic Aphasia Examination (BDAE; Goodglass & Kaplan, 1983) and the Western Aphasia Battery (WAB; Kertesz, 1980).

The BDAE has a Score Summary Profile that allows the raw score on each subtest to be plotted as a percentile score, so that the levels of performance on any measures can be directly compared with each other. It also provides a 5-level severity rating scale and a Profile of Speech Characteristics, all of which are useful in making diagnostic judgments. Most or all of the following criteria should be met for a diagnosis of conduction aphasia on the BDAE:

1. The Severity Rating is rarely below 2. Conduction aphasics are moderately to mildly aphasic, in the sense that they convey their intended message with little assistance.

2. The Profile of Speech Characteristics will usually show ratings of 5 or higher on Phrase Length, Articulation, and Variety of Grammatical Forms. The scale for Auditory Comprehension is at least 4—usually higher. The value on the Repetition scale must be lower than that for Auditory Comprehension. The scale for "Paraphasia in Running Speech" will show that such errors do occur—their frequency depending on the severity of conduction aphasia. The scale for word finding may range from the midpoint to "fluent without information" (i.e., conduction aphasia may be compounded by anomia, but it is rarely associated with output of the telegraphic or agrammatic type).

3. The Score Profile Summary will reflect a pattern similar to that of the Rating Scale Profile of Speech Characteristics. The triad of scores that is most distinctive is that Repetition of "High Probability" Sentences is lower than all the Auditory Comprehension subtests, whereas the count of phonemic paraphasias is elevated.

The user of the WAB is provided with a fixed set of numerical limits on critical subtests that can be applied to classify any score pattern unambiguously. By the standards of the WAB, a conduction aphasic has a Fluency rating of 5 to 10; a Repetition score of 0 to 6.9; a Comprehension score of 7 to 10, and a Naming score of 0 to 9. These scores nearly coincide with those for Wernicke's aphasics on all scales except Comprehension, where there is no overlap. On that scale, Wernicke's aphasics may score 0 to 6.9.

Optional and Occasional Features

Geschwind (1970), in his clinical teaching conferences, repeatedly called attention to a number of dependencies between the linguistic status of words to be repeated and the performance of conduction aphasics.

Lexical Versus Grammatical Words.   Conduction aphasics may experience their most spectacular failures when asked to repeat sentences composed primarily of grammatical functors (e.g., "He is the one who did it") as opposed to those dominated by lexical words (e.g., "John is the boy who drove"). Geschwind introduced the test phrase for repetition "No ifs, ands, or buts," which has continued in use in our center as a short screening task for conduction aphasia.

This phrase presents a double hazard. Not only is it constituted of grammatical functors, but it uses these terms as a word list, unsupported by their normal grammatical function in a sentence. As a result, this expression also proves difficult for patients who are not conduction aphasics. It is most convincing as a diagnostic tool if the individual failing on this item has met the "first line" criteria for conduction aphasia (i.e., runs of fluent, grammatically well-formed phrases, interrupted by phonemically disordered word production).

Selective difficulty in the repetition of sentences composed of grammatical morphemes is an occasional, but not a consistent, feature in conduction aphasia. We have never encountered a "false positive"—a patient who had this disparity but did not meet the other criteria for the diagnosis of conduction aphasia.

Paraphrasing.   The repetition of sentences by conduction aphasics is sometimes inaccurate only because they are paraphrased, but without a change in meaning. For example, "The car drove across the bridge" may be repeated as "The car drove over the bridge." Paraphrasing is most likely to affect grammatical functors, but a near synonym may also replace a noun, verb, or idiomatic expression. Paraphrasing is not, by itself, a strong diagnostic indicator of conduction aphasia. It is also encountered occasionally in anomic or Wernicke's aphasics. Provided that other indicators of the diagnosis are present, it may be taken as supporting rather than conflicting with it.

Paraphrasing is of special interest because it is unrelated to the primary symptom of disordered sequencing of phonemes or syllables. It may, instead, be a product of reduced auditory short-term memory in conduction aphasia. Whereas the patients' on-line auditory-processing of the sentence meaning may be adequate, verbatim retention of the morphological elements of grammar may be the most vulnerable to retention problems, because these elements do not carry a semantic tag and can therefore most readily be replaced without an effect on meaning.

Special Status of Numbers in Repetition. Following Geschwind's original observation, we have continued to note that conduction aphasics are much less likely to produce phonemic paraphasic errors in repeating numbers than non-number words. Single morpheme numbers are usually repeated perfectly, whereas two- and three-place numbers commonly elicit substitutions (e.g., "seven twenty-four" for "seven thirty-one"); that is, conduction aphasics usually make semantic substitutions in repeating numbers, but phonemic substitutions in repeating other words. This dissociation may be highlighted if the patient is asked to repeat an expression containing a number and a non-number word, such as "seventy-five dollars."

Borderline Cases

In the foregoing sections, we have dealt with the diagnosis of conduction aphasia solely on the basis of the signs to be expected in the typical case of moderate severity. We now place conduction aphasia in the context of mixed and borderline syndromes that share some of its features.

It has been noted that conduction aphasia rarely entails more than a moderate impairment of communication. One reason for this is that the lesion producing it is relatively small, compared to lesions associated with the most common neighboring syndrome—Wernicke's aphasia. Thus, in the prototypical instance of conduction aphasia, there is a lesion in the supramarginal gyrus, or in the insula, but Wernicke's area is either completely spared or only slightly involved. Proponents of the "disconnection" view of the anatomy of this disorder hold that the supramarginal gyrus lesion involves the *arcuate fasciculus,* which appears to carry fibres from Wernicke's area to the frontal speech zone. Thus, the arcuate fasciculus would be the actual anatomic realization of the connection postulated by Wernicke and Lichtheim between the auditory and motor speech areas. However, the clinical picture of conduction aphasia has also been observed with lesions in the temporal lobe, rather than in the supramarginal gyrus (Green & Howes, 1977).

Many patients who develop conduction aphasia present initially with the symptoms of Wernicke's aphasia: impaired auditory comprehension and copious paraphasic speech. In the course of the weeks immediately following their stroke, they show considerable recovery of comprehension, whereas semantic and neologistic paraphasias disappear from their output and they remain with the literal paraphasia that is the marker for conduction aphasia.

It is generally assumed that the regression from the more encompassing symptoms of Wernicke's aphasia to the restricted symptomatology of conduction aphasia corresponds to the subsidence of brain edema. Post-stroke edema is the initial tissue reaction to the injury of the stroke, and it involves a considerable area beyond the confines of the permanently damaged site.

Wernicke–Conduction Aphasia.   Upon regression of the most severe features of Wernicke's aphasia (i.e., dense comprehension defect and florid jargon paraphasia), the patients may still be left with an impairment of auditory comprehension that places them below the 50th percentile of aphasics' scores. At the same time, however, their output errors become largely confined to substitutions and transpositions of phonemes and syllables, whereas semantic and paragrammatic speech errors are rarely heard. On testing with picture naming and repetition, these patients show the characteristics of conduction aphasia in the form of multiple attempts to correct their literal paraphasias.

To some aphasiologists, the pattern signified that there was a continuum from the full-blown syndrome of Wernicke's aphasia to that in which speech errors consisted predominantly of phonemic paraphasia. In their terminology, these are all considered varieties of Wernicke's aphasia or jargon aphasia (Alajouanine & Lhermitte, 1964).

In cases that fall on the border, behaviorally, between Wernicke's aphasia and conduction aphasia, it is to be expected that the causative lesion is more extensive than in pure conduction aphasia, including both supramarginal and posterior temporal lobe areas.

Anomic–Conduction Aphasia.   This variant of conduction aphasia is quite different in its clinical presentation from the Wernicke–conduction type. The patient's speech output is severely anomic but otherwise fluent and grammatical, with little or no impairment of auditory comprehension. Phonemically distorted efforts are confined to the substantives that the patient has difficulty in retrieving, whereas the rest of the sentence is free of errors. These patients are totally unable to repeat the desired word when it is offered by the examiner and are unaided by any type of cue. Yet they are fully aware of the inaccuracy of their attempts, recognize the correct word when it is offered, and are highly frustrated by their inability to produce it.

Oral Reading in Conduction Aphasia. Conduction aphasics should always be tested for their oral reading. In some patients, the severe output impairment observed in free conversation, picture naming, and repetition disappears or is greatly ameliorated by the presentation of words or sentences in written form. There are, as yet, no data to indicate whether a difference in lesion site distinguishes those who have spared oral reading from those who do not.

Written Production. The status of writing, particularly spelling, in conduction aphasia has been a subject of theoretical interest. A number of investigators report that the spelling errors produced by their patients parallel the phonological errors of their speech production. The conclusion drawn from these observations is that the patients' retrieved phonological word representations are faulty, and that oral and written output both arise from the same defective phonology. However, as in the case of oral reading, written spelling ability varies among patients. For some conduction aphasics, writing is only minimally affected.

Theoretical Issues Relevant to the Assessment of Conduction Aphasia

Short-Term Auditory Memory. In 1969, Warrington and Shallice published the description of a patient who met the criterion for conduction aphasia, in that his repetition was extremely limited. Tests of auditory short-term memory showed that this patient had an extremely short span for immediate reproduction, whether of digits, word lists, or sentences. Even with short lists, he could produce only the last items on the list. The "primary effect," which also gives an advantage to the opening items on a list for normal individuals, was absent in this patient. Warrington and Shallice argued, on this basis, that conduction aphasia could be accounted for by a defect in auditory short-term memory.

This was a highly controversial position, particularly in view of the usual observation that severe conduction aphasics may be unable to repeat even single words; that they may retain the intended target through many attempts at self-correction and may then ultimately succeed in repeating it. It was suggested that Warrington and Shallice's patient did not have conduction aphasia but suffered from an auditory memory deficit that impaired repetition through a mechanism quite different from that of conduction aphasia.

Nevertheless, this paper prompted others to investigate the role of short-term verbal memory in this disorder. Tzortzis and Albert (1974), for example, found that conduction aphasics were deficient in auditory memory span for pointing sequentially to objects named by the examiner, in comparison with other aphasic patients. In 1971, Warrington, Logue, and Pratt reported two further cases who met the clinical criteria for conduction aphasia, in association with left parietal tumor removals. Both demonstrated a pattern of short-term auditory–verbal memory impairment, as did Warrington and Shallice's earlier patient. Clinical assessment of short-term memory in conduction aphasics in our program has so far revealed impaired retention of auditory–verbal input in every case.

Although decay of auditory memory does not account for failures in single-word repetition nor for phonemic paraphasia, it may well contribute to the severity of patients' failures in sentence repetition. The patient who processes a sentence correctly for meaning but cannot retain its phonological content is most likely to produce a paraphrase that preserves the meaning. As we noted earlier, such paraphrasing is commonly observed in conduction aphasia. The impact of fading phonological memory falls most heavily on grammatical morphemes, which cannot be encoded semantically; hence the propensity for paraphrasing to entail restructuring of syntax, with better preservation of the semantically "full" content words.

Conduction Aphasia as a Speech-Programming Disorder.   Dubois, Hécaen, Angelergues, Maufras de Chatelier, and Marcie (1964) concluded, from their psycholinguistic analysis, that conduction aphasia is a disorder of sequential programming of linguistic elements at the level of word, phrase, or sentence, but that it leaves intact the level of the phoneme. While acknowledging that repetition tasks exaggerate the disorder, they do not conceive of it as a disconnection phenomenon in any way—anatomic or behavioral.

According to the analysis of Dubois et al. (1964), conduction aphasics encounter difficulties when the computational load of ordering the next sequential grouping is too great. For this reason a polysyllabic word that is derived from several morphemes (e.g., "dismemberment") would be much more difficult than an equally long word that is monomorphemic (e.g., "arithmetic"). In the former, there are a series of points of low predictability at each juncture between morphemes; in the latter, the first vowel–consonant pair largely determines the rest of the program. By the same token, a multisyllabic nonsense word is much more difficult than a multisyllabic real word for repetition, because each syllable represents the starting point of a new segment of low predictability.

Dubois et al. provided suggestions that can prove useful in differential diagnosis, based on their interpretation of conduction aphasia. One is a test of antonyms. Conduction aphasics have little difficulty in supplying opposites that use a different root from the stimulus (e.g., true–false; open–close). They have great difficulty in coping with opposites derived by adding a negative prefix to the same stem (e.g., visible–invisible; tie–untie; polite–impolite). This is precisely the reverse of the pattern to be found with anomic aphasics.

At the sentence level, they suggest that compound sentences or short clauses joined by "and" prove more difficult than syntactically simple sentences of similar total length. Here again, their rationale is that each clausal juncture represents a peak of informational uncertainty that will provoke difficulties in programming. The ideas proposed by these authors have not been subjected to systematic study. It is worthwhile to incorporate them in diagnostic testing of conduction aphasics or suspected conduction aphasics for both investigative and clinical reasons.

Conduction Aphasia and Deep Dysphasia. As a final point in this discussion of diagnosis, we contrast conduction aphasia with a form of impaired repetition that has a somewhat different mechanism. Highlighting the differences between the disorders should sharpen the boundaries as to what constitutes conduction aphasia.

In 1983, Michel and Andreewsky described a form of repetition disorder marked by semantic word substitutions, even in single-word repetition. They called this disorder *deep dysphasia,* by analogy with *deep dyslexia.* The analogy lies in the fact that patients with deep dyslexia cannot access the phonological form of a word from its graphic presentation, but they do access the semantics sufficiently to activate a verbal response. Their verbal output sometimes coincides with the written stimulus but sometimes is only related to its meaning (e.g., page → "book") or to its graphic structure (pillar → "pillow"). The authors' analysis of their patient's repetition behavior showed many similarities to deep dyslexia. For example, he was more successful with nouns than with other parts of speech and totally unable to repeat grammatical words.

Katz and Goodglass (1990) reported a detailed case study of a second such patient. His repetition failures took the form of either semantic substitutions (e.g., rug for carpet) or substitutions of phonologically similar but unrelated real words. He did not show any evidence of *conduite d'approche* nor of having short-term retention of the stimulus to guide his efforts. In fact, like Michel and Andreewsky's patient, he complained of having immediately forgotten the sound of the word provided, but being clearly aware of its meaning. On the basis of their analysis, Katz and Goodglass attributed his repetition disorder to two interacting deficits. One was severely impaired short-term phonological memory, which left him, within seconds, without a phonological reference model for repetition. The second was a severe anomia that resulted in a large proportion of semantic paraphasias in visual confrontation naming. According to the authors' analysis, their patient was usually successful in processing the semantic content of the model provided and then trying to name the concept as he had decoded it. The result, as in his confrontation naming, was often a semantic paraphasia.

Deep dysphasia differs from conduction aphasia in the severity of the auditory-verbal memory deficit. The **symptoms** of conduction aphasia—

particularly prolonged self-corrective attempts and confident recognition of the target—are not compatible with the rapid disappearance of a phonological trace. Dubois et al.'s (1964) insistence that conduction aphasia is a disorder in the programming of phonemic or larger sized units goes to the heart of the clinical phenomenon. This is not explainable as a memory disorder. Although we have endorsed the observations that auditory-verbal memory is impaired, this impairment is at a level that interferes only with sentence-level repetition, in patients who meet the basic criteria for conduction aphasia.

The second differentiating aspect of deep dysphasia is the severity of semantic misnaming, which results in the intrusion of semantic paraphasia in repetition. Whereas conduction aphasics commonly have a degree of anomia, semantic misnaming is relatively uncommon; most naming failures involve partial phonological retrieval, or complete word finding failure, with circumlocution.

SUMMARY

The assessment of conduction aphasia is predicated on one's definition of the disorder. We have considered and set aside as unproven the concept that it is fundamentally a disorder of repetition due to a disconnection of the auditory phonological representation in Wernicke's area from the motor realization center (i.e., Broca's area). Rather, we have defined the disorder in terms of a symptom complex that is sufficiently distinctive to be discriminable from other forms of aphasia that share some of its features. Assessment is therefore based on techniques that are most likely to elicit the distinguishing symptoms.

The major and indispensible feature of conduction aphasia is literal paraphasia—transpositions, substitutions, deletions, or insertions of phonemes or syllables in the context of otherwise fluent aphasia. These appear in free conversation, and in tasks of object naming and repetition of words, phrases, and sentences. Conduction aphasia is distinguished from Wernicke's aphasia in the absence of paragrammatic jargon, the reduced number of semantic paraphasias, and the good preservation of auditory comprehension.

REFERENCES

Alajouanine, T., & Lhermitte, F. (1964). Composantes phonemiques et semantiques de la jargonaphasie International Journal of Neurology, 4, 277–286.

Dubois, J., Hécaen, H., Angelergues, R., Maufras de Chatelier, A., & Marcie, P. (1964). Etude neurolinguistique de l'aphasie de conduction [Neurolinguistic study of conduction aphasia]. Neuropsychologia, 2, 9–44.

Freud, S. (1891). Zur auffassung der aphasien: Eine kritische studie. Leipzig: Deuticke.

Geschwind, N. (1970). Unpublished manuscript.

Goldstein, K. (1911). Die amnestische und zentrale aphasie (leitungsaphasie) [Amnesic and central aphasia (conduction aphasia)]. Archiv fur Psychiatrie und Nervenkrankheiten, 48, 314–343.

Goodglass, H., & Kaplan, E. (1983). *Assessment of aphasia and related disorders* (2nd ed.). Philadelphia: Lea & Febiger.

Green, E., & Howes, D. H. (1977). The nature of conduction aphasia: A study of anatomic and clinical features and underlying mechanisms. In H. Whitaker & H. A. Whitaker (Eds.), *Studies in neurolinguistics* (Vol. 3, pp. 123–156). New York: Academic Press.

Katz, R. B., & Goodglass, H. (1990). Deep dysphasia: Analysis of a rare form of repetition disorder. *Brain and Language, 39,* 153–185.

Kertesz, A. (1980). *Western aphasia battery.* London, Ontario: University of Western Ontario Press.

Lichtheim, L. (1885). On aphasia. *Brain, 7,* 433–484.

Liepmann, H., & Pappenheim, M. (1914). Ueber einen Fall von sogenannte Leitungsaphasie mit anatomischen Befund [On a case of so-called 'conduction aphasia' with anatomic findings]. *Zeitschrifft fur Neurologie und Psychiatrie, 27,* 1–41.

Michel, F., & Andreewsky, E. (1983). Deep dysphasia: An analog of deep dyslexia in the auditory modality. *Brain and Language, 18,* 212–223.

Stertz, G. (1914). Ueber die Leitungsaphasie: Beitrag zur auffassung aphasischen Storungen [On conduction aphasia: contribution to the understanding of aphasic disorders]. *Monatsschrifft fur Psychiatrie und Neurologie, 35,* 318–359.

Tzortzis, C., & Albert, M. L. (1974). Impairment of memory for sequences in conduction aphasia. *Neuropsychologia, 12,* 355–366.

Warrington, E. K., Logue, V., & Pratt, R. T. C. (1971). The anatomical localization of selective impairment of auditory verbal short-term memory. *Neuropsychologia, 9,* 377–388.

Warrington, E. K., & Shallice, T. (1969). The selective impairment of auditory short term memory. *Brain, 92,* 885–896.

Wernicke, C. (1874). *Der aphasiche Symptomenkomplex* [The symptom complex of aphasia]. Breslau: Cohen & Weigert.

Chapter 4

CT Scan Lesion Sites Associated with Conduction Aphasia

Carole L. Palumbo
Boston University School of Medicine
Boston V.A. Medical Center

Michael P. Alexander
Braintree Hospital
Boston University School of Medicine

Margaret A. Naeser
Boston University School of Medicine
Boston V.A. Medical Center

Conduction aphasia is a clinical syndrome of impaired language. Patients with conduction aphasia produce normally articulated, sentence-length, grammatical (occasionally paragrammatical) utterances. Their auditory comprehension and reading comprehension are normal or near normal. Spontaneous speech is impaired, marked by word-finding deficits and paraphasic substitutions. Other areas of impairment include poor sentence repetition, recitation, naming, oral reading, and writing. Particularly prominent paraphasic substitution in repetition is sometimes considered to be the defining criterion of conduction aphasia. The paraphasic errors are predominantly phonemic but may be semantic for certain lexical categories (e.g., numbers and functors). Patients are generally aware that they are making paraphasic errors. In attempting to correct the phonemic errors, they may cut off incorrect utterances, or they may repeatedly attempt to produce the troublesome phoneme *(conduite d'approche)*.

The precise nature of the deficit(s) in linguistic operations that underlies this disorder is not known. Disruption of auditory short-term memory and disordered phonological output are the two most frequently suggested mechanisms. Berndt and Caramazza (1981) have even suggested that there may be two forms of conduction aphasia—one based on decreased auditory short-term memory and one based on disordered phonological output (the latter is sometimes called reproduction aphasia). Warrington and Shallice (1969) and Warrington, Logue, and Pratt (1971) studied the immediate memory span of three patients with probable conduction aphasia and lesions in the left supramarginal and angular gyrus areas. All three patients had a specific defect in auditory-verbal short-term memory. The authors concluded that, at least in some patients, the auditory-verbal short-term memory deficit could be responsible for the repetition deficit of conduction aphasia.

Strub and Gardner (1974) reported, however, several features of the repetition defect in conduction aphasia that were incompatible with a simple auditory-verbal span deficit. First, repetition improved when the stimuli were familiar. Second, span was normal when the task involved matching rather than speech production. Third, repetition errors were paraphasias or sequencing problems, not simple omissions beyond span. Strub and Gardner concluded that the repetition deficit associated with conduction aphasia is linguistic, not mnestic.

Heilman, Scholes, and Watson (1976) tested and compared the immediate memory of both Broca's and conduction aphasics. Both groups had a defect in auditory verbal immediate memory. They concluded that a modality specific defect in auditory-verbal immediate memory is not specific to conduction aphasics. Instead, auditory span deficits are common to all aphasics and have no direct relationship to paraphasic speech output.

Current evidence complements the finding of Heilman et al. (1976), insofar as there has been increased support for the notion that conduction aphasia involves disruption to the phonological output system (see Buckingham, this volume). For example, Kohn (1989) concluded that the characteristic production of phonemic paraphasias in conduction aphasia is due to a disruption of the phonemic output buffer.

Theories of the neuroanatomical basis of conduction aphasia have also undergone some evolution. Wernicke originally proposed the existence of conduction aphasia in 1874 based on a theoretical extension of his model of language organization.

Disconnection theories for the anatomical basis of conduction aphasia have been suggested ever since Wernicke (1874) (Benson et al. 1973; Damasio & Damasio, 1980; Geschwind, 1965; Kleist, 1934; Lichtheim, 1885; Liepmann & Pappenheim, 1914). Not all investigators have agreed on the critical disconnection for conduction aphasia. Wernicke believed that the essential connections would be in the insula. Dejerine (1901) subsequently demonstrated that there are connections in the arcuate fasciculus. The arcuate fasciculus is a white matter fiber bundle that originates in the superior temporal gyrus, runs through the white matter deep to the supramarginal gyrus, then continues anteriorly as the most inferior portion of the superior longitudinal fasciculus lying just above the insula and extreme capsule, and terminates in the dorsolateral frontal lobe including operculum. Others have proposed a shorter pathway connecting Wernicke's area to Broca's area. This shorter pathway runs deep to the insula, through the ventral portion of the extreme capsule and terminates in Broca's area. This fiber tract has been identified by Petrides and Pandya (1988). Lichtheim (1885), for example, believed that a lesion of these shorter fibers alone was responsible for conduction aphasia. Current evidence (Benson et al., 1973; Damasio & Damasio, 1980) suggests that both pathways may play a role in functional interactions between Wernicke's area and Broca's area, and that damage to the connections between these two areas is, in some manner, the lesion that underlies the characteristic speech output deficits of conduction aphasia.

Studies including postmortem examination (Benson et al., 1973), radionucleide scans (Kertesz, Lesk, & McCabe, 1977), and CT scan imaging (Damasio & Damasio, 1980, 1983; Kertesz, Harlock, & Coates, 1979; Mazzochi & Vignolo, 1979; Mendez & Benson, 1985) have all identified injury in the posterior perisylvian region as critical to the production of conduction aphasia. In the available reports, however, some variability in precise lesion topography has been observed. In this review, we describe the lesions of nine previously unreported cases of conduction aphasia, review the claims of prior investigators about the lesion of conduction aphasia, and analyze the possible relationship between variations in lesion site and variations in language findings.

SUBJECTS AND DATA COLLECTION

Subjects

We retrospectively examined the language data and CT–MRI scans of nine patients with conduction aphasia after left hemisphere infarcts. The gender, handedness, age at onset, and education of each patient are in Table 4.1.

Language Assessment

The diagnosis was made by criteria of either the Boston Diagnostic Aphasia Examination (BDAE; Goodglass & Kaplan, 1972, 1983) or the Western Aphasia Battery (WAB; Kertesz & Poole, 1974; see Table 4.2). All patients had impaired repetition. As production of paraphasic substitutions with repetition is often identified as the dominant deficit in these patients, specific details about repetition problems are summarized in Table 4.3.

Lesion Analysis

All nine cases had CT or MRI scans. Eight cases had scans done at more than 1 month post onset. Case 4 had only an early postacute scan (4 days post onset) that probably overestimated lesion size because of edema. All nine scans

TABLE 4.1.
Demographic Information for Each Conduction Aphasia Case

Case	Gender	Handedness	Age at Onset	Years of Education
1. CJ	M	R	53	15
2. CW	M	R	57	12
3. WL	F	R	81	12
4. CB	M	R	63	12
5. GA	F	R	71	12
6. NI	M	R	63	12 plus trade school
7. SM	F	R	76	11
8. BG	M	R	60	14
9. FJ	M	R	53	9, then high school equivalency degree

were studied for location of lesion in the major language areas that are represented on the diagram in Fig. 4.1. This diagram illustrates the major cortical language areas, as well as the deeper subcortical areas that contain the white matter pathways connecting the cortical language areas, using the slice labeling system described by Naeser and Hayward (1978). A brief description, and extent of lesion in specific cortical and subcortical areas, of each patient's lesion is provided in Tables 4.4 and 4.5, respectively.

Case Analyses

Case 1. CJ was tested with the BDAE at 1 and 6 months post onset. Spontaneous speech output was normal except for occasional phonemic paraphasias. Auditory comprehension and naming were normal, even at 1-month post onset.

Repetition was impaired. He made only rare phonemic paraphasias at the single-word level, but at the sentence level phonemic paraphasic errors were more prominent. The patient was aware of his errors and was often able to self-correct.

CJ's CT scan was performed at 6 months post-stroke onset (Fig. 4.2). The CT scan revealed a small left hemisphere infarct involving approximately half the insular cortex, with superior extension into the white matter deep to the lower sensory cortex. There is an additional small lesion present in the white matter deep to the anterior supramarginal gyrus.

Case 2. CW was tested with the BDAE at 1, 4, and 8 months post onset. Spontaneous speech output was fluent and grammatical with occasional pho-

TABLE 4.2

BDAE and WAB Phrase Length, Auditory Comprehension, and Naming Scores for Each Conduction Aphasia Case

| | | | BDAE Scores | | | WAB Scores | | |
Case	Testing MPO	Test Administered	Phrase Lenth (7)	Auditory Comprehension % z-score	Visual Confrontation Naming (105 or 114)*	Comprehension AQ (10)	Naming AQ (10)	Boston Naming Test (60)
1. CJ	1	BDAE	7	99%	105	n.a.	n.a.	n.a.
	6	BDAE	7	100%	103	n.a.	n.a.	n.a.
2. CW	1	BDAE	7	65%	70*	n.a.	n.a.	n.a.
	4	BDAE	6	77%	101*	n.a.	n.a.	n.a.
	8	BDAE	7	90%	108*	n.a.	n.a.	12
3. WL	3 weeks	WAB	7	n.a.	n.a.	8.15	4.2	8
	6 weeks	WAB	7	n.a.	n.a.	9.65	6.5	10
4. CB	1	BDAE	5	40%	89	n.a.	n.a.	n.a.
	4	BDAE	6	50%	n.a.	n.a.	n.a.	70/85
	13	BDAE	6	69%	104	n.a.	n.a.	n.a.
	20	BDAE	7	78%	105	n.a.	n.a.	n.a.
5. GA	3	BDAE	5	74%	64*	n.a.	n.a.	n.a.
	6	BDAE	5	82%	74*	n.a.	n.a.	8
6. NI	1	BDAE & WAB	7	incomplete testing	39*	5.9	n.a.	8
	2	WAB	7	n.a.	n.a.	9.45	9.0	51
	4	WAB	7	n.a.	n.a.	9.6	10	55
	7	BDAE & WAB	7	100%	114*	9.5	9.6	57
	8	WAB	7	n.a.	n.a.	incomplete testing	n.a.	59
7. SM	1 week	WAB	6	n.a.	n.a.	9.5	6.6	16
	2	WAB	7	n.a.	n.a.	10	8.3	30
8. BG	3	WAB	7	n.a.	n.a.	9.6	4.0	3
	7	WAB	7	n.a.	n.a.	10	8.9	34
9. FJ	2	BDAE	7	70%	76	n.a.	n.a.	n.a.
	4	BDAE	7	73%	n.a.	n.a.	n.a.	n.a.
	12	BDAE	7	88%	105	n.a.	n.a.	n.a.

*The first edition (1972) of the BDAE had a maximum score of 105 on the Visual Confrontation Naming subtest. The second edition (1983) of the BDAE had a maximum score of 114 on the Visual Confrontation Naming subtest. The subjects with an * next to the visual confrontation naming subtest score are those who were administered the second edition of the BDAE and, therefore, the scores are out of a possible 114 points.

Note: n.a. = > test not administered.

55

TABLE 4.3

BDAE and WAB Repetition Scores and Description of Errors for Each Conduction Aphasia Case

| Case | Testing MPO | Test Administered | BDAE Scores | | | WAB Repetition Score | Types of Errors |
| | | | Single Word Repetition | Phrase Repetition | | | |
			Total Correct (10)	High Prob. (8)	Low Prob. (8)	Total Score (100)	
1. CJ	1	BDAE	9	5	5	n.a.	mainly phonemic paraphasias at both the single-word and sentence level; often self-corrected
	6	BDAE	9	6	6	n.a.	
2. CW	1	BDAE	8	5	2	n.a.	phonemic paraphasias at the single-word level; mainly verbal paraphasias and an occasional neologism at the sentence level
	4	BDAE	8	5	1	n.a.	
	8	BDAE	8	4	2	n.a.	
3. WL	3 weeks	WAB	n.a.	n.a.	n.a.	39	mainly phonemic paraphasias at the single-word level; mainly verbal paraphasias and an occasional aborted attempt at the sentence level
	6 weeks	WAB	n.a.	n.a.	n.a.	52	
4. CB	1	BDAE	7	0	0	n.a.	phonemic paraphasia at the single-word level; mainly verbal paraphasias and some aborted attempts at the sentence level
	4	BDAE	9	0	0	n.a.	
	13	BDAE	9	2	0	n.a.	
	20	BDAE	9	3	1	n.a.	

Subject	Months	Test					Description
5. GA	3	BDAE	6	1	0	n.a.	mainly neologisms and an occasional phonemic paraphasia at the single-word level; mainly verbal paraphasias and an occasional phonemic paraphasia at the sentence level
	6	BDAE	6	0	0	n.a.	
6. NI	1	BDAE & WAB	5	1	2	10	no errors at the single-word level; a verbal paraphasia at the sentence level
	2	WAB	n.a.	n.a.	n.a.	72	
	4	WAB	n.a.	n.a.	n.a.	98	
	7	BDAE & WAB	10	8	6	100	
7. SM	1 week	WAB	n.a.	n.a.	n.a.	68	mainly phonemic paraphasias at both the single-word and sentence level;
	2	WAB	n.a.	n.a.	n.a.	88	
8. BG	3	WAB	n.a.	n.a.	n.a.	24	mainly phonemic paraphasias at the single-word level
	7	WAB	n.a.	n.a.	n.a.	72	both phonemic and verbal paraphasias at the sentence level and an occasional aborted attempt; some *conduite d'approche*
9. FJ	2	BDAE	8	2	0	n.a.	phonemic paraphasias at the single-word level; both phonemic and verbal paraphasias at the sentence level; some *conduite d'approche*
	4	BDAE	8	6	2	n.a.	
	12	BDAE	9	7	7	n.a.	

Note: n.a. = test not administered.

57

TABLE 4.4

CT/MRI Scan Information and Lesion Description
for Each Conduction Aphasia Case

Case	CT MPO	Lesion Description
1. CJ	6	approximately half of the insular region; small portion of the white matter deep to the lowest sensory cortex area and the white matter deep to the anterior supramarginal gyrus
2. CW	6	most of the insular region; small low density in the anterior half of the temporal isthmus; anterior-superior portion of the putamen; anterior supramarginal gyrus and the white matter deep to the supramarginal gyrus; the white matter deep to the lowest motor and sensory cortex and the deeper anterior periventricular white matter deep to the lowest motor cortex for face
3. WL	4 days	small portion of the insular region; approximately half of the anterior temporal isthmus; small portion of the white matter deep to the posterior half of Wernicke's area (less than half of total Wernicke's area is involved); anterior and posterior supramarginal gyrus areas and the white matter deep to the supramarginal gyrus
4. CB	20	very small portion of the insular region; most of the posterior half of Wernicke's area (less than half of total Wernicke's area); anterior and posterior supramarginal gyrus areas and angular gyrus, and the white matter deep to the supramarginal and angular gyrus areas.
5. GA	3	Left hemisphere: very small portion of the insular region; approximately half of the posterior half of Wernicke's area (less than half of total Wernicke's area); extensive involvement of the anterior and posterior supramarginal gyrus areas and the angular gyrus with deep extension into the white matter and periventricular white matter deep to the supramarginal and angular gyrus areas
		Right hemisphere: very small lowest motor cortex area for mouth
6. NI	3	Left hemisphere: approximately half of the insular region; anterior half of the temporal isthmus; patchy involvement of the posterior half of Wernicke's area (less than half of total Wernicke's area); anterior and posterior supramarginal gyrus areas, approximately half of the angular gyrus, and the white matter deep to the supramarginal and angular gyri;
		Additional Left Hemisphere Infarcts: small, lowest premotor cortex; small, white matter deep to lower motor cortex for mouth
		Right hemisphere: small lower premotor and motor cortex areas for mouth and face
7. SM	1	approximately half of the anterior supramarginal gyrus and the white matter deep to it, as well as portions of the periventricular white matter deep to the anterior supramarginal gyrus
8. BG	4	very small, patchy portion of the insular region; patchy involvement of the white matter deep to the anterior and posterior supramarginal gyrus areas
9. FJ	4	small low density across the temporal isthmus; part of the posterior supramarginal gyrus and all of the angular gyrus and the white matter deep to these areas

TABLE 4.5
Extent of Lesion for Each Patient for Specific Cortical and Subcortical Areas

Patient	Ant SMG	Deep to Ant SMG	Post SMG	Deep to Post SMG	Angular Gyrus	Deep to Ang Gyrus	Insular Region	Temporal Isthmus	Wernicke's Area	Other
1. CJ	—	< ½	—	—	—	—	½	< ½	—	WM deep to sensory cortex
2. CW	> ½	> ½	—	—	—	—	> ½	< ½	—	Ant. ⅓ PVWM and WM deep to motor and sensory cortex
3. WL	> ½	> ½	> ½	> ½	—	—	< ½	½	< ½	—
4. CB	> ½	> ½	> ½	> ½	< ½	< ½	< ½	—	< ½	—
5. GA	> ½	> ½	> ½	> ½	> ½	> ½	< ½	< ½	< ½	Right lowest motor cortex
6. NI	> ½	> ½	> ½	> ½	½	½	½	½	< ½	Left lowest premotor cortex; Left WM deep to lower motor cortex for mouth; Right lower premotor and motor cortex
7. SM	½	½	—	—	—	—	—	—	—	—
8. BG	—	½	—	< ½	—	—	< ½	—	—	—
9. FJ	—	—	< ½	< ½	> ½	> ½	—	½	—	—

Note. Ant SMG = anterior supramarginal gyrus; Post SMG = posterior supramarginal gyrus; Ang Gyrus = Angular Gyrus; — = no lesion present; < ½ = less than half of area has lesion; ½ = half of area has lesion; > ½ = more than half of area has lesion.

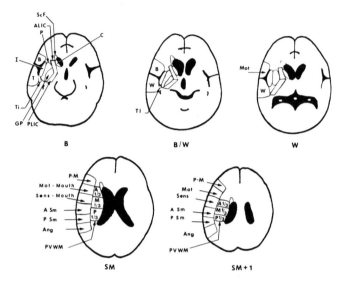

FIG. 4.1. Location of specific neuroanatomical areas on CT scan slices B, B/W,
W, SM, and SM + 1 (Naeser & Hayward, 1978, slice labelling system). Each
neuroanatomical area was visually assessed for presence and extent of lesion.
B = Broca's area (45 on slice B; 44 on slice B/W); T = temporal lobe anterior—
inferior to Wernicke's area on slice B; Ti = temporal isthmus; I = insular structures including insula, extreme capsule, claustrum, external capsule; P = putamen; GP = globus pallidus; ALIC = anterior limb, internal capsule; PLIC =
posterior limb, internal capsule; Sc F = medial subcallosal fasciculus; C = caudate;
W = Wernicke's area (22); Mot = motor cortex; P-M = premotor cortex; Sens
= sensory cortex; A Sm = anterior supramarginal gyrus; P Sm = posterior
supramarginal gyrus; Ang = angular gyrus; PVWM = periventricular white
matter area (A ⅓, anterior ⅓ PVWM; M ⅓, middle ⅓ PVWM; P ⅓, posterior
⅓ PVWM). (Reprinted by permission of Oxford University Press.)

nemic and semantic paraphasias and mild word-finding difficulties. His auditory comprehension was decreased initially, improved at 4 months post onset,
and within normal limits by 8 months post onset.

CW's repetition on the BDAE was good for single words at all test sessions
with the occasional errors being phonemic paraphasias. Repetition for sentences,
however, was impaired at each test session, particularly for the low probability phrases. He made both phonemic and semantic paraphasias and rarely attempted to self-correct.

CW's CT scan was performed at 6 months post-stroke onset (Fig. 4.3). The
CT scan revealed a left hemisphere low density area that involved most of the
insular region. The lesion also involved most of the putamen, and the most
superior portion of the anterior limb of the internal capsule. There was a small
posterior lesion extension across the anterior half of the temporal isthmus.
The lesion had a superior extension that involved the anterior supramarginal

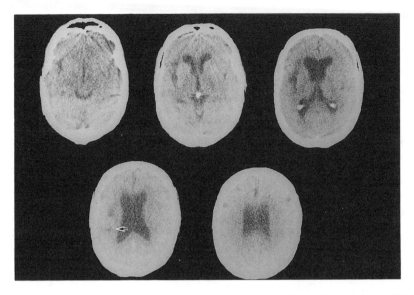

FIG. 4.2. Case 1, CJ. CT scan performed at 6 months post-stroke onset revealed a small left hemisphere infarct involving approximately half the insular cortex. There was superior extension into the white matter deep to the lower sensory cortex. There was additional small lesion in the white matter deep to the anterior supramarginal gyrus area (arrow).

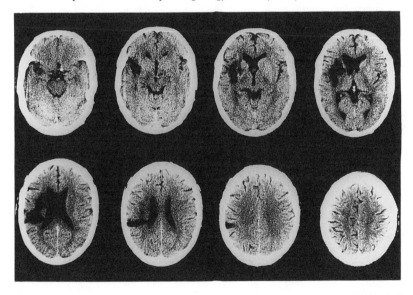

FIG. 4.3. Case 2, CW. CT scan performed at 6 months post-stroke onset revealed a left hemisphere lesion involving most of the insular region with posterior extension across the anterior half of the temporal isthmus. The superior portion of the lesion included the anterior supramarginal gyrus, as well as the white matter deep to the anterior supramarginal gyrus. There is additional deeper extension into the posterior periventricular white matter adjacent to the body of the lateral ventricle. There is additional white matter lesion deep to the lower motor and sensory cortex, as well as the deeper anterior periventricular white matter deep to the lower motor cortex for mouth and face.

61

gyrus. The supramarginal gyrus lesion extended into the white matter deep to the supramarginal gyrus and had an even deeper extension into portions of the posterior periventricular white matter, adjacent to the body of the ventricle. The superior portion of the lesion also involved the white matter deep to the lower motor and sensory cortex areas, as well as the deeper anterior periventricular white matter deep to the lower motor cortex for face and mouth.

Case 3.   WL was tested with the WAB at 3 weeks and 6 weeks post onset. Spontaneous speech output was fluent and grammatical. There were phonemic and semantic paraphasias. She often recognized her paraphasic errors and attempted to self-correct, occasionally doing so successfully.

Auditory comprehension was relatively preserved at 3 weeks post onset and normal by 6 weeks post onset. Naming was severely impaired at 3 weeks and at 6 weeks post onset. Naming errors were predominantly phonemic paraphasias.

Repetition was severely impaired at both tests. At the single-word level she made mostly phonemic paraphasias. At the sentence level she made both phonemic and semantic paraphasic errors.

WL's CT scan was performed at only 4 days post-stroke onset (Fig. 4.4). The CT scan showed evidence of slight pressure effects on the ventricles, probably due to edema surrounding this early post-stroke onset lesion. The lesion that was visible was present in a small portion of the insular area with a patchy posterior lesion extension across the anterior half of the temporal isthmus. The larger extent of the lesion began in the white matter deep to the posterior half of Wernicke's area and continued superiorly into the anterior supramarginal gyrus and the posterior supramarginal gyrus, as well as the white matter deep to the supramarginal gyrus.

Case 4.   CB was tested with the BDAE at 1, 4, 13, and 20 months post onset. Spontaneous speech output was effortful and hesitant, due to word-finding difficulties and paraphasias. It was grammatical and had good sentence length. The paraphasic errors were mostly phonemic.

Auditory comprehension was initially impaired and the diagnosis was on the boundary of conduction aphasia and Wernicke's aphasia. Comprehension improved and by 20 months post onset comprehension was normal. Naming was initially impaired but improved to near normal.

Repetition was severely impaired. Most single words were successfully repeated; errors were phonemic paraphasias. CB had much greater difficulty repeating phrases and sentences. He was unable to repeat any phrases until 1-year post onset. Sentence repetition had not improved, even at 20 months post onset. Errors at the sentence level were predominantly semantic, although occasional phonemic errors were also made.

CB's CT scan was performed at 20 months post-stroke onset (Fig. 4.5). The

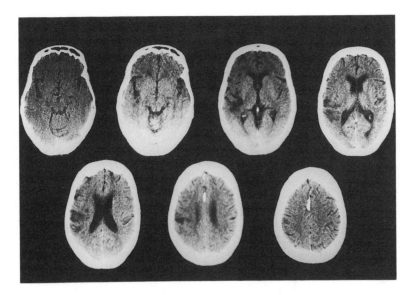

FIG. 4.4. Case 3, WL. CT scan performed at 4 days post-stroke onset, revealed evidence of slight pressure effects on the ventricles, probably due to edema surrounding this acute lesion. There was a left hemisphere infarct that involved
a small portion of the insular area with patchy posterior lesion extension across
the anterior half of the temporal isthmus. Lesion was also present in the white
matter deep to the posterior half of Wernicke's area with superior lesion extension into the anterior supramarginal gyrus and posterior supramarginal gyrus,
as well as the white matter deep to the supramarginal gyrus.

CT scan revealed a left hemisphere infarct that involved a very small portion
of the insular region and most of the posterior half of Wernicke's area (less
than half of total Wernicke's area). The lesion continued superiorly into the
parietal lobe and involved the anterior supramarginal gyrus, the posterior
supramarginal gyrus, and a small portion of the angular gyrus area. The parietal
lobe lesion extended into the white matter deep to the supramarginal and angular gyrus areas, as well as deeper extension into a portion of the posterior
periventricular white matter.

Case 5. GA was tested with the BDAE at 3 months and 6 months post
onset. At 3 months spontaneous speech output was fluent and grammatical
but empty with many phonemic paraphasias. At 6 months post onset speech
output had improved, but several phonemic paraphasias were still noted.

Auditory comprehension was initially moderately impaired but quickly improved to near normal. Naming was very impaired and did not improve significantly. Most naming errors were phonemic paraphasic errors.

Repetition was impaired. At the single-word level, GA made phonemic and

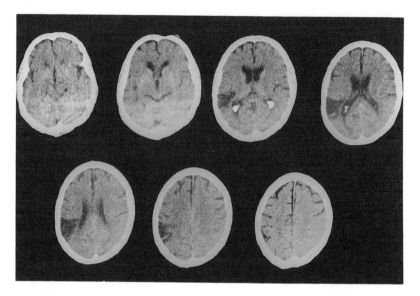

FIG. 4.5. Case 4, CB. CT scan performed at 20 months post onset revealed
a left hemisphere infarct that involved a very small portion of the insular region
and most of the posterior half of Wernicke's area. There is superior lesion extension into the anterior supramarginal gyrus, the posterior supramarginal gyrus, and a small portion of the angular gyrus. The lesion also involved the white
matter deep to these parietal lobe structures, as well as deeper extension into
a portion of the posterior periventricular white matter.

semantic paraphasias. Sentence repetition was nearly impossible due to abun-
dant phonemic and semantic paraphasias.

GA's CT scan was performed at 3 months post-stroke onset (Fig. 4.6). The
CT scan revealed a left hemisphere infarct that involved a very small portion
of the insular region. The larger portion of the lesion involved approximately
half of the posterior half of Wernicke's area (less than half of total Wernicke's
area). This lesion continued up into the parietal lobe and involved all the anterior supramarginal gyrus, the posterior supramarginal gyrus, and most of
the angular gyrus area. This parietal lesion extended into the white matter deep
to the supramarginal and angular gyrus areas, with even deeper extension into
the posterior third of the periventricular white matter adjacent to the body of
the lateral ventricle. This deepest periventricular white matter lesion was adjacent to the posterolateral corner of the body of the lateral ventricle and was
probably interrupting fibers of the auditory contralateral pathways from the
right temporal lobe. This parietal lesion continued up into the superior parietal lobule.

There was an additional very small area of patchy low density in the right
hemisphere that was in the lowest motor cortex area for mouth.

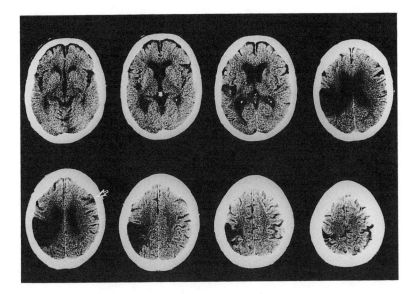

FIG. 4.6.   Case 5, GA. CT scan performed at 3 months post-stroke onset revealed bilateral lesions. The left hemisphere lesion involved a very small portion of the insular region. There was lesion present in a small portion of the posterior half of Wernicke's area with superior lesion extension into the anterior supramarginal gyrus, the posterior supramarginal gyrus, and the angular gyrus. The parietal lobe lesion extended into the white matter deep to the supramarginal and angular gyrus areas, as well as into the posterior periventricular white matter. There was an additional patchy, small right hemisphere lesion in the anterior periventricular white matter deep to the lower motor cortex area for mouth (arrow).

Case 6.   NI was tested with the BDAE at 1 month and 7 months post onset and the WAB at 1, 2, 4, 7, and 8 months post onset.

Spontaneous speech output was initially nonfluent and aggrammatic. He had severe word-finding difficulties and phonemic paraphasias. Over the next several months, speech output became fluent, sentence length, and grammatical, with less word-finding trouble but persistent phonemic paraphasias.

At 1-month post onset comprehension was impaired, but there was rapid improvement. At 2 months post onset auditory comprehension was normal.

Naming also improved rapidly. The errors made initially were mostly phonemic paraphasias. At 4 months post onset naming was within normal limits.

Repetition was initially severely impaired. Errors on single words were phonemic paraphasias. At the sentence level, NI made several phonemic paraphasias, but he also had occasional semantic paraphasias. By 2 months post onset, repetition had improved significantly. Errors were mostly at the sentence level and were mainly phonemic paraphasias. By 7 months post-stroke onset, NI showed no impairment on repetition.

NI's CT scan was performed at 3 months post-stroke onset (Fig. 4.7). The CT scan showed a left hemisphere infarct that involved approximately half of the insular region with posterior extension across the anterior half of the temporal isthmus. There was patchy lesion in the posterior half of Wernicke's area (slightly less than half of total Wernicke's area). The lesion continued superiorly into the parietal lobe and involved the anterior and posterior supramarginal gyrus areas and approximately half of the angular gyrus area. This parietal lobe lesion extended into the white matter deep to the supramarginal and angular gyri. The lesion continued up into the superior parietal lobule. Another area of low density was present in the left hemisphere in the lowest portion of the premotor cortex. There was an additional very small area of low density in the left hemisphere in the white matter deep to the lower motor cortex for mouth. An additional, small, right hemisphere lesion was present in the lower premotor and motor cortex areas for larynx and mouth.

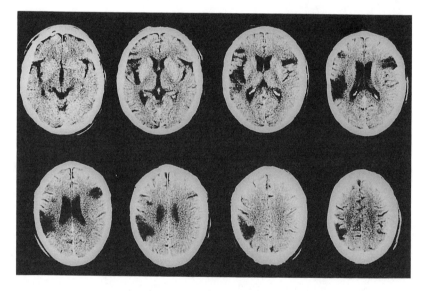

FIG. 4.7. Case 6, NI. CT scan performed at 3 months post-stroke onset revealed bilateral lesions. There was a left temporoparietal lesion that involved approximately half the insular region with posterior extension across the anterior temporal isthmus. There was patchy lesion present in the posterior half of Wernicke's area with superior lesion extension into the anterior and posterior supramarginal gyrus areas and approximately half of the angular gyrus, as well as the white matter deep to the supramarginal and angular gyri. There were two other small left hemisphere infarcts. One was present in the lower premotor cortex area; the other involved a small portion of the white matter deep to the lower motor cortex for mouth. There was an additional right hemisphere lesion that involved the lower premotor and motor cortex areas for mouth.

Case 7. SM was tested with the WAB at 1-week and 2 months post onset. At both testings spontaneous speech output was hesitant but grammatical. Phonemic paraphasias and word-finding difficulties were evident. She was aware of errors and made attempts to self-correct. Auditory comprehension was near normal at 1-week post onset and was certainly normal at 2 months post onset. Naming was impaired but improved by 2 months post onset.

Repetition was moderately impaired at both the single-word and sentence levels. Errors were primarily phonemic paraphasias. There was some improvement by 2 months post-stroke onset. Although her repetition was still impaired during follow-up testing, she did show some improvement.

SM's CT scan was performed at 1-month post-stroke onset (see Fig. 4.8) and revealed a small left hemisphere infarct that involved approximately half of the anterior supramarginal gyrus, as well as the white matter and portions of the deeper periventricular white matter, deep to the anterior supramarginal gyrus, almost to the border of the left lateral ventricle.

Case 8. BG was tested with the WAB several times between 3 and 7 months post onset. Spontaneous speech output was fluent and grammatical but somewhat empty. Phonemic paraphasias were prominent. He was aware of his paraphasic errors and often tried to self-correct but without success.

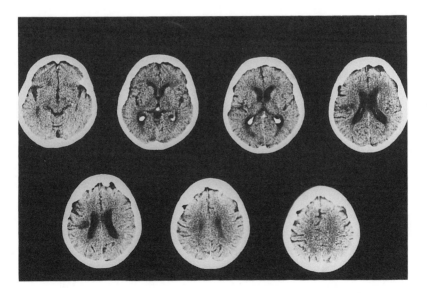

FIG. 4.8. Case 7, SM. CT scan performed at 1-month post onset revealed a small left hemisphere infarct in approximately half of the anterior supramarginal gyrus with deep extension into the white matter and portions of the periventricular white matter deep to the anterior supramarginal gyrus.

Auditory comprehension was within normal limits from the earliest testing session. Naming was initially impaired and, although there was improvement, a moderate deficit persisted to 7 months post onset.

Repetition was initially severely impaired but improved by 7 months post onset. There was phonemic paraphasias for single words and sentences and additional semantic paraphasias at the sentence level.

BG had an MRI scan that was performed at 4 months post-stroke onset (see Fig. 4.9, top and bottom). The T1 weighted axial and coronal images revealed a very small, patchy, hypointense area in a portion of the insular region. There was an additional small, very patchy, hypointense area in the white matter deep to the anterior and posterior supramarginal gyrus areas.

Case 9.   FJ was tested with the BDAE at 2, 4, and 12 months post onset. Spontaneous speech output was fluent and grammatical, but he had word-finding pauses and paraphasias. He was aware of his paraphasic errors and would attempt to self-correct, usually without success. By 4 months post onset, speech output had improved and there were few word-finding pauses and paraphasias. Auditory comprehension was initially mildly impaired, but by 12 months post onset, auditory comprehension was near normal. Naming was initially impaired but by 12 months post-stroke onset was normal.

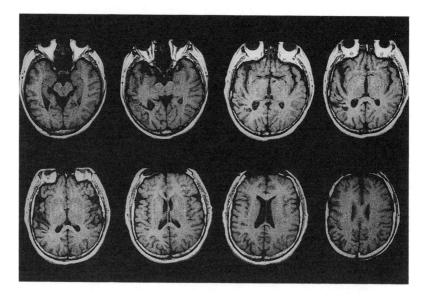

FIG. 4.9., Top.   Case 8, BG. T1 weighted axial MRI scan performed at 4 months post onset revealed a small left hemisphere lesion with patchy involvement in a portion of the insular region. There was very patchy lesion present in the white matter deep to the anterior and posterior supramarginal gyrus areas.

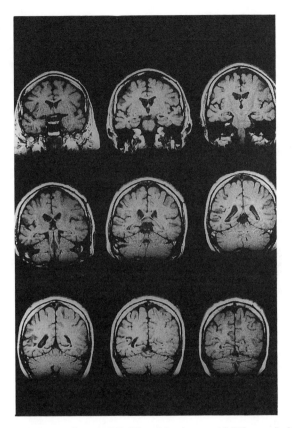

FIG. 4.9., Bottom. Case 8, BG. T1 weighted coronal MRI scan performed at 4 months post onset revealed the same lesion as was seen on the T1 weighted axial image. The coronal image, however, shows the supramarginal gyrus lesion extending deeper into the white matter than did the axial image.

Repetition was initially severely impaired at the sentence level. By 4 months post onset repetition of sentence-length material had improved significantly. At the single-word level, there were rare phonemic paraphasias. At the sentence level, there were both phonemic and semantic paraphasic errors. He recognized his errors and was sometimes able to self-correct. By 12 months post onset, repetition had recovered to near normal. The occasional errors were phonemic paraphasias.

FJ's CT scan was performed at 4 months post-stroke onset (Fig. 4.10). The CT scan showed a left hemisphere parietal lobe infarct in a small portion of the posterior supramarginal gyrus area and all of the angular gyrus area. This lesion extended into the white matter deep to the posterior supramarginal gyrus area and the angular gyrus area. There was an additional small area of low density across the temporal isthmus on the lowest slice of Fig. 4.10.

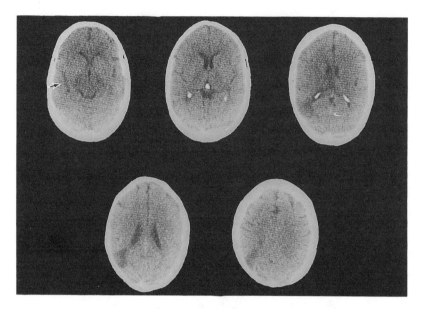

FIG. 4.10. Case 9, FJ. CT scan performed at 4 months post-stroke onset revealed a small lesion across the temporal isthmus on the lowest slice (arrow).
There was lesion present in a small portion of the posterior supramarginal gyrus
and in all of the angular gyrus with deep extension into the white matter deep
to the posterior supramarginal gyrus and angular gyrus areas.

SUMMARY

Aphasia Profile

All nine cases fit the clinical criteria outlined earlier for conduction aphasia.
They had fluent, grammatical speech output with word-finding deficits and
paraphasias, primarily phonemic. Auditory comprehension was normal or, if
impaired initially, rapidly became normal. Repetition of phrases and, in some
cases, single words were impaired. All cases had impaired writing. Of five who
received more detailed assessment, two had phonological agraphia (Cases 2
and 8) and three had mixed phonological and lexical agraphia (Cases 3, 5,
and 6; Roeltgen, 1985).

Lesion Profile

The key region of common lesion in these nine cases was in the inferior parietal lobule, largely centered in the anterior supramarginal gyrus area. Seven
of our nine cases had lesion in at least half of the anterior supramarginal gyrus

area, the white matter deep to this area, or the insula. In one case (Case 9), neither the anterior supramarginal gyrus area nor the insula was involved, but more than half of the angular gyrus area and a small portion of the posterior supramarginal gyrus area were involved, as well as the white matter deep to these areas. Case 1 had extensive lesion in the insula, and only a small lesion in the white matter deep to the supramarginal gyrus area. Thus, despite some local variability in lesion site, all cases had damage to neural systems centered in the shallow white matter system of the inferior parietal lobe. This would include short association pathways as well as the arcuate fasciculus deep to the supramarginal or postrolandic gyri.

In addition to repetition deficits, our patients had phonemic paraphasias that were prominent in spontaneous speech, recitation, naming, and oral reading. In the five cases studied in sufficient detail, similar errors were observed in writing, and none of the five cases could write even short pseudowords. Thus, they all had characteristics of phonological agraphia (Roeltgen, 1985), two in near isolation (Cases 2 and 8). Many of our patients had these pervasive phonological/phonemic deficits with near normal lexical and semantic capacities.

We conclude that the supramarginal gyrus area serves as a major neural focus for phonological/phonemic processes. Clinical deficits are directly related to deficient phonemic capacity caused by damage to parietal cortex or to short association pathways. Small variations in lesions may generate different profiles of impaired phonemics—in speech output, in visual/lexical to phonemic translations (paralexias), in auditory/lexical to phoneme translations (paraphasias), and so forth. Note that this is a different psychophysiological account than the usual one that damage to the arcuate fasciculus disconnects the conduction of phonemic information from temporal to frontal language zones. There are numerous reasons to suspect that explanation. One telling reason is the following: Geschwind (1965) emphasized that a disconnection explanation that supposes that the effect of disconnection is the same no matter what the location of the disconnection. If the frontal operculum or dorsolateral frontal convexity is the "target" of the arcuate fasciculus, then lesions in these regions should also result in prominent phonemic paraphasias, but this lesion is not associated with phonemic errors (Alexander, Benson, & Stuss, 1989).

Lesion localizations in the literature have all centered on the posterior perisylvian region, but some local variations have been described. Benson et al. (1973) described a patient with lesion restricted to posterior superior temporal gyrus. Partial injury to the posterior superior temporal gyrus with additional lesion in the inferior parietal lobe is more commonly reported (Benson et al., 1973; Damasio & Damasio, 1980, 1983; Kertesz et al., 1977). This is likely because the posterior superior temporal gyrus merges directly into the posterior supramarginal gyrus.

Conduction aphasia is sometimes thought to be a resolving stage of Wernicke's aphasia. Although some patients with Wernicke's aphasia will evolve into conduction aphasia profiles, conduction aphasia is not merely mild Wernicke's aphasia (Kertesz et al., 1977). The lesion profiles of conduction and Wernicke's aphasia differ most prominently in that the Wernicke's aphasics have a greater extent of lesion in the superior temporal gyrus than do the conduction aphasics. Results from recent studies have shown that a lesion involving the superior temporal gyrus, but with damage in less than half of Wernicke's area (Naeser, Helm-Estabrooks, Haas, Auerbach, & Srinivasan, 1987) or lesion involving only the subcortical white matter pathways of the temporal isthmus (Naeser, Gaddie, Palumbo, & Stiassny-Eder, 1990), may cause initial deficits in auditory comprehension, but some recovery will occur. Five of our cases had lesion in half or less than half of either the posterior superior temporal gyrus (Wernicke's area) (Cases 4, 5, and 6) or the subcortical temporal isthmus pathways (Cases 2 and 9). All five cases had initial modest impairments in auditory comprehension, but recovered. Four cases had no impairment in initial comprehension and/or lesions in temporal lobe. Hence, our conduction aphasia cases suggest that conduction aphasia patients who do have initial auditory conprehension deficits have lesions present in half or less than half of the superior temporal gyrus area or the temporal isthmus, in addition to parietal lobe lesion.

Only Case 3, WL, had some involvement of Wernicke's area on the CT scan and showed very little initial difficulty with auditory comprehension. There may be several explanations for the finding of relatively preserved auditory comprehension in the acute stages of Case 3, despite the presence of lesion in a portion of Wernicke's area. The most likely explanation is that she had only a very early post-stroke onset CT scan. Early CT scans are not acceptable for detailed analysis of *extent* of lesion within any specific neuroanatomical area. An early CT scan can be used only to determine the *approximate* location and etiology of the infarct. The early CT scan may be showing more low density than is actually involved as part of the infarct, possibly due to edema surrounding an early infarct. An early CT scan also may reveal less of the lesion than is actually present. In our Case 3, it may be that not all the low density that was visible in a small portion of Wernicke's area on the 4-day post onset CT scan was infarcted tissue, but some of it may have been edema that would resolve. In fact, there was evidence of pressure effects on the ventricles on this scan, which implies that there is some edema present at this early period post-stroke onset.

There have been patients reported with extensive lesions in superior temporal gyrus with preserved auditory comprehension but poor repetition (Benson et al., 1973; Kinsbourne, 1971, and our Case 3). Kinsbourne (1971) reported a patient with conduction aphasia including preserved auditory comprehension and a left temporoparietal infarct. Injection of Amytal into his right carotid artery produced a loss of auditory comprehension, but injection into the left carotid artery caused no deficit in auditory comprehension. Kinsbourne concluded that auditory comprehension was being processed by the right hemisphere in this patient. Benson et al. (1973) had described a similar case (their Case 2). In some patients, comprehension is apparently accomplished in the right hemisphere, but the left hemisphere is still essential for phonological output. Mechanisms for this anomalous functional lateralization are unknown.

Additional evidence that temporal pathways to the superior temporal gyrus are critical for comprehension whereas parietal pathways from the superior temporal gyrus are critical for output phonology (including repetition) comes from the literature on subcortical aphasia. Hemorrhagic lesions centered in the putamen can extend posteriorly or superiorly. When the lesion extends posteriorly across the temporal isthmus, comprehension deficits are observed. When the lesion extends superiorly into the parietal white matter, the result is a conduction aphasia profile (Alexander, Naeser, & Palumbo, 1987). Small, exclusively subcortical parietal white matter lesions produce conduction aphasia. This is true whether the lesion is deep to the posterior supramarginal gyrus area (Damasio & Damasio, 1980) or deep to the anterior supramarginal gyrus area (Benson et al., 1973; Damasio & Damasio, 1980; Poncet, Habib, & Robillard, 1987).

Although fluent speech output is a defining feature of conduction aphasia, some cases have had transient nonfluency. Our Case 6, for example, was initially nonfluent and agrammatic. He also had a small left hemisphere lesion in the lowest premotor cortex for mouth and a left subcortical lesion in the white matter deep to the motor cortex for mouth. There was additional lesion in the right motor cortex for mouth, although the relative contribution of this lesion to the initial nonfluency is unknown. Over a few weeks he had complete recovery of fluency. Other patients have a pattern of repeated attempts to correct phonemic paraphasias (i.e., *conduite d'approche*) that interrupts otherwise fluent utterances. The neuroanatomical basis for this speech output style is not known.

Some degree of naming deficit was consistently observed in our patients, but the clinical tests that were available (BDAE, WAB, and Boston Naming Test) do not allow definition of category-specific deficits or even clear measurement of overall severity. We observed no specific relationships between lesion site and severity of naming difficulties.

In summary, the conduction aphasia patients examined in this study had lesion in half or greater than half of at least one of the three following areas: (a) the anterior supramarginal gyrus area or the white matter deep to this area; (b) the angular gyrus area and the white matter deep to this area; or (c) the insular cortex area. Neuroanatomically, these lesions produce disruption between the auditory association cortex and the primary sensorimotor pathways for the bulbar muscles; and/or between the visual association cortex and the primary sensorimotor pathways for the bulbar muscles. Clinically, these lesions produce substantial impairment on the phonological/phonemic output level (both spoken and written), whereas producing less impairment, although variable, on the lexical/semantic level.

ACKNOWLEDGMENTS

This research was supported in part by the Medical Research Service of the Department of Veterans Affairs and by USPHS Grant DC00081, NIDCD.

REFERENCES

Alexander, M. P., Benson, D. F., & Stuss, D. T. (1989). Frontal lobes and language. *Brain and Language, 37,* 656-691.

Alexander, M. P., Naeser, M. A., & Palumbo, C. L. (1987). Correlations of subcortical CT lesion sites and aphasia profiles. *Brain, 110,* 961-991.

Benson, D. F., Sheremata, W. A., Bouchard, R., Segarra, J. M., Price, D., & Geschwind, N. (1973). Conduction aphasia: A clinicopathological study. *Archives of Neurology, 28,* 339-346.

Berndt, R. S., & Caramazza, A. (1981). Syntactic aspects of aphasia. In M. T. Sarno (Ed.), *Acquired aphasia* (pp. 157-181). New York: Academic Press.

Damasio, H., & Damasio, A. R. (1980). The anatomical basis of conduction aphasia. *Brain, 103,* 337-350.

Damasio, H., & Damasio, A. R. (1983). Localization of lesions in conduction aphasia. In A. Kertesz (Ed.), *Localization in neuropsychology* (pp. 231-243). New York: Academic Press.

Dejerine, J. (1901). *Anatomie des centres nerveux* [Anatomy of the nervous centers]. Paris: Reuff.

Geschwind, N. (1965). Disconnection syndromes in animals and man. *Brain, 88,* 237-294, 585-644.

Goodglass, H., & Kaplan, E. (1972). *The assessment of aphasia and related disorders.* Philadelphia: Lea & Febiger.

Goodglass, H., & Kaplan, E. (1983). *Assessment of aphasia and related disorders* (2nd ed.). Philadelphia: Lea & Febiger.

Heilman, K. M., Scholes, R., & Watson, R. T. (1976). Defects of immediate memory in Broca's and conduction aphasia. *Brain and Language, 8,* 201-208.

Kertesz, A., Harlock, W., & Coates, R. (1979). Computer tomographic localization, lesion size, and prognosis in aphasia and nonverbal impairment. *Brain and Language, 8,* 34-50.

Kertesz, A., Lesk, D., & McCabe, P. (1977). Isotope localization of infarcts in aphasia. *Archives of Neurology, 34,* 590-601.

Kertesz, A., & Poole, E. (1974). The aphasia quotient: The taxanomic approach to measurement of aphasic disability. *The Canadian Journal of Neurological Sciences, 1,* 7-16.

Kinsbourne, M. (1971). *Conduction aphasia.* Paper presented at the American Academy of Neurology, New York.

Kleist, K. (1934). Leitungaphasie (nachsprechaphasie) [Conduction aphasia (repetition aphasia)]. In K. Bonhoeffer (Ed.), *Handbuch der artzlichen Erfahrungen im weltkriege 1914/1918* [Handbook of medical experiences during the World War I period, 1914-1918]. Leipzig: Barth.

Kohn, S. E. (1989). The nature of the phonemic string deficit in conduction aphasia. *Aphasiology, 3,* 209-239.

Lichtheim, L. (1885). On aphasia. *Brain, 7,* 433-484.

Liepmann, H., & Pappenheim, M. (1914). Uber einem Fall von sogenannter Leitungsaphasie mit anatomischer Befund [On a case of so-called conduction aphasia with anatomical findings]. *Neurologie and Psychiatrie, 27,* 1-41.

Mazzochi, F., & Vignolo, L. A. (1979). Localization of lesions in aphasia: Clinical CT scan correlation in stroke patients. *Cortex, 15,* 627-634.

Mendez, M. F., & Benson, F. (1985). Atypical conduction aphasia: A disconnection syndrome. *Archives of Neurology, 42,* 886–891.

Naeser, M. A., Gaddie, A., Palumbo, C. L., & Stiassny-Eder, D. (1990). Late recovery of auditory comprehension in global aphasia: Improved recovery observed with subcortical temporal isthmus lesion vs. Wernicke's cortical area lesion. *Archives of Neurology, 47,* 425–432.

Naeser, M. A., & Hayward, R. W. (1978). Lesion localization in aphasia with cranial computed tomography and the Boston Diagnostic Aphasia Exam. *Neurology, 28,* 545–551.

Naeser, M. A., Helm-Estabrooks, N., Haas, M. A., Auerbach, S., & Srinivasan, M. (1987). Relationship between lesion extent in 'Wernicke's area' on computed tomographic scan and predicting recovery of comprehension in Wernicke's aphasia. *Archives of Neurology, 44,* 73–82.

Petrides, M., & Pandya, D. N. (1988). Association fiber pathways to the frontal cortex from the superior temporal region in the rhesus monkey. *The Journal of Comparative Neurology, 273,* 52–66.

Poncet, M., Habib, M., & Robillard, A. (1987). Deep left parietal lobe syndrome: Conduction aphasia and other neurobehavioural disorders due to a small subcortical lesion. *Journal of Neurology, Neurosurgery, and Psychiatry, 50,* 709–713.

Roeltgen (1985). Agraphia. In K. M. Heilman & E. Valenstein (Eds.), *Clinical neuropsychology* (pp. 75–96). New York: Oxford University Press.

Strub, R. L., & Gardner, H. (1974). The repetition defect in conduction aphasia: Mnestic or linguistic? *Brain and Language, 1,* 241–255.

Warrington, E. K., Logue, V., & Pratt, R. R. (1971). The anatomical localization of selective impairment of auditory verbal short-term memory. *Neuropsychologia, 9,* 377–387.

Warrington, E. K., & Shallice, T. (1969). The selective impairment of auditory verbal short-term memory. *Brain, 92,* 885–896.

Wernicke, C. (1874). *Der Aphasische Symptomencomplex* [The symptom complex of aphasia]. Breslau, Poland: Cohn & Weigart.

Chapter 5

Phonological Production Deficits in Conduction Aphasia

Hugh W. Buckingham
Louisiana State University

The purpose of this chapter is to present, evaluate, and interpret recent investigations of phonemic paraphasia as it is manifested in conduction aphasia (CA). Although phonemic paraphasia has been observed in other aphasic syndromes, it represents the *primary* linguistic deficit in conduction aphasia. The production model that serves as the primary vehicle for characterizing the phonemic paraphasias in CA is that of Merrill Garrett (e.g., 1988, 1990a). This model has been constructed on the basis of spontaneous speech in which slips-of-the-tongue have occurred, and so the spontaneous speech of CAs is considered. However, because much of the data on phonemic paraphasias in CA has been garnered at confrontation testing in neuropsychological and clinical laboratories, I also consider various stimulus–response elicitations collected experimentally. Some of the typical tasks utilized are repetition, object naming, and oral reading. Paraphasic production on these tasks is characterized as well by the Garrett model, with several distinct control factors taken into account, because responding to experimental stimuli is cognitively driven somewhat differently from responding to normal spontaneous speech stimuli in typical discourse settings; that is, the ideational–message level processing is different for spontaneous speaking versus responding on confrontational testing. I also consider the phonemic paraphasias produced in self-repairs of errors, either in spontaneous speech or on confrontation elicitation. Self-repair through self-monitoring has been studied under the heading of "sequential phonemic approximation" or "*conduite d'approche.*" Aphasia researchers have gained a great deal of information on phonemic paraphasia by the analysis of these self-repairs. The basic issue addressed, however, is whether and to what extent we can locate some level or levels in the Garrett model that serve to uniquely capture the phonemic paraphasic component in the language of conduction aphasics.

PHONEMIC PARAPHASIA AS THE SINE QUA NON
OF CONDUCTION APHASIA

What we have in CA is essentially a fluent disorder, by which I mean a disorder in the phonological system that is prephonetic. Put another way, the segmental paraphasias of CA arise prior to processes that impart greater motor-articulatory detail. Later in the chapter, however, I must temper this strict dichotomy.

I now provide a brief typology of phonemic paraphasias, greater detail for which can be found in Buckingham (1989). The basic accepted catalog of errors is substitution, addition, omission, and transposition. These types of derailments are considered to take place before any lower level allophonic or allomorphic accommodations are computed.

Many substitutive and additive errors involve segments that originate in the relatively close-order context of the error and therefore are, in reality, transposition errors. These must be clearly distinguished from substitutions and addition that have no such clear-cut sources.

The "no-source" substitution and addition errors have been relatively intractable, because the origin of those errors is much more recondite. Mac-Neilage, Hutchinson, and Lasater (1981) and Shattuck-Hufnagel (1979) suggested that the substituting segment's source is perhaps to be found in the representation of a competing or alternative word that somehow finds itself, albeit partially, in the speech plan. Shattuck-Hufnagel (1979) also considered the possibility that the intrusive segment was indeed in the context but was not recorded when the error datum was initially observed.

Three additional suggestions for the "no-source" error exist. First, Shattuck-Hufnagel (1979) considered the possibility that something derailed when the representative form was being "copied" (more on the mechanism that performs this operation later) onto utterance order, syllable templates. Second, and extremely difficult to demonstrate in a clear-cut way, Shattuck-Hufnagel (1979) considered the possibility that some feature of a segment in the surrounding segmental material interferes with, or in some way contaminates, the segmental array being processed. Note that recourse to the feature level in characterizing speech errors (whether in normals or in aphasics) is notably slippery business (Shattuck-Hufnagel & Klatt, 1979), except for some of the recent proposals from theories of "underspecification" in phonology, which I treat later.

In fact, the theory of underspecification now provides still another reasonable hypothesis for the no-source phonemic substitution (Beland, Caplan, & Nespoulous, 1990). If, at the underlying level, segments are minimally specified in terms of their ultimate feature values, there will be a point in any production model operating under this theoretical assumption where the additional features will be filled in or specified. At this point, any error in feature specification would result in a segment other than the target—the consequences resulting in a phonemic substitution.

Yet another possibility is that the phonemic substitution is created by the perceptual processes of hearers—the so-called "phonemic false evaluation" (see Buckingham & Yule, 1987), which I mention later when I discuss the more motorically involved CAs.

Omission errors also occur as phonemic paraphasia, but again the new context set up by the deletion of some segment will be accommodated by the later phonetic-level processes. Most often, consonants are deleted, especially when they occur in clusters. On the other hand, a consonant rarely, if ever, deletes if it is in intervocalic position (Beland, 1990).

The linear transposition error has been observed often in slips-of-the-tongue as well as in phonemic paraphasia. Transposed segments may move from left to right or from right to left. They may move, leaving their original position empty, or they may remain as well in their original slots, forming the so-called "doublet." Often a slot left unfilled by a movement will be filled by some other segment that moves into that position (see Lecours & Lhermitte, 1969, for one of the earliest investigations of doublet creations and phonemic paraphasia in general). Again, the linear phonemic paraphasias are produced prior to phonetic accommodation, and so newly created contexts will receive the required allophonic and allomorphic specifications.

Phonemic paraphasias do not occur haphazardly. In fact, there are very rigid constraints under which they are produced. In the first place, few if any phonemic paraphasias result in unpermitted morphotactic sequences. Second, when segments are transposed across word and syllable boundaries, those segments practically always end up in syllable slots analogous to the slot in which they originated. However, if there is a close-order consonantal transposition within a syllable, then some coda, for example, may move to the onset slot (Blumstein, 1978). Moreover, predictably, ambisyllabic consonants have a freer range over which to move. The very nature of the ambisyllabic consonant is such that it shares onset and coda properties, and therefore it would be reasonable for it to be capable of moving to either type of syllable slot (e.g., Stemberger, 1982). In addition, many of the so-called sonority constraints hold as well for phonemic paraphasias (Buckingham, 1990a).

The range of segmental material over which phonemic transpositions may move is of crucial importance to the analysis of ordering errors, and the establishment of this range (or ranges), as we see later, is of primary concern in the investigation of phonemic paraphasia in CA. Phonemic transpositions in aphasia have been noted to occur within syllables (e.g., Blumstein, 1978), within words (e.g., Buckingham, 1986; Caplan, Vanier, & Baker, 1986; Pate, Saffran, & Martin, 1987), and across contiguous words (e.g., Kohn & Smith, 1990), interphrasal (within noun phrases or verb phrases), and cross-phrasal (across the major NP–VP break in a clause (e.g., Buckingham & Kertesz, 1976). The question, of course, is do CAs reveal transpositions across all these ranges.

The Garrett Model

Merrill Garrett's (1990a) model for sentence production has increasingly come to be used as a way to capture the similarities, where they exist, between slips-of-the-tongue in normals and paraphasic derailments of aphasics (e.g., Buckingham, 1980; Caramazza & Hillis, 1989; Kohn, 1984; Nespoulous, Joanette, Ska, Caplan, & Lecours, 1987; Saffran, 1982; Saffran, Schwartz, & Marin, 1980; Schwartz, 1987) and Garrett, himself, has extended his model to characterize and locate the linguistic breakdowns in aphasics (e.g., Garrett, 1982, 1984).

The Message Level of this model does not concern us except for the fact that it is the driving force of sentence production in spontaneous speech. Message Level information contains the pragmatic specification of the production, items such as choice of speech act and the manipulation of the informational structure of the message such as ongoing information buildup, world knowledge (i.e., given vs. new information). Decisions such as how to get hearers to draw implicatures by flouting maxims in certain ways (irony, metaphorical usage, etc.; Grice, 1975) is established at this level. Practically everything that has been postulated to occur at the Message Level has been focused on accounting for normal, spontaneous, within discourse context sentence production (see Garrett, 1990b, for further comments). The question we ask later is how the Message Level is active in confrontation responses, and how that level interacts with the various sensory modalities to which stimuli may be presented in order to elicit a language production response: repetition, naming, oral reading.

The Functional Level of the Garrett model interacts directly with the information structure at the Message Level and sets out the specific argument structure. Here, the predicates and their arguments are selected (or "appreciated") solely on the basis of meaning, not form, and they are structured in purely functional and logical terms (selection here is often referred to as the "first lexical lookup"); that is, at the Functional Level, there is no phonological form, nor is there any utterance order syntax. The argument structure is in terms of f(x) formulations (see Grimshaw, 1990, for a full treatment of argument structure in linguistic terms). Once a lexical item at the Functional Level is established, a so-called "linking address" is set up that contains crucial information for ultimate form appreciation: initial phonetic shape of the word, stress location (at least tonic accent), and syllable length (Garrett, 1984). Thus, the linking address serves to connect the formless lexical item at the Functional Level with the phonological lexical item at the next lowest level, the Positional Level.

The computations that map the Functional Level onto the Positional Level are crucial for an understanding of aphasic breakdown, because it appears that many of these processes are disrupted as a consequence of brain damage. At the Positional Level, syntactic matrices, with superimposed intonational contours, are computed. The first question that arises is what is the range of these matrices? Are they all and only clausal length, are they basically computed phrase by phrase (i.e., first the NP, then the VP), is there a simultaneous unfolding of the full NP–VP clause? Could there be circumstances when the matrix to be built is for one lexical item? Because the driving–control capability rests at the Message Level, commands or one-word responses could be driven in such a way that the matrix set up at the Positional Level would be a slot for one word. At the Positional Level, there would certainly be no need for a fully specified matrix, with only one position filled. On the other hand, there would have to be some way to mark the so-called "empty categories" that have "traces," "PRO," and the like. Grodzinsky (1990) argued persuasively for trace markings at what must be the Positional Level to account for certain syntactic problems with patients exhibiting agrammatism. In any event, the maxima and minima for the matrix that is established at the Positional Level must be very carefully scrutinized.

Content word selection based on form is one of the principal computations that run off at the Positional Level (often referred to as the second lexical lookup). According to the model, the phonological form of the lexical item to be selected is accessed in some way through the linking address, originally established at the Functional Level at lexical lookup 1. Form must ultimately be linked to meaning in the production process; lookup 2 is a very reasonable juncture for this coalescence. The content words selected at the Positional Level are not only wholistically geared to be slotted in their respective matrix positions, but the individual segments of those content words must be undergoing manipulation for utterance ordering slotting onto something we understand to be syllabic templates. Most theories (e.g., Levelt, 1989) posit three syllable positions per underlying syllable specification—regardless of whether ultimately at the surface the syllable shape is V, CV, VC, CVC, or is V with an onset or coda cluster. Setting up the templates in this fashion will provide the so-called "empty slots," to which moved segments can transpose.

At this point in the Garrett model, I have claimed that the scan copier and checkoff monitor (and perhaps the error monitor) mechanisms suggested by Shattuck-Hufnagel (1979) must be added to actually carry out the computations that map those segments onto their utterance order positions at the Positional Level (see Fig. 5.1). For purposes of accounting for abstruse neologisms, I have suggested elsewhere that Butterworth's Random Generator be placed among the computations at this level (e.g., Buckingham, 1985, 1987, 1990b;

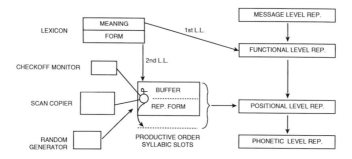

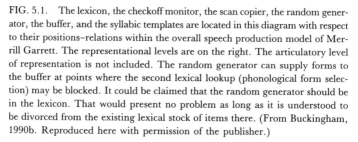

FIG. 5.1. The lexicon, the checkoff monitor, the scan copier, the random generator, the buffer, and the syllabic templates are located in this diagram with respect
to their positions–relations within the overall speech production model of Merrill Garrett. The representational levels are on the right. The articulatory level
of representation is not included. The random generator can supply forms to
the buffer at points where the second lexical lookup (phonological form selection) may be blocked. It could be claimed that the random generator should be
in the lexicon. That would present no problem as long as it is understood to
be divorced from the existing lexical stock of items there. (From Buckingham,
1990b. Reproduced here with permission of the publisher.)

see Fig. 5.1). The syntactic slotting for lexical-sized units is tightly bound to
the processes that order the individual segments of those lexical items.

The segments are still abstract at the Positional Level, even though they
may have picked up additional redundant features not present in the underlying minimally specified level of lexical representation. For example, if some
coronal consonant such as /t/ (of the word *ten*) does not have [+ cor] in its underlying specification, it will pick that feature up in the mapping process at
this level. Note, however, that an even lower level feature of /t/ (providing
we are deriving a syllable-initial /t/ of a stressed syllable in English), such as
[+ aspirated], will *not* be specified at the Positional Level. The further specification of allophonic features must await the Phonetic Level. This is an important point to consider later in the chapter.

The range over which the scan copier manipulates phonemic segments becomes very important in the analysis of CA, which we see later. There is a
good deal of evidence that segmental ordering errors in slips-of-the-tongue cover
ranges from phrases (NPs, VPs) to clauses (NP + VP); that is, segments can
move within phrases as well as across major NP + VP boundaries (e.g., Fromkin, 1980; Garrett, 1980). Aphasic movement errors may also cross these spans
(e.g., Buckingham, 1985). In CA, as we see later, there is evidence that segments may move at least between contiguous words. Some investigators have
observed a tendency to restrict the transposition range to a single lexical item.
Some see more left to right movement; others see more right to left movement.

It is also not clear that the productive mechanism for segmental ordering
in all cases must be obliged to operate across phrase or clause boundaries. For

example, for holophrastic productions (the phonological word, which under-lies, is comprised of more than one lexical unit) or for any other single word production, the syntactic range at the Positional Level will have one slot, and, consequently, any ordering derailment will be restricted to that word. This can obviously be the case in spontaneous speech where the Message Level control, given the pragmatics of the situation, drives a single-word production. I argue later that confrontation testing will, itself, force the restriction of the matrix range down to the level of the word (single-word repetition, object naming, single-word oral reading, and other such tasks that focus on isolated lexical items).

The final point to emphasize is that at the Positional Level any derailment of lexical segments will be preallophonic and preallomorphic; that is, every-thing will be prior to phonetic accommodation, which brings us to the Phonet-ic Level in the Garrett model.

As Garrett put it, "regular" phonological processes map the Positional Level onto the Phonetic Level. These are understood to be the processes that specify the required shapes for allophones and allomorphs. For example, morpheme shifts at the Positional Level will pick up their accommodated allomorphic reali-zation at the Phonetic Level. If for some reason, the third person singular verb morpheme in *He hits ten* moves to the end of *ten,* then the phonetic shape of that morpheme will be /-z/, not the /-s/. This accommodation *must* wait for the error to take place, so to speak. Likewise, if the /s/ of *stick* deletes at the Positional Level, the /t/ will pick up its allophonic feature [+ aspirated] at the Phonetic Level. Normal processing at the Phonetic Level will also make sure that syllable initial consonants are produced with the proper voice onset tim-ing constraints, that vowels preceding nasals are nasalized, and that vowels preceding final voiced consonants are longer than those same vowels in front of final voiceless consonants. Underlying /t/ versus /d/ contrasts in certain pho-netic environments will be neutralized to the alveolar flap at the Phonetic Lev-el, and a whole host of additional phonetic phenomena.

As a consequence of the processes that are localized at the Phonetic Level, any derailments here will, by definition, result in phonetic abberations and will predictably sound apraxic (see Rosenbek, McNeil, & Aronson, 1984). True phonetic disintegration, aphemia, or anarthria (e.g., Lecours & Lhermitte, 1976) will be the result of computation breakdowns at the Phonetic Level. Fur-thermore, the resulting speech output will not be typically fluent in any sense.

Finally, to round out the Garrett production model, the Phonetic Level maps onto the Motor–Articulatory Level. These processes involve the various com-mands to the neural centers of the lower nuclei, which result in signals to the motor neuron groups that subsequently innervate the muscular structures of the speech track. Derailments here involve the full range of dysarthric abberations—spastic and flaccid, well treated recently in McNeil, Rosenbek, and Aronson (1984). It goes without saying that this level is not involved in the syndrome of CA.

Extensions and Refinements of the Garrett Model

For a full discussion of CA within the Garrett model, certain refinements and extensions to that model must be considered. As mentioned previously, S–R confrontation tasks have provided so much of the data points in the analysis of the aphasias that any message-level-driven production model must allow for stimulus intervention at some point. Models set up to account for confrontation elicited responses are like those in Caplan, Vanier, and Baker (1986) or Rapp and Caramazza (1991). Caplan et al. (1986) established a component for modality-neutral underlying phonological representations as a revision of the classical connectionist model of the 19th-century diagram makers (see Fig. 5.2). In the Caplan et al. (1986) study of a reproduction CA, the authors looked at single-word productions on naming, repetition, and reading aloud. Essentially, they found quite similar errors on all three types of confrontation tests. This led to the positing of auditory and visual inputs into a model, with no mention of Functional or Message Levels above. The visual input was mediated by an abstract letter identification component, which in turn feeds into

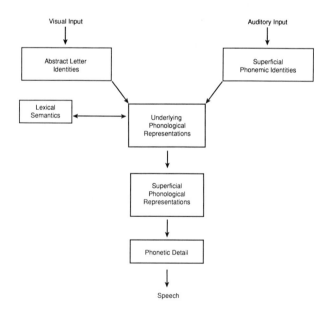

FIG. 5.2.   This is a revision of Wernicke's model. In this revised model, abstract letter identities, superficial phonemic identities, and lexical semantics are all necessarily linked to the underlying phonology. Here, word recognition and production map onto a common stage of phonological representations. However, these representations are far more abstract than those of the older connectionist models of the "diagram makers." (From Caplan, Vanier, & Baker, 1986. Reproduced here with permission of the publisher.)

the underlying phonological representation component. That component is also accessed by auditory input, mediated through a component responsible for superficial phonemic identifications. The underlying phonological representations have access to lexical semantic knowledge, which is connected but separate. These authors located the CA breakdown in the mapping between the underlying phonological representations (again, modality neutral) and the superficial phonological representations, which in turn are mapped onto a level of phonetic detail.

Clearly, Garrett must admit to more detail in the lexicon, showing components containing lexical semantic representations as well as the underlying phonological representations. Of course, these types of components are understood to be there by Garrett, for without them there could be no lexical lookup 1 or 2. What must be added are the sensory–perceptual routes to the underlying phonological representations through the graphemic and phonemic perceptual recognition (identification) systems.

Rapp and Caramazza (1991) have three input sources: orthographic, phonological, and visual (nongraphemic; see Fig. 5.3). All sensory inputs run through a semantic system, which in turn feeds into either an orthographic or a phonological output lexicon. Again, all the inputs seem to be located below any Message or Functional Level components, although the semantic system is certainly

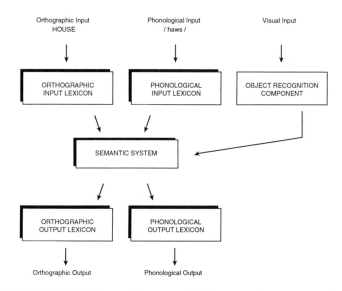

FIG. 5.3. The lexical processing system, including processing components that allow for the mapping of graphemes to phonemes in reading as well as for the assembly of graphemes from phonemes in writing. A component for object recognition is also depicted for nonlinguistic visual input. (From Rapp & Caramazza, 1991. Reproduced here with permission of the publisher.)

understood to be located in Garrett's scheme at the Functional Level. Rapp and Caramazza's (1991) input lexicons (phonological and orthographic) are there to handle all the experimental confrontation testing that involves the various kinds of stimuli introduced to the subject to elicit a language production response. Their object recognition component mediates the visual presentation of objects or other visual (nongraphemic) items such as scenes to be named or described. That component feeds into the semantic system, which in turn feeds into the two typical output lexicons: orthographic (for writing) and phonological (for speaking). Rapp and Caramazza's (1991) phonological output lexicon, Caplan et al.'s (1986) underlying phonological representations that lead to "speech," and Garrett's form lexicon are basically the same. Rapp and Caramazza (1991) made a crucial point when they write:

> It is not the case that different components exist to perform different tasks, but rather that each component has a certain FUNCTION and whenever that function is required for any task, the component is utilized. Thus, the same phonological output component is recruited in the tasks of oral reading and spontaneous speech, although the former task involves the use of the orthographic input lexicon whereas the latter does not. (p. 186)

Their point is that damage to some component would give rise to impaired performance on *any* task that may require that component.

In any event, Caplan et al.'s (1986) mapping between the underlying phonological representations and the superficial phonological representations or Rapp and Caramazza's (1991) output lexicons would involve mechanisms such as the scan copier and the checkoff monitor (or some kind of equivalent selection and ordering cognitive metaphors). Again, the ranges over which ordering errors take place are discussed later.

In Kohn's (1984) study of phonological disorders of CA, feedback loops from prearticulatory and articulatory programming are set up to loop back through the working memory component. Feedback looping in this manner has always been a possibility for Garrett's model to handle any type of self-repairing or monitoring. Kohn was studying self-repairs on confrontation naming in the "single-word paradigm." She located the CA breakdown among the processes of prearticulatory programing that involved selection and copying. The CAs in her study appeared to access the form from the output phonological lexicon (the underlying representations) at the second lexical lookup but had selection and/or copying errors.

Beland, Caplan, and Nespoulous (1990) would add more linguistic specificity to the processing of segments of the form lexicon in Garrett's model, now having established that Garrett's lexicon must have form component and a meaning component. These authors posit two word-level phonological processes. One involves the computations that fill in redundant distinctive features of segments. Note again that these are redundant *distinctive* features, and, even at this point of filling in of features, features such as [+ aspiration] for English /p/, /t/, and /k/ would not be involved. In actuality, there are three levels of feature specification in this theory: underlying representation (minimal specification), lexical representation (roughly enough specification for phonemic distinction), and surface representation (full specification of all features, redundant and nonredundant, that will map more directly onto articulatory commands).

The second process is that of syllabification. The algorithm used by Beland et al. (1990) is not unlike other syllabic algorithms that have been proposed (e.g., Clements, 1990). Generally, the algorithm begins with rime identification, given skeletal slots marked minimally. Rimes are most often identified when a feature that is typically vocalic is recognized. The algorithm then checks for default rime identification–syncopation and checks for adjacent rimes. At this point, sigma formation establishes the supraordinate syllable node category. Subsequently, onset formation is computed, and lastly coda formation is processed.

Consonantal substitutions in Beland et al.'s (1990) CA (the same reproduction CA as studied in Caplan et al. (1986)) seemed to arise at points in *each* of these processes: at the underlying level, with the minimally specified features, at the point of redundant feature specification, or during the processes of syllabification. An intriguing example of phonemic paraphasia at the level of underspecification involves the special status of [+ coronal] segments (Beland & Favreau, 1989). The feature [+ coronal] is not specified in the underlying structure, and, according to Beland and Favreau (1989), this explains the findings in one of their patients that coronal targets were more likely to be replaced by segments of other places of articulation (i.e., by labials or velars). The phonemic substitution would arise from the specification process where the empty place node (empty for coronal at the underlying level) would be filled with the velar or labial feature. Beland and Favreau (1989) drew an analogy from acquisition data where they noted a strong tendency for the underspecified place of articulation to be replaced by a specified place of articulation. The observation was that in *early* stages of language acquisition coronals are replaced by velars and labials. Beland and Favreau (1989) also noted that doublet creations involving substitution are often characterized by errors where some velar or labial moves and substitutes for a coronal. Viewed in the logic of underspecification phonology, nothing would be able to spread from an underspecified segment, while, on the other hand, something would obviously be able to spread from a specified segment. Therefore, what we see more of are linear assimilations and paradigmatic substitutions of more specified features for less specified features.

When this specified–nonspecified distinction is not observed in other paraphasias, it is likely the case that they have arisen during the syllabification processes; that is, there may be a derailment in laying out a two-syllable word with a structure of CV\$VC, whereby the initial C is erroneously copied again intervocally to form a CV\$CVC, thus leading to a less marked form. The error, however, conforms with syllabic constraints, and thus the reasoning is that errors that respect syllable constraints must at least occur during or after syllabification.

Underspecification and syllabification algorithms as put forth in Beland et al. (1990) are rather recondite processes that do not easily map onto the psycholinguistic mechanisms, such as the scan copier that we have discussed so far. Scan copiers select and order; checkoff monitors erase used items from the buffer, and error monitors may delete items. As I indicated earlier, the errors usually abide by the phonotactic constraints of the language of the aphasic, and in many cases the error reduces the markedness of the target form, although it is not invariably the case. It certainly could be said, and indeed has been said (Buckingham, 1990a), that these psycholinguistic production mechanisms "have knowledge" of markedness, phonotactics, sonority, and the like and operate under their constraints. The result is that the errors will mirror those constraints. Beland et al. (1990, p. 142) seem ready to dispense with these mechanisms. They reason that errors that are predictable in terms of simplifying marked forms indicate that the speakers are using "repair strategies" (provided by phonological competence) to circumvent any problem they may be experiencing in producing the form. The use of the less marked form seems to indicate that the subject has either the underlying knowledge of the syllable structure of the lexical representation or the skeletal (number of slots) or melodic (specific segment types) structure of the underlying representation. As a consequence, Beland et al. (1990) wrote: "To the extent that errors reflect natural processes that reduce markedness, there will be less need for a special 'error-generator' to account for paraphasias" (p. 142). Presumably, these authors are talking about scan copiers, and so forth—the typical psycholinguistic production mechanisms in most models I am familiar with. They continued:

> That is, given a specific problem a subject has either with the computation or with the mapping of a representation, he uses repair strategies provided by his knowledge of phonological processes. The form of error depends on the level of the accessed representation (underlying rep., lexical rep. or surface rep.) and on the limited choice of phonological processes available at that particular moment (omission, substitution, epenthesis, assimilation, addition). (p. 142)

Although they add that not all phonemic paraphasias reduce markedness, they seem to be calling for linguistic theory to supplant psycholinguistics. Whether or not we fully accept Beland et al.'s (1990) call for less performance and more competence, if we keep our mechanisms and the overall models in which they operate, we must certainly claim that in some sense they have the knowledge handed down from representative theories of phonological competence—theories that characterize underspecification and syllabification. The issue here is not unlike the typical tension in parsing theory, where the question is often how much of the grammar does the parser know? Our question here is how much phonological competence knowledge do our production mechanisms have? I doubt that many parsing theorists would relinquish their mechanisms for the competence-oriented, logical time processes of formal syntactic theory. Nevertheless, there is good reason to assume that grammars can help parsers (Crain & Fodor, 1985), and likewise that underspecification theory can help scan copiers.

Conduite d'Approche in the Garrett Model

Conduite d'approche is the French phrase for successive approximation and is the term for the set of attempts on the part of the patient at the production of some linguistic form—usually an isolated word. Most often, these sequential sets of attempts are collected on confrontation testing, usually on repetition, naming, and oral reading of isolated printed words. Less often, the *conduites d'approche* appear and are studied in spontaneous speech when, in running discourse, patients make a sound form error, catch themselves in midstream, and attempt a self-repair. This, of course, happens in the speech of nonbrain-damaged subjects as well (Levelt, 1989), but the string of attempts does not tend to be as lengthy as those of the aphasics. Because many of the studies of this phenomenon have been with items elicited at confrontation, the models to characterize the productions necessarily have the stimulus intervention that bypasses the message and most likely the functional levels of most models and feeds directly into the lexicon and levels below it. When examining *conduites d'approche,* one can glimpse (a) the initial error, (b) whether it is monitored (caught) or not, and (c) whether *and how* the error can be repaired.

Phonemic approximations to target forms are in most cases relatively tractable in this paradigm, and several studies have appeared in print in the last 10 years or so in which attempts have been made to distinguish the major aphasic syndromes with regard to the various patterns of these sequential attempts at successfully producing target words. The first is the investigation by Joanette, Keller, and Lecours (1980), in which they studied Broca's, CAs, and Wernicke's aphasics in spontaneous speech, in repetition of words and nonwords, in reading aloud, and in automatized sequences. The CAs, in general, exhibited the "most regular trend towards the target" (p. 30). However, the authors very importantly noted that on repetition, the CAs did not demonstrate this continuous trend toward the target, and they were even worse when attempting to repeat a nonword. The investigators also noted that on longer sequences there was a less decisive trend toward the target than there was with shorter sequences. Another interesting result was noted with the CAs. When repeating nonwords, they were actually closer to that nonform initially, but at the end of the approximation sequence were quite far from it. This finding adumbrated a decay of the nonsense word representation over time; that is, the CAs had a marked difficulty keeping in mind the perceived phonemic string presented to them auditorily and gradually lost hold of it as they attempted repeatedly. Therefore, Joanette et al. (1980) hypothesized that the CAs impairment may very well not be with the production mechanism itself, but rather with the input to the mechanism. Obviously, a weak, fuzzy, hazy (or however one wishes to characterize a trace that is vanishing in some fashion) representation will cause great production difficulties down the line. In fact, the authors (Joanette et al., 1980) wrote: "The initial strength and permanence of the internal representation of the target emerge as important factors required for the good functioning of this mechanism" (p. 30).

The next major study of *conduite d'approche* focused exclusively on the nature of the phonological disorder in CA and again compared that group with Broca's and Wernicke's (Kohn, 1984—a prelude to Kohn's doctoral dissertation, 1985). This also was the first in-depth study of CA with the backdrop of Garrett's model and Shattuck-Hufnagel's mechanisms. Kohn (1984) looked at confrontation naming in the "single-word paradigm" and closely analyzed the conduites d'approche when they occurred on this task. She noted that the CAs, as opposed to the other two groups, demonstrated a prevalence of phonologically oriented sequences where the error forms in the sequence resembled the targets "in outline form"; that is, the CA usually had the correct number of syllables in the error forms, and, when considered in their totality, all the segments of the target form were in one or another of the error forms in the sequence. Sometimes there were full target word fragments in the error productions. Often, the initial part of the target was revealed. Note, too, that the intonation of many of the errors in the sequence (i.e., tonic accent placement) was that of the target. So, in terms of the "linking address" discussed earlier, it looked as though the CAs had at least this much information. This was not unlike what Joanette et al. (1980) had found as well, because the task Kohn used was naming—not repetition. In any event, although the CAs had the "outline" form of the target, they could not close in on the target at the end. The errors were also fluent, and accordingly, Kohn (1984) concluded that the essential breakdown of the CAs was not one of lexical selection, nor one of phonetic implementation; that is, in terms of Garrett's model, the breakdown came at the Positional Level and involved the processes of selection and copying—computations imputed to the scan copier.

The *conduites d'approche* on naming in CA did not seem to reveal any difficulty with short-term auditory–verbal memory, which would expectedly occur more often when the input was in the auditory modality (i.e., on repetition). Kohn reasoned that a sequence based on fading phonological representation (such as that observed in Joanette et al., 1980 with repetition, especially of nonwords, in CA) would not predict the remarkable stability of form outline over a long series of attempts. Kohn (1984) concluded by hypothesizing that CA is a disruption of prearticulatory programming involving the mechanisms of selection and ordering, which are operating under conditions of weakened acoustic-motor integration, and that the lesions responsible for such a breakdown are most likely of parietal or temporoparietal origin.

In a very recent study, Valdois, Joanette, and Nespoulous (1989) further investigated the intrinsic organization in *conduite d'approche* in on-line repairs in conversational speech of one CA (who, it was noted, had recovered from Wernicke's aphasia) and two Wernicke's aphasics. They made special note that the CA made many linear transpositions of segments as well as substitutions (some of which may themselves have been of a linear nature). Several analyses were carried out, the first of which demonstrated that the CA was closer to the target then were the Wernicke's at the end of the sequence of approximations.

Recall that we are not talking about repetition, but rather about on-line monitorings and repairs during conversational speech. This, then, implies that the control system is quite different from the control of stimulus–response confrontation elicitation. Conversational speech is driven normally by the Message Level, which obviously does not so crucially depend on some isolated auditory stimulus presented by an examiner to be repeated. As Hughlings Jackson (1874/1931) claimed, the repetition control system is quite different from the system that drives spontaneous speech. A higher degree of volition is involved in the confrontation repetition setting, whereas spontaneous speech is less volitional in this sense. It might therefore be expected that, in spontaneous speech, the CA could hold on to the material better than when repeating.

The second analysis revealed that when the *conduites d'approche* were longer, only the Wernicke's patients were further away from the target. This was not the case for the CA. The third analysis demonstrated that *both* groups were sensitive to the number of syllables in the target. The authors considered this to be "global" information concerning the target. Note, as well, that the number of syllables is part of the information of Garrett's linking address.

The fourth analysis was an extensive study of the actual accessing and processing of phonological information across the whole range of successive sequences. Four major findings from this analysis were presented. First, the CA, when the total count of the sequences of errors was tabulated, had produced all the target segments, a trait of CA that had been observed in Kohn (1984). The Wernicke's successfully generated their share of segments, but not as many as the CA.

The second finding from this analysis was that the CA got progressively more segments of the target as he went through the successive sequences—getting most, if not all, in the last attempt. This was not the case for the Wernicke's, who on the other hand would often get *all* the segments somewhere in the middle of the sequence but would lose many of them by the end of their series of attempts. The CA, then, was getting the target segments in a "bit-by-bit" incremental fashion, until at the end when he seems to get most, if not all, of them.

Two further findings involve the nature of syllable outline access and maintenance. Both the Wernicke's and the CA are very good at accessing the number of target syllables initially, but only the CA holds on to this information to the end of the sequence. As it concerns the constituent structure of target syllables, it appeared that the Wernicke's aphasics got this information initially better than the CA, but again lost that information by the time the successive sequence came to an end.

Three major conclusions were drawn from this study. First, and most obvious, was that the CA demonstrated a constant progression toward the target. The Wernicke's patients revealed a very irregular progression toward the target. The second conclusion was that the Wernicke's patients, unlike the CA, got worse in their attempts as the sequence grew longer. And, finally, it appeared that the CA had a better capacity to use monitoring feedback to compare his errorful repairs and to use that comparison to approximate—in a stepwise fashion—the target structure. The Wernicke's seem able only to access and compare global information concerning the target.

One thing therefore seems certain. As Wernicke's aphasics recover in the direction of a CA, their ability to progressively repair errors as they approximate correction productions is enhanced. All the errors of the CA seem to indicate that the problem is postlexical, but prephonetic, and involves the computations of the scan copier, aided by the ability to monitor and repair errors by feeding back information on each error to the buffer, whereby another attempt is produced, iteratively, until the target is, in most cases, correctly produced. Further, all the processing that seems to be going on in the *conduites d'approche* appears to be somewhere among the processes that map to the Positional Level in the Garrett model. I would now like to explore further the question of the location or locations in the Garrett model that might best characterize the phonological production breakdown in CA.

Where Is Conduction Aphasia In The Garrett Model?

Since its inception with the work of Wernicke (1874/1977), CA has been considered a "fluent" disorder where the articulatory output did not give the impression of motor–phonetic disruption. Garrett's model keeps this distinction by separating the Positional Level from the Phonetic Level. In addition to the issue of fluency in CA, there is the question of the range (the encoding unit) over which segmental transpositions move. Both of these areas of concern have a direct bearing on localizing the disorder of CA in the production model.

To begin with, Caplan (1987) outlined various distinct model locations where phonemic paraphasia (no matter which aphasia type) could arise:

1. Phonemic paraphasia could take place at the juncture where the patient is manipulating the "linking address" from lexical semantics (1st Lexical Lookup) to lexical phonology (2nd Lexical Lookup). Because the linking address is presumed to have the more "global" aspects of representations (initial segments, number of syllables, intonation pattern), paraphasia here would presumably involve these more wholistic aspects of words. It is not clear how problems with the linking address would result in transposition errors, however, because there seems to be no kind of ordering process inherent in the notion of the linking address.

2. Phonemic paraphasia could arise during *accessing* of superficial phonological representations, where the linking address is intact. Errors here would presumably be restricted to segmental selection errors, not linear ordering. Selection and ordering are quite distinct computations. Feature specification of more redundant values may be taking place at this point, and consequently mis-specifications of features would result in phonemic paraphasia of a substitutive nature.

3. Phonemic paraphasia could also arise as the lexical phonological representations are being simultaneously scan copied for utterance order onto syllabic templates and placed into their respective matrix slots. Again, depending on the speaking situation, the encoding units will have different sizes, usually words, phrases, or clauses. Few if any linear errors cross major sentential boundaries, and therefore the maximum range over which the scan copier may work is usually considered to be the clause (i.e., the major NP + VP structure). Linear errors have been observed to travel within syllables, across syllables in single words, across two contiguous words, within phrasal confines (NPs, VPs, PPs, and the like), and across major phrases (i.e., within the clause, but across, say, the major NP–VP boundary).

4. Caplan would no doubt now add the distinct locations of feature specification computation (underlying—minimally specified level [UR], the lexical level [LR], and the superficial—maximally specified level [SR]; Beland et al., 1990).

5. Also, given the Beland et al. (1990) contribution, phonemic paraphasias could arise before, during, or after syllabification.

Location 4 is actually several locations. Obviously, the phonemic paraphasias located at the underspecified level would be occurring somewhere in the form lexicon at a rather deep level. Phonemic errors at the level of lexical representation would also be very abstract. Lower level feature specification at the surface phonological representation level appears to still be abstract and phonemic in nature as far as *some* of the features go. For instance, the French example (Beland et al. 1990, p. 132) of UR, LR, and SR features for the vowel /i/ show that the specifications for [nasal] and [voice] are computed at SR. If the marking for [nasal] had been [+ nasal], everything else remaining the same, the resulting switch would have been at the phonemic level (given the phonemic status of nasal vowels in French), but a marking for [voice] of [– voice] would have resulted in a more phonetically abberant production. Therefore, the specifications at the level of SR may or may not result in a phonemic paraphasia. I now discuss some major papers concerned with locating the principal phonological breakdown in CA.

One of the earliest attempts to do this was by Dubois, Hecaen, Angelergues, Maufras de Chatelier, and Marcie (1964/1973). Initially, these authors ruled out anomia as the primary disorder underlying CA. They observed that CAs could usually find the word, but they could not verbally realize it, and consequently this is one of the earliest claims for the CA breakdown to be post-selectional. Very importantly, the authors noticed that the more global aspects of the lexical representation were intact and not nearly as subject to error as were the specific segments of the form. They claimed that the CAs, despite their rampant phonemic paraphasia, still held on the "syllable image, program, or configuration," and so they had the outline or skeleton form of the word in mind. Recall that Valdois et al. (1989) showed that Wernicke's as well as CAs tended to hold faster to the more global aspects of lexical items. Recall as well that it is these more global aspects of words that are usually imputed to the linking address. It is also this kind of wholistic information of underlying word forms that is evident in the tip-of-the-tongue phenomenon as well as in the production of malapropisms.

Caplan, Vanier, and Baker's (1986) report mentioned earlier analyzed the errors on single-word productions of a patient with reproduction CA, who was asked to name objects, repeat words, and read printed words aloud. Although this patient was far worse on the repetition of nonwords, his phonological errors were qualitatively the same throughout all these tasks. Again, as mentioned before, this is why the authors felt that the phonological problem was modality neutral—and thus, purely linguistic.

This CA was somewhat atypical, because the authors (Caplan et al., 1986) reported that the "errors consisted mainly of substitutions and omissions of single consonants" (p. 102), with only occasional misorderings. Recall that this is the same patient reported on in Beland et al. (1990). Such paucity of linear transpositions would obviously eliminate the need for ranges of errors of more than one segmental slot and would accordingly place less emphasis on ordering mechanisms such as the scan copier.

After considering various possible accounts for their patient's disruption, Caplan et al. (1986) wind up in essential agreement with the Dubois et al. (1964) explanation that the CA's problem concerns encoding or output rather than decoding or word selection. Caplan et al. (1986) also feel that the CA has a rather firm grasp of the syllable image or configuration, and that, rather than being tied to any certain perceptual modality, it is a *linguistic* disorder that involves *planning* processes. It is a sensory problem only to the extent that any output motor speech planning mechanism requires an input from auditory representations.

Caplan et al. (1986) have certain problems with previous explanations of CA. Whereas Dubois et al. (1964/1973), in terms of the linguistics of Andre Martinet (1964), claimed that the CA's problem is with the construction of words, phrases, and sentences (i.e., Martinet's "1st articulation" level), Caplan et al. feel that the CA's problem rests more with the construction of phonemes (i.e., Martinet's "2nd articulation" level). Caplan et al. do not believe that the CA's problem concerns the linking address necessarily, because the linking address hypothesis hooks semantic representations to phonological representation, whereas these authors see no reason to assume that their patient invariably incorporates a semantic route to arrive at the phonological form.

Caplan et al. (1986) do not feel that the breakdown arises with the scan copier as it imparts ordering to the segments as they are being inserted into clausal matrix slots, for the simple reason that their patient's phonemic problem seemed to rest at the level of single words. There may be two reasons for this. First, most of the tasks were on single-word confrontation testing, which as I mentioned before, would really only require a matrix range of a single word in the Positional Level processing. Second, the patient studied in this work was not a CA who made many linear transpositions. There are, however, many CAs who produce large numbers of misorderings. There simply seems to be no reason why this patient's errors cannot be described in terms of misfirings during the scan copying of the underlying phonological representations onto syllable templates, the output being the superficial phonological representation. The problem would then be exactly what Caplan et al. (1986) said: the mapping from the underlying modality neutral phonological representations to the superficial phonological representations. In the single-word paradigm of confrontation testing, the production of the matrix slot into which the segments ultimately find themselves is the size of a word—no more. I see no reason to restrict scan copying and placement into Positional Level slots to the level (and hence the range) of the clause. Again, there are many situations where the matrix at the Positional Level need be no larger than a word.

The recent study by Nespoulous et al. (1987) makes more direct use of the Garrett model with the scan copier. These authors compared Broca's aphasics (BA) with CA on repetition and oral reading of single words of one to four syllables—same words on both tasks for comparative purposes. Several conclusions were drawn.

First, as would be expected, the BAs revealed a low-level phonetic deficit not observed in the CAs. The second conclusion was that the CAs were deficient with mechanisms that compute linear phonological representations at Garrett's Positional Level. Clearly, the authors had the scan copier in mind. The computational derailments occurred subsequent to successful access of the deeper, more abstract, and probably nonlinear lexicophonological representation from the lexicon. In line with Caplan et al. (1986), the CA's errors were "roughly" the same for repetition (auditory stimulus input) and for oral reading (visual stimulus input). Nespoulous et al. (1987), in line with Caplan et al. (1986), felt that the CA errors could have arisen at several possible junctures in the model (discussed earlier). The BA's breakdown was at a lower level—most likely at the Phonetic Level.

In an interesting and very important footnote (16, p. 74), Nespoulous et al. (1987) broached the issue of the window size of the scan copier's misfirings. Recall that much disagreement surrounding CA deals precisely with the range over which the segmental ordering computations of the scan copier can or does operate in that syndrome. They began the footnote by citing Blumstein (1978): "The maximal unit of encoding, then, must at least be several words, and more likely is the syntactic phrase" (p. 199). Blumstein's (1978) study predates the work on processing models discussed here and thus makes no reference to Shattack-Hufnagel, nor, obviously, to the scan copier, but she was nevertheless talking about ordering processes. Blumstein's range limit appeared to stop at the maximum of a phrase, which would then prohibit a segmental transposition from crossing a major NP–VP boundary, an unwanted move because errors have been observed that do precisely that (see Buckingham, 1985). Nespoulous et al.'s (1987) footnote goes on to say that in single-word production the window size is probably limited to the target lexical item itself, a larger phrasal frame being unnecessary for such tasks. My point, earlier, was that even in spontaneous conversational speech there may be several occasions for which Message Level control would only require a phrasal frame at the Positional Level of one word (e.g., as a response to the question: "Where did you go last night?" Answer: "Home."). The authors continued the footnote noting that several questions remained. For instance, to what extent in the repetition and oral reading of isolated words would there or could there be partial "remnance" of the structural attributes of a preceding lexical item, when the subject comes to encode the following one? This certainly is a crucial question to ask, because there is so much perseveration observed in these fluent populations. The last question considered in this footnote is extremely significant. Nespoulous et al. ask to what extent may aphasics modify window size in order to better control their sequential production. In other words, could an aphasic, in this case a CA, develop some kind of adaptive strategy to gain better control over his or her speech production? This may very well be possible, and in fact it has been shown to be the case in anterior motor aphasia (Baum, 1990).

In an excellent overview article on neuropsychological approaches to the study of language, Saffran (1982) assessed recent accounts of CA and evaluated two possible sources for the phonemic paraphasic component of that syndrome. Having outlined Morton's (1979) logogen theory, Saffran suggested that the CA impairment may rest at the "morphemic" level (presumably content morphemes), the phonemic paraphasia arising during the retrieval of phonological information at the level of the output logogen. This would be a purely lexical phenomenon whereby the phonemic manipulation would be restricted to occur in one-word, whole units. Alternatively, she considered that the phonemic paraphasias could arise at the point where the phonologically specified lexical elements (having been successfully selected at the 2nd lexical lookup) are being inserted into the phrasal frames at the Positional Level of the Garrett model. Saffran then reasoned that each proposal makes different predictions of the paraphasias in CA. If the former hypothesis is correct, then CAs should not produce phonemic errors that cross word boundaries, whereas if the latter holds, then CAs would be expected to make both within-word and transword errors. She (Saffran, 1982) claimed that, "To my knowledge, the requisite analysis of error types in the connected speech of conduction aphasics has yet to be done" (p. 331). Pate, Saffran, and Martin (1987) is just such an analysis.

Pate et al. (1987) examined, in great detail, one reproduction CA and used Garrett's model (1984) to locate the breakdown. This was a 64-year-old male, who had suffered a left CVA. An unenhanced scan revealed a rather large lesion of the middle and inferior temporal gyri that extended from the mid-temporal region to the temporo–occipital junction. Atypical of CA lesions (Damasio, 1991), the posterior portion of the superior temporal gyrus (Wernicke's area) was also affected in the patient. Testing did not begin until approximately 1 year postinsult, and it could be the case that this patient was a CA who had recovered from Wernicke's aphasia.

Unfortunately, the stage was set for some confusion regarding CA in a Garrett (1984) paper, one that apparently influenced Pate et al.'s (1987) reasoning. Before examining the Pate et al. study, a few remarks on Garrett (1984) are, therefore, in order. First, Garrett claimed (p. 188) that CAs have linking address information available to them but are impaired in the use or manipulation of that information. There is some confusion here because it now appears to be the case from the *conduite d'approche* studies that CAs actually *do* use this information and can, indeed, hold on to it while they are working on the rest of the segmental (melodic) information to produce some target item. Recall that linking address information is mostly suprasegmental, containing number of syllables and tonic stress information. The only segmental information that is usually included is the first segment or two of the target. In 1984, Garrett had not yet placed ordering mechanisms, such as the scan copier of Shattuck-Hugnagel (1979), among the processes at the Positional Level, something that had only been hinted at in Buckingham (1980) but developed further in Buckingham (1985). Garrett (1988, p. 83) now appeared ready to incorporate Shattuck-Hufnagel's scan copier into his Positional Level operations, if for no other reason than for its "descriptive power." Nevertheless, in 1984, Garrett clearly realized that the segmental errors in slips occurred when lexical items were being placed into their respective phrasal frame slots. Having claimed that CAs have linking address information, Garrett leaped to the suggestion that the phonemic paraphasias of CA might be best understood in terms of the processes of segmental interpretation of word forms in the phrasal frame. But, as Garrett reasoned, if those words are already in their matrix slots at the Positional Level, then they are in the input to the phonological specification of the details of phonetic form (i.e., the so-called "regular phonological processes" that map the Positional Level onto the Phonetic Level. Garrett (1984) therefore claimed that "The commonly reported failures of conduction aphasia seem best understood as a disorder of the phonological interpretation of the lexically specified positional frames" (p. 189); that is, Garrett is claiming that the phonemic paraphasia of CA is located at the Phonetic Level. This, then, turns out to be what Pate et al. (1987) ended up claiming, based on their results.

Garrett (1984) reasoned the same way that Pate et al. (1987) did. He claimed (p. 189) that if the location of CA derailments took place at the point of assigning segmental information to a phrasal frame, then one would expect to see frequent sound-exchange errors, but he said: "no current observations indicate such an exacerbation of exchange errors for conduction aphasics" (p. 189). He also noted that repetition failures in CA occur on single-word testing as well as for phrasally integrated words; that is, Garrett had not observed CAs committing cross-lexical transpositions in sentence (or phrasal) repetition. This, of course, is what Pate et al. showed as well.

Garrett seemed to be placing too much emphasis exclusively on the sound-exchange error, which everyone knows is very rare in aphasia. However, many have observed anticipations and perseverations that fluent aphasics produce, which certainly seem to be prephonetic. In any event, the location of the phonemic paraphasic component in CA among the phonetic computations below the Positional Level was indicated by Garrett 3 years prior to the Pate et al. study. One point I raise when discussing the Pate et al. study is that Garrett and several others have been somewhat loose in defining the specification of phonetic detail by the "regular phonological processes" that map from the Positional Level to the Phonetic Level.

Experiment 1 in Pate et al. had the CA read a paragraph aloud in chunks: words, phrases, and word blocks (holophrastic units containing more than one word in the underlying form). Within isolated words as they appeared alone or as they were read in larger phrasal units, as the number of syllables in words increased, the phonemic paraphasias increased. This increase did not occur as more words were added to phrases, but only as individual words increased in the number of syllables. The authors noted that phrases from four to eight syllables (i.e., phrases with many mono and bisyllabic words) were much easier to handle for the CA than were single words with four to eight syllables.

The results of Experiment 1, however, showed that the CA was doing some interesting things. First, there are several within-word, cross-syllabic phonemic transpositions: *stanitation* (sanitation), *ferpumz* (perfumes), *dimaneter* (diameter), *decradation* (declaration), *instist* (insist), *windwill* (windmill), *skelekon* (skeleton), *thruth* (truth), *kask, tacks, ask, tackst* (task). I have seen no proposal to date, not even by Garrett, for an ordering mechanism to operate among the phonetic processes at this level. After Experiment 4, Pate et al. suggested a ''segmental read-in'' ordering mechanism. In any event, that mechanism would have to be very much like the scan copier, and, even more importantly, the output would still have to be prephonetic. It seems that all the errors in Pate et al. (1987) are computed at a prephonetic level, except for the second interesting behavior of this CA. Like an apraxic, this CA often deleted unstressed syllables. This is something a motor aphasic, or a less fluent apraxic, is likely to do. Why this patient does it, I do not know. It would be helpful to have more medical information on this CA, for it may turn out that the patient is one of the more motorically involved CAs, an issue we discuss later in this chapter.

Experiment 2 was an interesting one. The subject had to read pairs such as *murderous* versus the two-word phrase *murder us.* Both these forms were embedded in larger phrasal units and presented to the patient to read aloud. The prediction, of course, was that the polysyllabic words would cause more difficulty than the phrases with the same number of syllables. The prediction held. Again, the CA's difficulty seemed to be within #____#s (word boundaries). At this point, Pate et al. considered the possibility, mentioned earlier, that their patient's aphasia forced him to process word by word, which may certainly have been the case. To test this, Experiment 3 was performed.

In this experiment, the authors looked at ''beat movement'' processing in the patient. Beat movement (see Levelt, 1989, p. 374, and references there) prevents the unwanted situation of contiguously stressed syllables in English. In any production model, and at a postlexical level, there must be a mechanism that scans intonation contours and points of major pitch change in sentences to ensure that stress does not occur on any two adjoining syllables. The mechanism would therefore need a window size of more than one word. For instance, in its citation form (the lexical representation, roughly), the word *abstract* has its stress (tonic) on the second syllable, but if that word is encountered in the phrase *abstract art,* with the phrasal tonic stress on *art,* a beat movement to the left on *abstract* will be required so that stress will fall on the first syllable. The result is ABstract ARt. When Pate et al.'s patient read phrases that required beat movement in this fashion, he was able to make the shift, thus indicating that he was in fact not performing in a word-by-word fashion exclusively.

Experiment 4 investigated the CA's ability to read multiword units. These were "familiar" word groups that were comprised of several separate words but that, according to the authors, function as single chunked units. They were of three types: fixed phrases ("letter of the law"), proper nouns ("Death Valley"), and famous people ("Thomas Jefferson"). The authors found far more transpositions across items in this experiment than they found on the first experiment. The kinds of transpositions observed are items like *between the lines* being read as *betwain,* and *kick off* being read as *kif.* At this point, the authors make an analogy with certain slips-of-the-tongue reported in Fromkin (1973) that seem to involve overlearned word units like those in Pate et al. (1987). As examples from Fromkin, they cite the slips: *mirrage immer* (mirror image), *pat aus* (pass out), and *heft lemisphere* (left hemisphere). One problem with all this is the somewhat open-ended question of just which groups are automatized (routinized), which are not, what is the degree of automatization, and the very thorny decision as to how to know whether and when a multiword phrase achieves its chunked status.

At this point, Pate et al. (1987) suggested a "sequential reading" processing mechanism, which operates on single words and on multiple-word units. They appear to set up this ordering mechanism as something for the oral reading task. They furthermore place the mechanism at the Phonetic Level in the Garrett model, because at that point the words have already been positioned into their Positional Level matrix slots. Nevertheless, that ordering mechanism does the same thing as the scan copier does at the Positional Level, except its input range is the word or multiple-word unit.

For all their zeal, the major problem with the Pate et al. (1987) conclusions is that they locate the *phonemic* paraphasic component of CA at the *phonetic* level, without seeming to realize the serious consequences for that stand. First, they must essentially duplicate the operations of the scan copier, that for numerous reasons must be placed among the Positional Level operations. It is simply not the case that all transposition phonemic errors are restricted to the single-word or multiword unit ranges. The outputs of scan copier errors are predictably accommodated at the Phonetic Level. The puzzle with the Pate et al. (1987) position is that they predict that there will be much phonetic abnormality in CAs, because the phonological processes imputed to this level are involved in deriving phonetic level representations, which can then more directly feed into the motor command system for actual articulation. Therefore, if the problem in CA is at this level, one would expect many phonetic aberrations: unaspirated syllable initial /p,t,k/, non-nasalized vowels prenasally, no flapping neutralization of underlying /t/and /d/, haphazard allophonic variation of the English lateral approximate /l/, and a whole host of other phonetic types of errors. This simply does not happen in the typical CA, unless of course we broaden the scope of the syndrome and consider whether or not there are more motorically and less motorically involved types of CA, a point we consider later.

Several items lead me to wonder whether the CA in Pate et al. (1987) was more motorically involved than other types of CA. They noted a selective vulnerability of unstressed syllables to be omitted. This kind of deletion propensity is not typical of CA. They also noted that phoneme omission errors were the most frequent type of error in their patient. Again, this is not typical of the CA.

On the issue of beat movement assignment, I would have no trouble locating that process among the other kinds of accommodation computations at the Phonetic Level. In fact, Levelt (1989) locates this operation far below the lexicon, because the "no contiguous stressed syllables" dictate of English must wait for the Positional Level matrices to be filled. In this way, the beat movement processor must be understood to be some type of filter or accommodator. Again, in the previous example, the word *abSTRACT* has the tonic accent (therefore, obviously stressed) on the second syllable in its lexical representation, but if that word ends up in a sentence at the Positional Level, such as *I bought some abstract art,* with the major pitch change (i.e., tonic sentence accent) over *art,* then beat movement will move the underlying stress from the second to the first syllable in *abstract.* Obviously, this process must operate subsequent to the Positional Level. The Positional Level matrix will indeed have the intonation contour superimposed, but in the preceding case *abstract* will likely have its citation form stress pattern. Given the Positional Level input, the beat movement operation at the Phonetic Level will shift the tonic to the left one syllable. Consequently, this type of accommodation operation will have to be able to scan over a range of more than one word. Again, the CA is *expected* to have normal accommodation capabilities, but that is because the problem does not rest at the Phonetic Level. CA is simply not primarily a phonetic abnormality, at least not like a limb kinetic apraxia or a dysarthria.

The Pate et al. (1987) investigation, although one of the most detailed case studies of CA I have seen, still leaves many interesting puzzles unsolved, not only for CA, but also for models of speech production in general. In an interesting footnote (2) early in their paper, Pate et al. admitted that "conduction aphasics do not form a homogeneous group . . ." and that their "conclusions about NU's impairment may not generalize even to all conduction aphasics with reproduction disorders." In fact, they wrote, "Whether they do or not is an empirical question beyond the scope of this case study." What Pate et al. are emphasizing is that "the implications of NU's deficit for models of speech production do not depend on the degree to which his behavior is characteristic of 'conduction aphasia' " (p. 76). It should be clear from the discussion in this chapter that the claims of Pate et al. indeed do have as much to do with general issues concerning speech production and Garrett's levels and computations as they do with characterizing CA specifically.

It was not long after the Pate et al. (1987) study that another investigation of CA indeed demonstrated between-word phonemic transpositions. That investigation was carried out by Kohn and Smith (1990). In this case study, the authors analyzed 140 sentences that their patient had repeated; repetition was the only type of task in the study. The CA in this report produced both left-to-right and right-to-left movement errors, and most of the segments involved originated in syllable rhymes and moved to syllable rhymes, as would be expected given the syllable position law that stipulates that transposed segments respect their original (target) syllable specifications. Kohn and Smith considered these movement errors as "copies," and they considered both left to right and right to left to be perseveratory in nature. The movements are generally appreciated as "copies," because they move to other slots but are not often erased from their original positions. I have referred to these kinds of transpositions as doublet creating errors, whether the phenomena take place within words or across word boundaries (see footnote 2 in Kohn & Smith, 1990, p. 139, for a discussion of our differences in point of view). Most previous studies (e.g., Lecours & Lhermitte, 1969) have dealt with doublets as they result from copies within words exclusively. In any event, in both cases, one segment X moves without being deleted in its original site, thus producing double the amount of X's (Buckingham, 1990a).

Kohn and Smith noted that rhyme constituents or whole rhymes are copied but that rarely if ever do onset C's of CVs move. The binary constituent structure of the syllable into Onset and Rhyme, with Rhyme bifurcating into Peak and Coda would explain why the C's of VCs are more glued to the V than the C's of CVs, but it would certainly not explain why onset consonants rarely moved in this patient (see Shattuck-Hufnagel, 1987), or why onset consonants are less attached to syllables and therefore more likely to strip off from them in speech errors. In addition, because we have already established that the basic window size the matrices at the Positional Level is the clause (i.e., NP + VP) and that the scan copier operates normally on the clause, we can use that mechanism and the buffer out of which it works to handle the transpositions of the CA patient in this study. There is no need to worry about restricting ordering operations to one phrase at a time. This being the case, the Positional Level computations and mechanisms I outlined earlier will account for the errors listed in Table 5 of Kohn and Smith (1990, p. 145). Seven of the 11 errors in that table involve right-to-left (anticipatory) transposition of segments from the VP across the major boundary and into the subject NP, whereas 3 comprise linear switches from the subject NP into the VP. One error has a transposition within the NP that is contained within the VP. Again, as the authors point out, most all the segments involved are rhyme elements. If the scan copier is not drawing on elements from a buffer with a clausal window size, none of these errors can be accounted for, because, again, they cross the major clausal NP–VP boundary. Of course, the process could work phrase by phrase, but then something puzzling would arise. Left-to-right copies would be normal, because some segment may not be erased from the buffer and would be copied again with the next phrase. The right-to-left anticipatory error, on the other hand, would force us to claim that the second phrase was computed first, with a segment or segments failing to be erased and thus copied in the first phrase. A simultaneous view by the scan copier of *both* major phrases of the clause (NP + VP), however, would more easily capture the possibility of transpositions moving in either direction. This, therefore, would require that we postulate the clause as the basic encoding unit for segmental ordering.

In order to account for their CA's preponderance of coda instability, Kohn and Smith (1990) suggested, following recent work by Shattuck-Hufnagel (1987), that if rhymes are constructed before onsets, rhymes will be in place longer and perhaps for this reason receive more activation and thus be more prone to being perseverated. This pattern of copy errors contrasts with that of many fluent aphasics that involves transposed (i.e., moved, as opposed to perseverated) onset consonants (see the alliteration and assonance reported in Buckingham, Whitaker, & Whitaker, 1978). It follows that onset consonants are most loosely tied to the rest of the syllable, and, therefore, are subject to more instability than coda consonants, the latter being more glued to the body of the syllable (i.e., rhyme; Shattuck-Hufnagel, 1987). Still, the notion proposed by Kohn and Smith (1990) contradicts recent evidence (e.g., Beland et al., 1990; Clements, 1990) that, in fact, syllabification algorithms construct *onsets* before codas, with the peaks being established prior to either consonant type. Very importantly, the maximal onset principle (Goldsmith, 1990) is insured by assigning onsets to syllable units before codas. In any event, the Kohn and Smith (1990) investigation shows quite clearly that CAs can and do produce phonemic paraphasic errors that cross not only word boundaries but also major NP–VP constituent boundaries.

Yet another major paper on CA is Kohn's (1989), where much evidence is garnered to argue that CA represents a breakdown with the computations that manipulate strings of segments postlexically, and that this type of phonological difficulty is consistent across tasks such as repetition, naming, and oral reading (in agreement with Caplan et al., 1986). Of course, this finding is in disagreement with Joanette et al. (1980), who, as aforementioned, noted a sharp drop in CA's performances on repetition in their conduites d'approche. The patient in Kohn (1989) was the same as that reported on in Kohn and Smith (1990), so there is some overlap in the discussion of those two papers.

That patient, however, presented with many transposition errors, which to Kohn's way of reasoning, represented perseveration because those errors were "copies." Both the left-to-right and the right-to-left moved segments remained in their target positions as well. The left-to-right error involved the correct target production initially, but the uncleared buffer resulted in that segment being produced later on. The right-to-left error involved an erroneously anticipated copy of the segment, but again the uncleared buffer resulted in the production of the segment in its original target position. There is no reason to suspect that the operations involved here are any different from those reported in other studies such as Buckingham (1990a), with the scan copier working postlexically at the Positional Level with clausal buffer windows, and with a "checkoff" monitor" (see Fig. 5.1 earlier) to erase the segment from the buffer once it is copied onto syllabic templates—the whole operation taking place as the contentives are being positioned into their respective matrix slots. "Buffer clearing" or "checkoff monitoring" are metaphors that can be reasonably interchanged one for the other (see Hoffman, Cochran, & Nead, 1990, for an excellent treatment of cognitive metaphors throughout the history of psychology). In addition, Dell (1988) pointed to the metaphorical similarity of activated segments returning to their "resting levels" in parallel distributed processing (PDP) theory and of segments being "checked off" by Shattuck-Hufnagel's mechanism. The additional point is, of course, that there need be no a priori restriction as to the size of the matrix. For different purposes, it may vary from the single word (the highly eliptical response) to the clause. Otherwise, one ends up being obliged to posit segmental ordering mechanisms, buffers, and erasure devices at several different levels.

Six major conclusions concerning CA are offered by Kohn (1989), in combination with Kohn and Smith (1990). The first is that the patient never produced a sound exchange error. The full segmental exchanges seen in slips-of-the-tongue rarely if ever occur in aphasia. This, however, should not be taken to imply that the transposition errors in CA could not occur at the Positional Level through derailments of the scan copier and–or the checkoff monitor. The second conclusion, which seems to be an idiosyncracy of this CA and not necessarily diagnostic of all CAs, is that the transpositions involved whole rhymes or rhyme constituents, but few if any onsets. The third was that the transpositions not only crossed word boundaries, but they also crossed the major NP–VP clausal constituents. The fourth conclusion was that practically all the linear errors were doublet creating (copy errors), which indicated that there was a problem clearing the buffer (checking off) of ordered segments, giving rise to repeated segmental production. The fifth conclusion emphasized the importance of establishing the window size of the buffer, whereas the sixth conclusion admits that, in all likelihood, CA is in reality a heterogeneous syndrome. One group of CAs would be those who have recovered from an initial Wernicke's aphasia, but who were still very fluent in their output. The other group, who will functionally test out as CAs on aphasia batteries, will be those with a more dysfluent paraphasic speech output.

Is There One Conduction Aphasia?

Kertesz (1979) carried out a clustering analysis of aphasics by numerical taxonomy, using the Western Aphasia Battery (WAB) as the diagnostic battery. Functionally, CAs divided into two distinct clusters. This functional bimodal distribution divided into an "afferent conduction" group (high fluency, with relatively low comprehension and repetition scores) and an "efferent conduction" group (lower fluency and higher comprehension). In addition, Kertesz (1979) performed an isotope lesion localization composite study for the same patients who were tested on the WAB. The CA's lesions were "primarily between Broca's and Wernicke's areas, although some appeared right over these areas as well" (p. 149). The lesion composite showed that there was greatest overlap around the superior lip of the Sylvian fissure, comprising the inferior portions of the precentral, postcentral, inferior partietal, and supramarginal gyri. Kertesz also points out that some of the CA lesions were small, but often quite deep, involving insular cortex as well as the white fiber tracts connecting the frontal and temporal lobes. In addition, Kertesz (1979) observed that "The less fluent patients . . . had more anterior lesions. Those with higher fluency scores had uptakes situated more posteriorly" (p. 149). The parallel functional and anatomical bimodal distinctions in the CA group demonstrated by Kertesz (1979) offer very convincing evidence that, in fact, there is a certain degree of heterogeneity in the syndrome.

This heterogeneity will have a significant impact on our evaluation of the production breakdown in CA. In actuality, there are distinctions along two dimensions in CA: repetition versus reproduction CA and afferent (fluent) versus efferent (less fluent) CA. The latter distinction will fall out differently in terms of breakdown locations in our production model, whereas the former distinction may show up only in terms of type of confrontational tasks. To my knowledge, no one has attempted to see if a four-way CA distinction would ever be possible: (a) + reproduction, + fluent; (b) – reproduction, – fluent; (c) + reproduction, – fluent; (d) – reproduction, + fluent.

Two recent studies have variously treated the afferent–efferent issue in CA (Ardila & Rosselli, 1990; Valdois, Joanette, Nespoulous, & Poncet, 1988). Valdois et al. (1988) published an in-depth analysis of the relationship between "afferent motor aphasia" (AMA) (Luria's CA) and CA, as it is understood by those of the non-Russian school of aphasiology. To arrive at the two populations, these authors selected 6 CAs (French speaking) on a French version of the BDAE. Furthermore (Valdois et al., 1988), "Subjects were all clinically labeled as conduction aphasics, according to the definition of Lecours, Lhermitte, & Bryans (1983)" (p. 66). Out of this group of 6, 3 were further identified as subjects likely to be classified by Luria's scheme as AMA (afferent motor aphasia; hypoesthesia of the upper right limb [hand], no hemiparesis of visual defect, a severe buccolingual apraxia with no involvement of speech muscles, and lesions located in at least the anterior part of the left inferior parietal lobule). The task in this study was the repetition of 170 French lexical items from 1 to 4 syllables in length (of CVCV, etc. structure). Eighty-five were French words, and 85 were nonwords, respecting French phonotactics.

Although Valdois et al. (1988) feel that both AMA and CA are essentially premotoric, the buccofacial apraxia and the anterior parietal lesion location of the AMAs would argue for at least some further involvement of a phonetic nature for the AMAs. In any event, the authors observed several differences in the patterns of phonological errors in the two groups. Because 71% of all the phonemic paraphasias from both groups were substitutions, the substitutive errors formed the basis for much of the comparison. The first important difference noted was that the CAs had more errors of one feature distance, whereas the AMAs had more errors differing in two features. For both groups, [place] and [manner] were more prominent than errors involving the feature [voice]. However, [voice] and [manner] seemed to be less a problem for the AMA group. The feature [place] suffered equally in each group. In 42% of their substitution errors, the AMAs modified both [place] and [manner]. CAs did this in only 32% of their errors. In addition, the [place] substitutions ended up further away from the target more often in AMA. However, the AMA [place] substitution errors had the effect of decreasing the syntagmatic distance relations with other consonants in the word. For instance, the velar /k/ in *become* may be substituted for a consonant that was closer to the bilabial place of articulation because the other consonants in that word /b/ and /m/ are bilabials. This tendency to reduce spatial place differences among the consonants of words was not observed in the CAs, and therefore the claim is that the AMA substitutions were motivated on the syntagmatic axis. The CA errors were focused more along the paradigmatic axis. A cluster analysis of these kinds of distinctions resulted in a dendrogram that clearly grouped the AMAs and the CAs differently (p. 77).

Valdois et al. (1988) then considered the origins of the substitutions. They considered a motor hypothesis along the lines of the "gesture reduction" notion suggested in Keller (1984) but rejected this because the problem seemed to them to involve motor *planning* rather than motor *execution*. To Valdois et al., the problem seemed to be more abstract.

At the premotor level of planning, these authors considered two mechanisms: ordering or accessing. Ordering was ruled out as the essential breakdown, because most of the errors observed were substitution of the nonlinear type; that is, the substitutions in this corpus were paradigmatic and were not those kinds of substitutions that result from misordering segments from somewhere in the context; The substitutions in this corpus were of the so-called "no source" kind. So, the authors turned to the processes of access.

Wholistic access of phonological form is not the problem because few if any of the phonemic paraphasias obliterated target word recognition. Therefore, Valdois et al. (1988) argued that the problem *for both* groups is a failure to access (from the lexicon) phonemic information such that only an incomplete specification of a target segment is available to be placed into the operating buffer (p. 87). At this point, the AMAs and the CAs repair the problem at different rates. The CAs, according to the authors, repair immediately and select another segment for compensation. The AMAs, on the other hand, repair more slowly. By the time their deficit (or underspecified) segment gets to the buffer, the repair mechanism has had time, in some way or another, to consider the contextual material, which would then, according to this line of reasoning, make it more likely that the repair to further specify the features of the deficit segment would include some of those neighboring features, bringing that segment more in line with the others in the word. This is how the authors account for the tendency of AMAs to reduce syntagmatic distance relations by their phonemic substitutions. So, the CAs actually make a full segmental substitution, whereas the AMAs are essentially filling in additional features from the other segments in the context.

Only time will tell whether this view of the distinction between AMA and CA will withstand scrutiny, but one item does merit some discussion. Notice that Beland et al. (1990) and Valdois et al. (1988) share an interest in having segments underspecified at the point where phonemic paraphasia arises, but they arrive at their positions quite differently. Beland et al. (1990) are incorporating an independently motivated phonological theory that posits underspecified segments, and they claim that phonemic paraphasia arises at various points where further—and more redundant—features are being specified. Valdois et al. (1988) claim that the underspecified segments are that way as a consequence of the brain damage. They claim that, at least for the AMAs, the paraphasias come about through the migration of neighboring features into the deficiently specified feature matrix of the problematic phonemic segment. A very detailed microanalysis of phonemic substitutions could perhaps tease these two positions apart. At least for the AMA-type errors that reduce syntagmatic distance, one could look to see whether the features involved were more likely to be switches of plus or minus on place features that would indeed reduce syntagmatic distance, and whether or not the change would be at chance level or not, given the other feature marking changes that could have taken place at the lexical or surface feature specification levels, given the theory of underspecification. Note that the Valdois et al. (1988) view predicts the direction of the substitution error of the AMA, that direction that will lessen syntagmatic feature distance. I see no kinds of prediction of this kind from the phonological theory of underspecification. In any event, much more work is needed in this arena.

The other recent treatment of CA as a nonunique syndrome is found in Ardila and Rosselli (1990). These authors studied one patient and titled their paper ''Conduction Aphasia and Verbal Apraxia.'' One immediately realizes that this is a study of a CA who would quite likely fall into the AMA category of Luria. The patient had an insular and parietal operculum infarct and demonstrated an apraxia for buccofacial movements as well as an apraxia for performing meaningless and symbolic movements with the hands. According to these authors, the best way to characterize this patient is to attribute to him an overriding ideomotor apraxia for speech articulatory segments. This form of CA, then, would represent an apraxia for performing the highly skilled, symbolic, intransitive, distal, very rapid, and complex movements of the articulatory "limbs" (as Liepmann called them; Buckingham, 1991) that transmit language. The apraxic component in one form of CA does not shift the burden onto the Motor Level of the Garrett model, but rather to the Phonetic Level. Again, the dysarthrias, not the apraxias, would involve the Motor Level of that model.

It is quite obvious that the division within CA of more versus less fluent output will fall out along different lines in a production model. The primary question is whether the buccofacial apraxic component gives rise to phonemic level errors or not. Although Valdois et al. (1988) noted this kind of apraxia to be present in their three AMAs, the paraphasias they discussed did not seem to be phonetic disruptions but rather phonemic disruptions; that is, at least for these patients with buccofacial apraxia, there did not seem to be many asynchronies with, say, voice onset timing, abnormal syllable lengthening, fricative elongation, or the like. Disruptions that cause these kinds of disintegrations would have to be placed at the Phonetic Level. It may very well turn out to be that a buccofacial apraxia can accompany an AMA type of CA or a Broca's aphasic. A lower level phonetic problem might then be more likely in the latter group.

Finally, the other dimension along which CA bifurcates is that of repetition versus reproduction. Up to the early 1970s, many aphasiologists came to feel that the repetition problem in CA was simply due to short-term verbal–acoustic memory span. The patients could not repeat because they could not hold onto the acoustic stimulus presented to them. Nor could these patients repeat more than two or three digits. In 1974, however, Strub and Gardner submitted the mnestic account of repetition in CA to experimental test. Among other things, they found that their patient could improve repetition when the stimulus was presented more slowly and when the item to be repeated was familiar. The patient made many linear as well as transposition errors, but on testing revealed no primary short-term auditory–verbal memory deficit. Strub and Gardner (1974) concluded, therefore, that the CA had what is essentially a linguistic problem in "proceeding from a phonological analysis [by which they meant from the appreciation of the lexical segmental form representation—HWB] to the selection and combination of target phonemes" (p. 253). This provided strong support for the Dubois et al. (1964/1973) position.

Two years later, Heilman, Scholes, and Watson (1976) failed to find any significant differences for digit span immediate memory in both the oral and the visual modes of presentation for a group of Broca's aphasics and CAs. They also observed that there was a correlation between immediate memory capacity and comprehension. The more the former was compromised, the more the latter was. However, they concluded the article by taking a familiar stand in the philosophy of science: Correlation does not demonstrate causation. They wrote:

> Although intuitively the relationship is apparently causal [i.e., a reduced immediate memory span caused reduced comprehension of sentences], it is possible that both are indication of underlying linguistic incompetence. Therefore, these experiments do not provide us with sufficient evidence to make any definite statements regarding causal relationships. (p. 208)

They, therefore, appear to consider the possibility that the CA's major problem is one with language and not with short-term auditory–verbal memory.

Warrington and Shallice (1969) had published an influential study on short-term auditory–verbal memory, which gave rise to many memory studies of CA, but the definitive work by these two researchers did not appear until Shallice and Warrington (1977), where they introduced for the first time the pair of terms *reproduction* and *repetition* to sharply distinguish the CAs, whose problem is linguistic in nature in the former case (again, vindicating studies such as Dubois et al., 1964/1973, and those that support such a view) and memorial in the latter. The functional distinction was that the reproduction CA had a phonological manipulation (or recoding) problem on all kinds of confrontation situations, in addition to repetition such as naming and oral reading and where the errors produced were qualitatively the same across all tasks.

Caramazza, Basili, Koller, and Berndt (1981) published a case study of a repetition CA. This patient had a selective deficit on repetition but had no other speech output problems. Other types of tests revealed that this patient did, indeed, have a severe pathological limitation on auditory-verbal short-term memory. Although many reports on CA previously had claimed that this population had relatively intact comprehension, Caramazza et al. (1981) submitted this patient to more rigorous assessment of syntactic comprehension. The assessment revealed that the patient had poor comprehension when, in more complex sentences, material had to be held for analysis at a later point. Local analysis in simple sentences was not a problem, so the authors could rule out a primary deficit with the syntactic parser itself. "Holding on" to material was the problem, and this was attributed to the short-term auditory-verbal memory deficit. This was the first major study that showed a concomitant problem in CA with repetition and syntactic comprehension, both arising from limited short-term auditory-verbal memory.

Friedrich, Glenn, and Marin (1984) went as far as to claim that because general verbal short-term memory is so linked to phonological code manipulation, any assessment of this kind of memorial system could in truth actually be an assessment of phonology. They noted that short-term memory for sequences of tones was unimpaired. Other short-term verbal memory tasks all involved phonological coding of one form or another. Their patient had very little trouble with the repetition of familiar, high-frequency terms but had a severe breakdown in repeating nonsense words, indicating to these authors that their CA had two routes for repetition: lexical and direct auditory–articulation linking through nonlexical phonological coding processes. In this study the onus is placed on phonological coding abilities in CA, and that it is the deficit in this ability that gives rise to all the trouble these patients have with short-term auditory–verbal memory tasks.

Obviously, the issue of repetition versus reproduction CAs and their phonological–memorial deficits pertain to the decoding side, but they have consequences for production as well, albeit at the confrontation setting exclusively. It is not clear just how much a role short-term auditory-verbal memory plays in spontaneous speech, where there is no intervening stimulus item to be perceived, buffered, and manipulated for confrontation responding.

CONCLUSIONS

It should not be surprising that this chapter has revealed a great deal of heterogeneity in the CA syndrome. The number of single case studies and studies with small numbers of subjects in aphasia research today is steadily increasing, as is the psychological and linguistic analytic sophistication with which those studies are being carried out. As the findings of case studies accumulate, it becomes practically impossible to speak of "the typical" Broca's aphasic, Wernicke's aphasic, and so on. At best, we are left with category coherency in aphasia at a *theoretical* level of understanding (Caplan, 1991), rather than at the level of this or that patient. When our goal is to understand theoretical coherency of some syndrome, then group studies are more appropriate (Caplan, 1988). Nevertheless, some have argued quite vehemently against doing any study in aphasia with an *n* larger than one (e.g., Caramazza, 1984, 1986; Caramazza & McCloskey, 1988; McCloskey & Caramazza, 1988). After all is said and done, most participants in the argument come to the conclusion that the field can support case studies, multiple case studies, and even group studies with reasonable numbers of subjects. A recent statistic has been suggested that would allow us to combine both strategies by determining how good or bad a certain subject fits into an aphasic category (Bates, McDonald, Mac-Whinney, & Appelbaum, 1991; also see Bates, Appelbaum, & Allard, 1991; but see Caramazza's (1991) remarkable reply).

CA most often, if not always, arises as a consequence of lesions to the left perisylvian region, which actually is not diagnostic of very much. Within some reasonable degree, *all* aphasias arise from lesions of this zone. Damasio (1991) noted that the perisylvian lesions of CAs usually involve areas 41 and 42 (primary auditory cortex), a portion of area 22 (temporal lobe association cortex surrounding primary auditory cortex), and variably parts of insular cortex, subcortical white matter deep to that cortex, as well as area 40 (supramarginal gyrus). Damasio (1991) pointed out quite correctly that not all these regions need to be lesioned to produce a patient who will be classified as a CA on one or another aphasia battery. Damasio (1991) finally stressed that CA lesions typically do not extend to the posterior sector of the superior temporal gyrus (Wernicke's area—that is, if we can come to some agreement as to exactly what may or may not encompass Wernicke's area; Bogan & Bogan, 1976).

Given the fact that the plenum temporale (e.g., Galaburda, 1982) is located in the region often included in the lesion of the CA, given the fact that there is so much acoustic cortex in these regions, and given the fact that important memorial structures are located deep to this region in the temporal lobe, it is not surprising that there is so much functional heterogeneity observed in patients who test as CAs. Furthermore, slight shifts along the anterior–posterior axis of the Sylvian Fissure will result in greater or lesser motor involvement along with any other functional deficits that may appear. Fiber tracts, with bidirectional and multisynaptic structures, appear to be continually involved in mediating acoustic representations with motor representations, as they course through temporal, parietal, and frontal opercular regions, which form the underlying rim of perisylvian cortex. Therefore, from an anatomical point of view, it would be totally unreasonable to expect uniform homogeneity in CA. Of course, the gnawing puzzle to all this is the observed fact (again, see Valdois et al. 1988) that such heterogeneity characterizes a large number of patients who are all of the same category—CA, in this case. Obviously, if we are to continue talking about CA, it must be at the idealized and theoretical level of category description of which Caplan (1991) spoke.

What does all this mean in terms of locating CA breakdowns in a psycholinguistic model of language production? One thing for sure is that there will be some disagreement as to which components and which levels are involved. This chapter has outlined several suggestions. Much evidence has been garnered to suggest that the primary level of disruption in CA is the Positional Level, and that the computational breakdowns involve the processes that operate there. That, of course, does not imply that other aphasic symptoms may not involve one or more of those processes (e.g., Buckingham, 1985; Caramazza & Hillis, 1989). One of the crucial computations at this level is that of manipulating phonemic strings in the mapping procedure that takes lexical representative segments and imparts an ordering to those segments that more closely approximates utterance order. The range over which these ordering mechanisms operate is a very important issue, because some CAs appear to reveal a breakdown in the operations as they perform within words, across words, within phrases, or across phrases. Some investigators (e.g., Pate et al. 1987) have argued that ordering mechanisms that operate exclusively on isolated words must be located below the Positional Level. The argument then becomes one of whether or not segmental ordering processes at the Positional Level must be restricted to operate across phrases. We questioned this restriction and suggested that ordering processes at the Positional Level may operate over units as short as the word or as long as the clause.

Somewhere above the Positional Level is the lexicon, and any breakdown there, short of total access failure, will result in phonemic paraphasia. Researchers such as Beland et al. (1990) have suggested that the paraphasias of CAs can be accounted for by certain problems with operations that ostensibly occur within the lexicon, such as certain feature specification processes and procedural algorithms that construct syllables. Others (e.g., Kohn, 1989) argue that the CA's breakdown is postlexical. Much of the disagreement rests with the theoretical stances taken at the outset by individual investigators. Note that Beland et al. (1990) opt for the theory of underspecification, which assumes that syllable algorithms and feature specification (underlying and lexical) are in the lexicon. These investigators naturally characterize many CA paraphasias, therefore, as phenomena of the lexicon.

Whether one is at the level of the lexicon, or among the Positional Level postlexical operations, one can easily expect that the output of the error—wherever it may be—will be a fluent one, and one that has proper allophonic, allomorphic, and suprasegmental properties; that is, all errors will be accommodated. This accommodation takes place through the phonological process that are post-Positional Level and that are located at the Phonetic Level in the Garrett model. If one is to locate the breakdown of CA at the Phonetic Level, then one should expect to see a lack of accommodation, improper allophonic production, abberant allomorphic realizations, and the like. One should expect to see phonetic derailments that result in abnormal vowel lengthening, fricative elongation, VOT asynchronies, abnormal nasality, and so forth. Much of this kind of disintegration may very well cause productions that hearers may feel are simply phonemic category shifts, but the speakers would be experiencing clear-cut phonetic problems—something that takes place below the Positional Level.

The puzzle we must work out ultimately is that of the observed dysfluencies in some CAs, especially those who present with buccofacial apraxias or other kinds of ideomotor-like articulatory abnormalities. Their lesions are predictably more anterior in the perisylvian region, but what must be clearly demarcated is to what extent the articulatory errors of these CAs truly encroach on the allophonic level. Recall that, although the AMA types of CA in the Valdois et al. study (1988) had buccofacial apraxias and had more anterior parietal lesions, their paraphasias as measured by the investigators were different from the CAs but did not appear to reveal abnormal allophones; that is, the AMAs had an apraxic component but did not seem to have a Phonetic Level problem. Clearly, much more research is needed here.

In sum, the cross-cutting functional complexities and extreme heterogeneity seen in conduction aphasia present some of the most intriguing and challenging puzzles for language and speech production modelling in aphasiology today, and it would not be surprising if that syndrome ultimately goes the way of agrammatism, holding together as it does at the level of a theoretical category and resisting much patient-to-patient homogeneity.

REFERENCES

Ardila, A., & Rosselli, M. (1990). Conduction aphasia and verbal apraxia. *Journal of Neurolinguistics, 5,* 1-14.

Bates, E., Appelbaum, M., & Allard, L. (1991). Statistical constraints on the use of single cases in neuropsychological research. *Brain and Language, 40,* 295-329.

Bates, E., McDonald, J., MacWhinney, B., & Appelbaum, M. (1991). A maximum likelihood procedure for the analysis of group and individual data in aphasia research. *Brain and Language, 40,* 231-265.

Baum, S. R. (1990). Acoustic analysis of intra-word syllabic timing relations in anterior aphasia. *Journal of Neurolinguistics, 5,* 321-331.

Beland, R. (1990). Vowel epenthesis in aphasia. In J.-L. Nespoulous & P. Villiard (Eds.), *Morphology, phonology, and aphasia* (pp. 235-252). New York: Springer-Verlag.

Beland, R., Caplan, D., & Nespoulous, J.-L. (1990). The role of abstract phonological representations in word production: Evidence from phonemic paraphasias. *Journal of Neurolinguistics, 5,* 125-164.

Beland, R., & Favreau, Y. (1989). On the special status of coronals in aphasia. *Tapuscrits CHCN Working Papers,* No. 22, 52-66.

Blumstein, S. E. (1978). Segment structure and the syllable in aphasia. In A. Bell & J. B. Hooper (Eds.), *Syllables and segments* (pp. 189-200). Amsterdam: North-Holland.

Bogen, J. E., & Bogen, G. M. (1976). Wernicke's region—where is it? *Annals of the New York Academy of Sciences, 280,* 834-843.

Buckingham, H. W. (1980). On correlating aphasic errors with slips-of-the-tongue. *Applied Psycholinguistics, 1,* 199-220.

Buckingham, H. W. (1985). Perseveration in aphasia. In S. Newman & R. Epstein (Eds.), *Current perspectives in dysphasia* (pp. 113-154). Edinburgh: Churchill Livingstone.

Buckingham, H. W. (1986). The scan-copier mechanism and the positional level of language production: Evidence from aphasia. *Cognitive Science, 10,* 195-217.

Buckingham, H. W. (1987). Phonemic paraphasias and psycholinguistic production models for neologistic jargon. *Aphasiology, 1,* 381-400.

Buckingham, H. W. (1989). Phonological paraphasia. In C. Code (Ed.), *The characteristics of aphasia* (pp. 89-110). London: Taylor & Francis.

Buckingham, H. W. (1990a). Principle of sonority, doublet creation, and the checkoff monitor. In J.-L. Nespoulous & P. Villiard (Eds.), *Morphology, phonology, and aphasia* (pp. 193-205). New York: Springer-Verlag.

Buckingham, H. W. (1990b). Abstruse neologisms, retrieval deficits and the random generator. *Journal of Neurolinguistics, 5,* 215-235.

Buckingham, H. W. (1991). Explanations for the concept of apraxia of speech. In M. T. Sarno (Ed.), *Acquired aphasia* (2nd ed., pp. 271-312). San Diego: Academic Press.

Buckingham, H. W., & Kertesz, A. (1976). *Neologistic jargon aphasia.* Amsterdam: Swets & Zeitlinger.

Buckingham, H. W., Whitaker, H., & Whitaker, H. A. (1978). Alliteration and assonance in neologistic jargon aphasia. *Cortex, 14,* 365-380.

Buckingham, H. W., & Yule, G. (1987). Phonemic false evaluation: Theoretical and clinical aspects. *Clinical Linguistics and Phonetics, 1,* 113-125.

Caplan, D. (1987). *Neurolinguistics and linguistic aphasiology*. Cambridge, England: Cambridge University Press.

Caplan, D. (1988). On the role of group studies in neuropsychological and pathopsychological research. *Cognitive Neuropsychology, 5,* 535-548.

Caplan, D. (1991). Agrammatism is a theoretically coherent aphasic category. *Brain and Language, 40,* 274-281.

Caplan, D., Vanier, M., & Baker, C. (1986). A case study of reproduction conduction aphasia I: Word production. *Cognitive Neuropsychology, 3,* 99-128.

Caramazza, A. (1984). The logic of neuropsychological research and the problem of patient classification of aphasia. *Brain and Language, 21,* 9-20.

Caramazza, A. (1986). On drawing inferences about the structure of normal cognitive systems from the analysis of patterns of impaired performance: The case for single-patient studies. *Brain and Cognition, 5,* 41-66.

Caramazza, A. (1991). Data, statistics, and theory: A comment on Bates, McDonald, MacWhinney, and Applebaum's "A maximum likelihood procedure for the analysis of group and individual data in aphasia research." *Brain and Language, 41,* 43-51.

Caramazza, A., Basili, A., Koller, J. J., & Berndt, R. S. (1981). An investigation of repetition and language processing in a case of conduction aphasia. *Brain and Language, 14,* 235-271.

Caramazza, A., & Hillis, A. E. (1989). The disruption of sentence production: Some dissociations. *Brain and Language, 36,* 625-650.

Caramazza, A., & McCloskey, M. (1988). The case for single-patient studies. *Cognitive Neuropsychology, 5,* 517-528.

Clements, G. N. (1990). The role of the sonority cycle in core syllabification. In J. Kingston & M. Beckman (Eds.), *Papers in laboratory phonology I: Between the grammar and the physics of speech* (pp. 283-333). Cambridge, England: Cambridge University Press.

Crain, S., & Fodor, J. D. (1985). Can grammars help parsers? In D. R. Dowty, L. Karttunen, & A. M. Zwicky (Eds.), *Natural language parsing: Psychological, computational, and theoretical perspectives* (pp. 94-128). Cambridge, England: Cambridge University Press.

Damasio, H. (1991). Neuroanatomical correlates of the aphasias. In M. T. Sarno (Ed.), *Acquired aphasia* (2nd ed., pp. 45-71). San Diego: Academic Press.

Dell, G. S. (1988). The retrieval of phonological forms in production: Tests of predictions from a connectionist model. *Journal of Memory and Language, 27,* 124-142.

Dubois, J., Hecaen, H., Angelergues, R., Maufras de Chatelier, A., & Marcie, P. (1973). Neurolinguistic study of conduction aphasia. In H. Goodglass & S. Blumstein (Eds.), *Psycholinguistics and aphasia* (pp. 283-300). Baltimore: Johns Hopkins University Press. (Original work published 1964)

Friedrich, F., Glenn, C. G., & Marin, O. S. M. (1984). Interruption of phonological coding in conduction aphasia. *Brain and Language, 22,* 266-291.

Fromkin, V. A. (Ed.). (1973). *Speech errors as linguistic evidence*. The Hague: Mouton.

Fromkin, V. A. (Ed.) (1980). *Errors in linguistic performance: Slips of the tongue, ear, pen, and hand*. New York: Academic Press.

Galaburda, A. M. (1982). Histology, architectonics, and asymmetry of language areas. In M. A. Arbib, D. Caplan, & J. C. Marshall (Eds.), *Neural models of languages processes* (pp. 435-445). New York: Academic Press.

Garrett, M. F. (1980). Levels of processing in sentence production. In B. Butterworth (Ed.), *Language production: Vol. 1, Speech and talk* (pp. 177-220). London: Academic Press.

Garrett, M. F. (1982). Production of speech: Observations from normal and pathological language use. In A. Ellis (Ed.), *Normality and pathology in cognitive functions* (pp. 19-76). London: Academic Press.

Garrett, M. F. (1984). The organization of processing structure for language production: Applications to aphasic speech. In D. Caplan, A. Lecours, & A. Smith (Eds.), *Biological perspectives on language* (pp. 172-193). Cambridge, MA: MIT Press.

Garrett, M. F. (1988). Process in language production. In F. Newmeyer (Ed.), *The Cambridge survey, III. Language: Psychological and biological aspects* (pp. 69–96). Cambridge, England: Cambridge University Press.

Garrett, M. F. (1990a). Sentence processing. In D. Osherson & H. Lasnik (Eds.), *Language: An invitation to cognitive science* (pp. 133–175). Cambridge, MA: MIT Press.

Garrett, M. F. (1990b). A review of Levelt: *Speaking. Language and Speech, 33,* 273–292.

Goldsmith, J. A. (1990). *Autosegmental and metrical phonology.* London: Basil Blackwell.

Grice, H. P. (1975). Logic and conversation. In P. Cole & J. L. Morgan (Eds.), *Syntax and semantics: Speech acts* (Vol. 3, pp. 41–58). New York: Academic Press.

Grimshaw, J. (1990). *Argument structure.* Cambridge, MA: MIT Press.

Grodzinsky, Y. (1990). *Theoretical perspectives on language disorders.* Cambridge, MA: MIT Press.

Heilman, K. M., Scholes, R., & Watson, R. T. (1976). Defects of immediate memory in Broca's and conduction aphasia. *Brain and Language, 3,* 201–208.

Hoffman, R. R., Cochran, E. L., & Nead, J. M. (1990). Cognitive metaphors in experimental psychology. In D. E. Leary (Ed.), *Metaphors in the history of psychology* (pp. 173–229). Cambridge, England: Cambridge University Press.

Jackson, J. H. (1931). On the nature of the duality of the brain. In J. Taylor (Ed.), *Selected writings of John Hughlings Jackson* (Vol. 2, pp. 129–145). London: Hodder & Stoughton. (Original work published 1874)

Joanette, Y., Keller, E., & Lecours, A. R. (1980). Sequences of phonemic approximations in aphasia. *Brain and Language, 11,* 30–44.

Keller, E. (1984). Simplification and gesture reduction in phonological disorders of apraxia and aphasia. In J. C. Rosenbek, M. R. McNeil, & A. E. Aronson (Eds.), *Apraxia of speech: Physiology, acoustics, linguistics, management* (pp. 221–256). San Diego, CA: College-Hill Press.

Kertesz, A. (1979). *Aphasia and associated disorders: Taxonomy, localization, and recovery.* New York: Grune & Stratton.

Kohn, S. E. (1984). The nature of the phonological disorder in conduction aphasia. *Brain and Language, 23,* 97–115.

Kohn, S. E. (1985). *Phonological breakdown in aphasia.* Unpublished doctoral dissertation, Department of Psychology, Tufts University, Boston, MA.

Kohn, S. E. (1989). The nature of the phonemic string deficit in conduction aphasia. *Aphasiology, 3,* 209–239.

Kohn, S. E., & Smith, K. L. (1990). Between-word speech errors in conduction aphasia. *Cognitive Neuropsychology, 7,* 133–156.

Lecours, A. R., & Lhermitte, F. (1969). Phonemic paraphasias: Linguistic structures and tentative hypotheses. *Cortex, 5,* 193–228.

Lecours, A. R., & Lhermitte, F. (1976). The "pure form" of the phonetic disintegration syndrome (pure Anarthria): Anatomo-clinical report of a historical case. *Brain and Language, 3,* 88–113.

Lecours, A. R., Lhermitte, F., & Bryans, B. (1983). *Aphasiology.* London: Bailliere Tindall.

Levelt, W. J. M. (1989). *Speaking: From intention to articulation.* Cambridge, MA: MIT Press.

MacNeilage, P. F., Hutchinson, J. A., & Lasater, S. A. (1981). The production of speech: Development and dissolution of motoric and premotoric processes. In J. Long & A. Baddeley (Eds.), *Attention and performance* (Vol. 9, pp. 503–519). Hillsdale, NJ: Lawrence Erlbaum Associates.

Martinet, A. (1964). *Elements of general linguistics.* Chicago: University of Chicago Press.

McCloskey, M., & Caramazza, A. (1988). Theory and methodology in cognitive neuropsychology: A response to our critics. *Cognitive Neuropsychology, 5,* 583–623.

McNeil, M. R., Rosenbek, J. C., & Aronson, A. E. (Eds.). (1984). *The dysarthrias: Physiology, acoustics, perception, management.* San Diego: College-Hill Press.

Morton, J. (1979). Word recognition. In J. Morton & J. C. Marshall (Eds.), *Psycholinguistics 2: Structures and processes* (pp. 107–156). Cambridge, MA: MIT Press.

Nespoulous, J.-L., Joanette, Y., Ska, B., Caplan, D., & Lecours, A. R. (1987). Production deficits in Broca's and conduction aphasia: Repetition versus reading. In E. Keller & M. Gopnik (Eds.), *Motor and sensory processes of language* (pp. 53–81). Hillsdale, NJ: Lawrence Erlbaum Associates.

Pate, D. S., Saffran, E. M., & Martin, N. (1987). Specifying the nature of the production impairment in a conduction aphasic: A case study. *Language, and Cognitive Processes, 2,* 43–84.

Rapp, B. C., & Caramazza, A. (1991). Lexical deficits. In M. T. Sarno (Ed.), *Acquired aphasia* (pp. 181–222). San Diego: Academic Press.

Rosenbek, J. C., McNeil, M. R., & Aronson, A. E. (Eds.). (1984). *Apraxia of speech: Physiology, acoustics, linguistics, and management.* San Diego: College-Hill Press.

Saffran, E. M. (1982). Neuropsychological approaches to the study of language. *British Journal of Psychology, 73,* 317–337.

Saffran, E. M., Schwartz, M. F., & Marin, O. S. M. (1980). Evidence from aphasia: Isolating the components of a production model. In B. Butterworth (Ed.), *Language production Vol. 1: Speech and talk* (pp. 221–241). London: Academic Press.

Schwartz, M. F. (1987). Patterns of speech production deficit within and across aphasia syndromes: Application of a psycholinguistic model. In M. Coltheart, G. Sartori, & R. Job (Eds.), *The cognitive neuropsychology of language* (pp. 163–199). London: Lawrence Erlbaum Associates.

Shallice, T., & Warrington, E. K. (1977). Auditory–verbal short-term memory impairment and conduction aphasia. *Brain and Language, 4,* 479–491.

Shattuck-Hufnagel, S. (1979). Speech errors as evidence for a serial-ordering mechanism in sentence production. In W. E. Cooper & E. C. T. Walker (Eds.), *Sentence processing: Psycholinguistic studies presented to Merrill Garrett* (pp. 295–342). Hillsdale, NJ: Lawrence Erlbaum Associates.

Shattuck-Hufnagel, S. (1987). The role of word-onset consonants in speech production planning: New evidence from speech error patterns. In E. Keller & M. Gopnik (Eds.), *Motor and sensory processes of language* (pp. 17–51). Hillsdale, NJ: Lawrence Erlbaum Associates.

Shattuck-Hufnagel, S., & Klatt, D. H. (1979). Minimal use of features and markedness in speech production. *Journal of Verbal Learning and Verbal Behavior, 18,* 41–55.

Stemberger, J. P. (1982). The nature of segments in the lexicon: Evidence from speech errors. *Lingua, 56,* 235–259.

Strub, R. L., & Gardner, H. (1974). The repetition defect in conduction aphasia: Mnestic or linguistic? *Brain and Language, 1,* 241–255.

Valdois, S., Joanette, Y., & Nespoulous, J.-L. (1989). Intrinsic organization of sequences of phonemic approximations: A preliminary study. *Aphasiology, 3,* 55–73.

Valdois, S., Joanette, Y., Nespoulous, J.-L., & Poncet, M. (1988). Afferent motor aphasia and conduction aphasia. In H. A. Whitaker (Ed.), *Phonological processes and brain mechanisms* (pp. 59–92). New York: Springer-Verlag.

Warrington, E. K., & Shallice, T. (1969). The selective impairment of auditory–verbal short-term memory. *Brain, 92,* 885–896.

Wernicke, K. (1977). The aphasia symptom-complex: A psychological study on an anatomic basis. In G. Eggert (Ed.), *Wernicke's works on aphasia: A sourcebook and review* (pp. 91–145). The Hague: Mouton. (Original work published 1874)

Chapter 6

Issues Arising Regarding the Nature and Consequences of Reproduction Conduction Aphasia

David Caplan
Harvard Medical School

Gloria Waters
McGill University

In 1977, Shallice and Warrington drew a distinction between two types of disturbances of repetition, which had previously been grouped together under the heading of *conduction aphasia* (Shallice & Warrington, 1977). They argued that one reason for a patient's failure to repeat a verbally presented stimulus was a disturbance of auditory–verbal short-term memory. They labeled this disturbance *repetition conduction aphasia*. A second reason they identified for a patient's failure to repeat was a disturbance in formulating the phonological form and the sequence of articulatory gestures associated with a single word. They termed this impairment *reproduction conduction aphasia*. In this chapter, we discuss a number of issues that arise regarding the nature and consequences of this latter disturbance.

Our presentation is organized as follows. In the first section of this chapter, we deal with the nature of reproduction conduction aphasia itself, discussing the functional architecture of the word production mechanisms, and the nature of lexical phonological representations and how they are activated. In this part we suggest that reproduction conduction aphasia might be divisible into a number of different disturbances affecting word (and nonword) sound production. In the second section of this chapter, we consider reproduction conduction aphasia as a single disturbance and outline several possible consequences of reproduction conduction aphasia in five areas: speech sound discrimination and spoken word recognition, recognition of written words, auditory–verbal short-term memory, metalinguistic phonological processing, and sentence and discourse comprehension. Although it is possible the different forms of reproduction conduction aphasia that we suggest may exist may each have different consequences for these different psycholinguistic functions, we do not pursue the discussion to this level of detail.

Although all the questions that we raise are unresolved (and there is no evidence of which we are aware that bears on many of them), we hope that the framework we provide for approaching this disturbance may prove helpful in thinking about the implications of particular results and even in guiding future research.

THE NATURE
OF REPRODUCTION CONDUCTION APHASIA

Possible Loci of Deficits in the Functional Architecture of the Word Sound Production System

Phonological errors that arise in repetition tasks could have many possible sources. These include disorders affecting the discrimination or identification of phonemes, disorders of recognizing spoken words, and disorders affecting the ability to produce the forms of words. An initial challenge is to identify the functional component(s) of the word-processing system that are affected in a patient who makes these errors in repetition. An important clue can come from the tasks in which these errors are made. Contemporary cases that fall into the category of reproduction conduction aphasia have all had disturbances affecting the production of single words in confrontation naming and reading tasks, as well as repetition. The fact that phonological errors occur in all these speech production tasks, and that errors are at least grossly similar in these three tasks in affected patients described in the literature, has led many authors to argue that the disturbance found in reproduction conduction aphasia affects what might be called a "final common pathway" that is part of the speech production mechanism used in not only repetition but in reading and confrontation naming as well. One way to illustrate this hypothesis is presented in Fig. 6.1.

The rationale for postulating a disturbance at the stage of phonological output processing in these patients is essentially as follows: The inputs in the tasks of confrontation naming, repetition, and reading are all extremely dissimilar, and, therefore, similar types of errors occurring on these tasks must be secondary to a disturbance in some output-oriented mechanism. Given that the errors made by these patients are phonological in nature, a reasonable inference is that the disturbed output processing component is one that involves the formulation and/or specification of the sound of a word (or nonword).

This characterization of the functional locus of the impairment in reproduction conduction aphasia immediately raises the question of whether the syn-

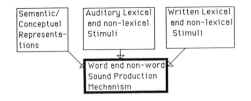

FIG. 6.1.   A simple model of word sound production in which the locus of impairment in reproduction conduction aphasia is viewed as a disturbance in the final sound production mechanism common to all speech tasks. The damaged component is indicated by a dense outline.

drome fractionates along task lines; that is, whether there are disturbances with the output characteristics of reproduction conduction aphasia that arise in one or two of the tasks of confrontation naming, repetition, and reading but spare the remaining task(s). The classic neurological literature suggests that this is the case. In the classical neurological view (Lichtheim, 1885; Wernicke, 1874; see Geschwind, 1965, for a modern analysis), conduction aphasia in general is characterized by a disturbance affecting repetition that is greater than a disturbance affecting auditory comprehension. Classical neurologically oriented theorizing hypothesized that conduction aphasia arose because of a "disconnection" between the representations of the phonological forms of words used to identify and understand spoken words and the motor speech-planning mechanisms. A patient with a deficit in the "transmission pathway" between word recognition and word production would be able to discriminate speech sounds and identify words and would also be able to read words and nonwords aloud and produce appropriate names for visually presented objects but would show a disturbance of phonological output in word and (possibly nonword) repetition. Such a disturbance is illustrated in Fig. 6.2.

Experimental results in normal subjects provide evidence for a "direct" or "privileged" route between processing phonological input and output phonological planning that is involved in repetition and therefore offer a reason to believe that a patient with a disturbance of this route might exist. The finding that repetition can proceed while a subject is performing secondary tasks, whereas other language functions are affected by these secondary tasks, provides evidence for a direct/privileged repetition route. For instance, McLeod and Posner (1984) found that repeating the words "high" and "low" was not affected by performing a visual letter-matching task that required a manual response, whereas saying "high" and "low" in response to the stimuli "up" and "down" or in response to a high or a low tone was affected by this secondary task (see also Freidrich, Glenn, & Marin, 1984; Shallice, McLeod, & Lewis, 1985; Monsell, 1984; Barnard, 1985; and others regarding a "privileged" or "direct" route between auditory verbal input and oral verbal output). If repetition of words (and possibly nonwords) were to proceed by

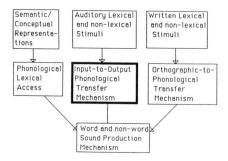

FIG. 6.2. A more detailed model of word sound production in which specialized mechanisms are postulated that mediate the activation of sound patterns
as a function of input. The locus of impairment in "neurologically classic"
reproduction conduction aphasia is viewed as a disturbance in the mechanism
transferring phonological input representations to the final sound production
mechanism common to all speech tasks. The damaged component is indicated
by a dense outline. The model suggests that there could be other "route-specific"
forms of reproduction conduction aphasia.

this privileged route, a disturbance of this route would correspond to the classical neurological view of reproduction conduction aphasia.[1]

It is not clear, however, whether an isolated disturbance consisting of phonological paraphasias and other errors attributable to word sound planning exists in repetition tasks without a co-occurring disturbance in naming and
reading.[2] Kinsbourne (1972) suggested that a patient he examined had a disturbance of the route between input and output phonological planning. JO
was unable to repeat single words or digits accurately but could match two-
digit strings. Kinsbourne argued that this showed that JO's deficit lay in transferring information from an input to an output system. However, this patient's
output problems were not presented in detail, and it is possible that he had
a disturbance in a sound production component common to several tasks.

A disturbance of the direct/privileged repetition route would not be expected

---

[1]There is some uncertainty as to whether there are separate "routes" or cognitive mechanisms
underlying the repetition of words and nonwords. The direct/privileged "status" may apply to
both a lexical and a nonlexical input-to-output route, or there may be a single mechanism underlying the transmission of phonological forms from the input side to the output side.

[2]Note that although this disturbance is one of repetition, it falls into the category of "reproduction" conduction aphasia in the Shallice and Warrington (1977) classification scheme because it
affects repetition of single words and (ex hypothesi) is not due to a short-term memory (STM)
deficit. Shallice and Warrington (1977) reserve the term *Repetition* Conduction Aphasia for disturbances of repetition due to STM impairments. These disturbances show up in repeating lists of
words and sometimes sentences, not single words. Shallice and Warrington (1977) discuss the possibility that STM problems contributed to the poor single-word repetition performances of several
patients. The issue of whether and how STM disturbances can affect repetition of single words
(i.e., of the role of STM in single-word repetition) is a complex matter that is not discussed here.

to be discernible unless the patient were forced to use this route to repeat words and nonwords. Aside from repetition routes based on form alone, repetition of words may proceed via a semantic route, in which words are recognized and understood and their phonological forms reconstituted from the semantic representations thus extracted. Word repetition via this semantic route would, in essence, consist of the combination of single-word auditory comprehension and single-word oral production from semantics, as shown in Fig. 6.3.

Evidence for the existence of this semantic route comes in part from the existence of brain-damaged patients who apparently use this route to repeat. Such patients make numerous semantic paraphasias in repetition tasks (Michel & Andreewsky, 1983). Assuming that this semantic route does in fact exist, a disturbance of the direct/privileged route would only lead to the production of phonological paraphasias if a patient was not able to compensate for this disturbance by employing the semantic route in repetition. Accordingly, a disturbance of the direct/privileged repetition route would only show up as reproduction conduction aphasia if a patient were somehow constrained to use this damaged direct/privileged mechanism. There are two possible reasons that this might happen: Alternate routes—in particular, the semantic route—might be impaired, and/or strategic considerations might make the patient continue to rely on the direct/privileged repetition route. If a patient were to be discovered who showed evidence of impairment of repetition via the direct/privileged route, it would be important to know why he or she did not use the semantic route to compensate for this impairment.

If we accept the possibility that there may be a disturbance that corresponds to the classical neurological notion of reproduction conduction aphasia— namely, an impairment to the transfer of phonological information from input to output processing mechanisms (in different terms, a disturbance of the direct/privileged repetition route)—we may ask whether there could be corresponding disturbances affecting the transfer of information from input to out-

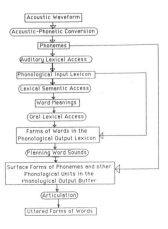

FIG. 6.3.   A model repetition incorporating sequential processing stages involving a Phonological Output Lexicon and a Response Buffer. Different repetition routes are indicated by the sequences of arrows between representations.

put processors in single-word oral reading and confrontation naming. The literature is suggestive, but far from definitive, on this point.

Phonological paraphasias in oral reading are extremely common, but whether they occur in single-word reading tasks without also occurring in repetition and confrontation naming tasks is unclear. In the contemporary literature, the best studied examples of phonological errors in single-word oral reading are the errors made by so-called surface dyslexics (Patterson, Marshall, & Coltheart, 1985). Patients with surface dyslexia can read both words and nonwords but make a variety of errors, of which the characteristic and defining type is the "regularization" error. In a regularization error, a patient produces a more common phonological value for a grapheme or other spelling unit than that associated with the grapheme or spelling unit in that particular word. Thus, a surface dyslexic may read the word PINT with a short, rather than a long, I because the usual phonological value for I, especially when followed by two consonants at the end of a word, is a short, rather than a long, vowel (Bub, Cancelliere, & Kertesz, 1985). One theoretical position regarding the origin of these errors is that they reflect disturbances of the translation of whole-word orthography to whole-word phonology, with over-reliance on sublexical spelling-sound correspondences, in particular grapheme–phoneme correspondences (Coltheart, Masterson, Byng, Prior, & Riddoch, 1983).[3] Such a mechanism is obviously to be distinguished from those that are involved in the direct/privileged repetition route and any translation/transfer process that occurs between picture or object visual recognition and spoken word production. Accordingly, we should be prepared to include disturbances such as surface dyslexia and other phonological segmental errors in reading as route-specific forms of reproduction conduction aphasia occasioned by disruption of a pathway from input orthographic forms to output phonological representations.[4]

The fractionation of reproduction conduction aphasia along route-specific lines includes the possibility that there may be a disturbance of the transmission of semantic values to phonological output representations that affects picture naming and, possibly, the activation of phonological forms of words from concepts that have been evoked by thoughts. Many theories of the activation of phonological forms of words from concepts specify that various aspects of the forms of words become available to the speaker in an incremental fashion

---

[3]See Patterson, Seidenberg, and McClelland (1989) for an alternative account of surface dyslexia in terms of a single-route reading mechanism based on parallel distributed processing principles. We review this model briefly in our discussion of reading and word recognition.

[4]There are other possible accounts of these errors. In particular, it is possible that at least some of these errors arise because of a disturbance in the hypothesized final sound planning mechanism common to all speech output tasks, as shown in Fig. 6.1. Not all errors made by surface dyslexics are attributable to regularization effects or visual confusions (Marcel, 1980); some may arise due to disruptions of sound planning processes that occur after orthographic-to-phonological conversion has taken place.

(Levelt, 1989), and it is possible that the activation of lexical phonological forms might be arrested at any one of these stages. Because some of these stages are unique to the activation of the phonological forms of words from semantic representations and are not found in either the direct/privileged repetition route or the various mechanisms involved in transcoding lexical or nonlexical orthographic representations to phonological representations, it is possible that a patient have a disturbance affecting one or another of these stages of word form activation from concepts.

One form such a disturbance might take is to put a patient in the tip-of-the-tongue state in confrontation naming tasks and spontaneous speech (Brown & McNeill, 1966). Such patients, who can verbally or otherwise indicate that they have a reasonably complete semantic/conceptual representation at their disposal but who cannot "find" the complete form of the word that corresponds to this representation, have been described by many authors (Goodglass, Kaplan, Weintraub, & Ackerman, 1976). It is extremely likely that the disturbance these patients have consists of a failure to activate complete lexical phonological representations on the output side, and this must include or entail a failure to activate some segmental phonological elements (phonemes) in output-side tasks. These disturbances thus may be seen as a type of route-specific reproduction conduction aphasia. In addition to patients whose performances resemble the normal tip-of-the-tongue state, it is possible that there are patients whose phonological segmental planning disturbances only affect single words in tasks in which the forms of single words are activated from semantic/ conceptual representations. To our knowledge, however, no patients have been described who only make phonemic paraphasias in confrontation naming and naming to definition tasks, but not in either repetition and/or reading.

An important aside that is relevant at this point is that disturbances that show up as phonological paraphasias in spontaneous speech may not represent the same disturbance that affects the activation and planning of phonological forms of words from lexical semantic representations in single-word production tasks, such as naming pictures or providing words for definitions. The reason that these types of disturbances may not be equivalent is that phonological errors that arise in spontaneous speech could occur during the insertion of the phonological forms of words into sentence structures. In fact, most researchers who have studied phonemic errors in normal subjects have documented these errors as exchange errors between words in connected speech, not as phonological errors within individual words. These researchers have generally agreed that most of these phonological segmental errors in normal subjects arise during some process of sentence construction—in particular, Garrett (1976, 1978, 1980, 1982), Shattuck-Hufnagel (1985, 1986), Dell (1984, 1986, 1988), Dell and Reich (1981), Stemberger (1982, 1983a, 1983b, 1985), Stemberger and MacWhinney (1986), Stemberger and Treiman (1986), and others have all produced variants of the hypothesis that these errors arise during lexical insertion into sentential structures. Patients who make phonological errors only in sentence production—that is, in spontaneous speech—are therefore not necessarily to be considered as cases with reproduction conduction aphasia as defined by Shallice and Warrington (1977), because their disturbances may not involve the formulation of the phonological forms of single words, but rather the insertion of phonological forms into syntactic structures (Buckingham, 1980).

A final possibility is that the form of the phonological errors seen in one task may differ from those in another (e.g., one author [DC] has seen a patient who made phonological paraphasias in repetition and more complex phonological neologisms in spontaneous speech). The implications of such a pattern are unclear: Does the patient have a single disturbance in a component of the speech production system common to the affected tasks, which is manifest differently because of the way that component is influenced by the other aspects of each task, or does the patient have a set of different impairments in the transfer functions between different inputs and some part of the phonological planning mechanism? At present, there are no good data documenting such qualitative dissociations in sound planning as a function of task. Future work will hopefully resolve the question of whether and how these types of dissociations occur.

Models of the Word Production Mechanism I: Implications of Lexical Effects

The second set of issues that arise regarding the nature of reproduction conduction aphasia pertains to the status of lexical effects on the production mechanism. The first issue in this area is whether there are separate mechanisms involved in the production of words and nonwords. This question can be seen as one that relates to the functional architecture of the word production system, and its discussion might properly belong in the previous section. We have grouped it together with issues regarding the role of word classes and other lexical effects in word sound production because we think it is more properly conceived of as being related to the effects of lexical variables on a single component of the phonological production system.

Virtually all studies of conduction aphasics have shown that the production of nonwords is worse than the production of words (Bub, Black, Howell, & Kertesz, 1987; Caplan, Vanier, & Baker, 1986; Dubois, Hecaen, Angelergues, Maufras de Chatelier, & Marcie, 1964/1973; Miceli, Giustolisi, & Caramazza, 1990; Miller & Ellis, 1987; but see Kohn, 1989). In some cases, repetition of words is almost normal, whereas virtually no nonwords are correctly repeated (Miceli et al., 1990). In other cases the dissociation is not so extreme (Caplan et al., 1986; Bub et al., 1987). The consistent difference between words and nonwords, however, requires explanation.

The most extreme analysis that would account for this discrepancy would be one in which separate word and nonword production mechanisms were postulated. On the basis of the performance of their patient, Miceli et al. (1990) in fact postulated the existence of a "lexicoarticulatory" process, which converts whole-word phonological forms into articulatory gestures, bypassing any process involved in the activation and production of sublexical sound units. In the absence of the reverse dissociation, however, models that make for less drastic separations between word and nonword production mechanisms are theoretically more desirable. In some such models, a word production advantage would be derived from the increased familiarity associated with words. Interactive activation models of the kind described by Dell (1986) have a bias toward producing words when they generate errors because of complex interactions between word- and phoneme-level activation mechanisms. In the Dell model, for example, words activate phonemes that then feed back to lexical representations; errors that arise at the level of phonemic planning are thus subject to a "corrective" influence from the lexical level. Whether lesions can be produced in computer-implemented models of this kind that simulate the full range of differences between word and nonword production in repetition tasks in brain-damaged patients remains a subject for further research.

The word advantage in word production tasks seen in patients with reproduction conduction aphasia (and in other patients) rules out any strictly serial model of the word production process, such as that proposed by Morton and Patterson (1980), as discussed by Caplan et al. (1986). Morton and Patterson's model (1980), shown in its essence in Fig. 6.3, postulates a Phonological Output Lexicon, which is activated from cognitive representations and from input lexical representations (either phonological or orthographic), and which feeds a Response Buffer in which articulatory plans for phonemes and sequences of phonemes are developed. Nonwords cannot activate items in the Phonological Output Lexicon and therefore activate representations in the Response Buffer directly. Any disturbance of the Response Buffer would be expected to affect words and nonwords equally; disturbances of the Phonological Output Lexicon would be expected to affect words but not nonwords. Without some interactive mechanism, or a separate mechanism for words and nonwords, there is no way to account for word advantages over nonwords in repetition (and oral reading) tasks. As noted earlier, however, a major research question is what the nature of this interaction may be.

A whole host of lexical factors other than lexical status itself may be important in determining patients' performances on word production tasks. Two of these factors are frequency of occurrence of lexical items and grammatical class.

Word frequency has a ubiquitous effect on psycholinguistic tasks, but its effects have not always been documented in the relationship to the generation of phonemic paraphasias in word production. Thus, for instance, Pate, Saffran, and Martin (1987) reported a conduction aphasic whose phonological errors did not seem to be frequency sensitive. These errors appear to have arisen at the individual word level (though the patient was primarily tested in sentence production tasks). Why lexical frequency did not affect this patient's performance, whereas it did affect the incidence of phonemic errors in other patients (Bub et al., 1987), requires further modeling of the speech production process.

Word class effects are of potentially great interest in reproduction conduction aphasia. Normally occurring phonological speech errors almost entirely spare the function word vocabulary, even for vocabulary items matched for frequency with "open class" items (Garrett, 1976, 1980, 1982, 1990). Accordingly, it is reasonable to ask whether phonemic paraphasias also arise predominantly on one or more vocabulary classes, defined grammatically or in some other way. Caplan et al. (1986) reported that their patient with reproduction conduction aphasia did not make phonological errors on function words. Other patients' performances in this respect have not been reported.

In patients with deep dyslexia, different word classes within the content word vocabulary are differentially susceptible to semantic paralexias (Coltheart, 1980). Nouns are spared relative to adjectives and verbs in many of these patients. Whether there are comparable differences in the production of phonemic paraphasias as a function of word class within the content word vocabulary is unknown. Prepositions are another interesting category with respect to phonemic errors. Although prepositions are subject to word substitution errors in naturally occurring speech errors, suggesting that they are treated as members of the open class vocabulary set at certain stages of lexical activation and/or sentence planning, they are not subject to phonological segmental errors and thus, in this latter respect, pattern with closed class vocabulary elements (Garrett, 1982). Whether or not phonological paraphasias arise in prepositions in patients with reproduction conduction aphasia is not known.

Finally, semantic factors influence certain types of word production errors in brain-damaged patients. Once again, patients with deep dyslexia are cases in point. In these patients, abstractness appears to be a variable that influences the frequency of occurrence of semantic paralexias, with abstract nouns tending to not be read at all, and concrete nouns tending to produce semantic paralexias (Coltheart, 1980). Whether or not abstractness and other lexical semantic variables affect word production in repetition, reading, and naming to definition tasks in reproduction conduction aphasia is unknown.

The question of the role that these lexical factors might play in generating phonemic paraphasias speaks to essentially the same question as that raised by the differential performance of patients in repeating words and nonwords; namely, the question of whether different word production mechanisms need to be postulated for different vocabulary types or, more reasonably, how to model the nature of the interaction of different information types in the word sound production process within a single-word production mechanism. Much empirical research remains to be done regarding the degree of association and dissociation found in individual patients and series and groups of patients with respect to the effects of the variables listed previously on word production. In addition, a considerable theoretical and simulation enterprise will be needed to describe and explain observed patterns of performance as a function of these variables.

A real possibility is that these lexical variables may interact singly or in various combinations with the various input-to-output routes that we have discussed above. If this were to be found, it would imply that the different mechanisms involved in activating phonological forms as a function of different types of input are all individually subject to different types of influences coming from lexical variables. A priori, this seems like an extremely likely state of affairs. Hopefully, detailed studies of patients' performances on different tasks in which these lexical variables are manipulated will indicate whether this is in fact the way the output system deals with different types of lexical items.

Models of the Word Production Mechanism II:
The Nature of Lexical Phonological Representations
and Their Activation

The study of reproduction conduction aphasia has led researchers to draw conclusions about the nature of lexical phonological representations and their processing. Phonemic paraphasias have classically been thought to reflect a patient's inability to "plan" the sound pattern of a word. The notion of planning refers to the conversion of the representation of the sounds of a word that is accessed in a mental lexicon into a form appropriate for articulatory production. This raises the question of what lexical phonological representations are, and whether (and how) they differ from the representations of the sounds of a word that are used in directly planning articulatory gestures.

Several everyday observations indicate that a speaker must access a representation of the sound pattern of a word that is modified before it is actually articulated. Words can be uttered with various intonation contours, at different loudness levels, in whispered form (i.e., without any voicing), and in many other ways that lead to very different articulatory gestures being associated with their constituent sounds. The level of formality of speech, the rate of speech, and other factors also lead to different realizations of the same phonemes in a given word. Although we do not know the storage capacity of the human brain, it is unlikely that all these articulatory forms are permanently stored for each word in a speaker's vocabulary. What is much more likely is that a speaker accesses a standard (or "canonical" or "citation") form of a word, which is then modified as a function of speech loudness, speed, and so forth. The *minimal* phonological information that must be lexically specified is that which allows the speaker to assign the surface forms of each of the segments in the word in any discourse context. Although the principle of parsimony is obviously not a definitive basis on which to decide what lexical phonological representations consist of, it is worthwhile to consider what this minimal phonological representation might be.

Linguistic (phonological) theory can contribute to this issue. Aside from the nonlinguistic factors just mentioned that change the citation form of a word before its actual production, linguistic theory has identified language-universal and language-specific phonological processes that make it unnecessary for every feature of each segment to be lexically specified. The debate in theoretical phonology is not over whether lexical phonological representations are more abstract than the phonological representations needed to capture the surface form of a word: All phonologists agree that they are. The issue that remains is how abstract these phonological representations are (see Kiparsky, 1978, for discussion). To understand these models, a certain familiarity with phonological theory is needed. The following is a brief review of some of the relevant phenomena and theories.

There is widespread agreement among phonologists that the phonological representations of words consist of phonemes (defined in terms of distinctive features) that are organized into higher order phonological structures (Clements & Keyser, 1983; Goldsmith, 1976; Halle & Vergnaud, 1987; McCarthy, 1979; Selkirk, 1984). The most commonly appreciated higher order structure is the syllable. Syllables consist of a sonorant peak surrounded by less sonorant borders. Syllables have constituents: Most theories divide syllables into onsets and rimes, and the rime into a nucleus and a coda (Liberman & Prince, 1977). In multisyllabic words, the syllables are further organized into feet (Selkirk, 1984).

Lexical phonological representations are abstract at all these levels of representation. For instance, at the level of phonemes and distinctive features, most phonological theories represent each distinctive feature along a binary axis. Thus, they cannot represent point of articulation differences as different values of a single distinctive feature representing "point of articulation." For instance, in a binary distinctive feature framework, the differences between /p/, /t/, and /k/ are represented in terms of binary values of two distinctive features, such as [± anterior] and [± coronal]. Thus, even a representation of the superficial phonemic content of a word is an abstraction—an idealization of the articulatory and acoustic content of the phonemes of languages.

The phenomena of coarticulation and allophonic variation make for additional variation in the articulatory gestures involved in producing phonemes, because every phoneme is affected in some way by every different context in which it occurs, and allophonic variants are predictable on the basis of their context. Most phonologists do not believe that allophonic variation is indicated in the lexical phonological representation of a word, and, to our knowledge, no one believes that coarticulatory phenomena are lexically represented. Thus, phonemic representations are abstract on these grounds as well.

What needs to be represented lexically is also affected by other redundancies in the sound system. For instance, the sequences of phonemes that constitute the words of a language are partially determined by universal and language-specific laws regulating syllable structure in a language. Universal factors dictate that syllables tend to become more "sonorant" from onset to nucleus, and less sonorant from nucleus to coda. Language-specific rules further constrain the internal organization of syllables and thus the order of phonemes in the words of a language. Certain distinctive features can be eliminated from lexical phonological representations because they are predictable given these influences on sound patterns in a language.

Other phonological features of words include stress and tone. In English and many other languages, word stress contours are determined by the phonemes in a word and their organization into syllables (Halle & Vergnaud, 1987; Liberman & Prince, 1977) and thus do not need to be represented lexically. In turn, stress assignment affects phonemic distinctive feature content. In English, all vowels that have not been assigned any stress whatsoever during the process of stress assignment in a word are reduced to a neutral vowel known as "schwa" (/ə/). Thus, the vowel sounds almost the same in the second syllables of *anecdote, matador, Canada,* and so on. However, morphological phenomena indicate that these vowels are not all the same at *some* level of phonemic representation. For instance, the second vowel in the word *Canada* is related to the second vowel in the word *Canadian.* Other instances of changes in underlying distinctive features include the diphthongization of tense vowels in English (that is, tense vowels are followed by glides: *cry, bay, bow, blue*), and a process known as "vowel shift" that affects the features [high] and [low] in tense diphthongized vowels. Phonologists have argued that these phenomena can be described by postulating underspecified lexical phonological segmental representations, which are affected by syllabification, stress assignment, and certain morphological processes. These representations can be sparse indeed. For instance, some theories maintain the underlying representation of the phoneme /t/ in a language like French contains no information about its distinctive feature content at all, because all the information that determines the surface value of a phonemic segment that has no distinctive features specified at the underlying level of phonological representation is available from a combination of language-universal and language-specific considerations (see Grignon, 1984; Halle & Mohanan, 1985; Mohanan, 1982; Pesetsky, 1979; and Pulleyblank, 1986, for discussion).

Linguists have argued that, if words consist of these abstract and underspecified representations of phonological structures, learning the words of a language is easier in certain respects. For instance, if the stress patterns of English words can be partially determined by general rules, children do not need to learn the stress pattern of each word of English individually. Rather, they can learn the rules that determine the assignment of stress and apply them to each new word that they acquire. They will have to learn that words consist of phonemes, defined in terms of distinctive features, that are organized into higher order structures such as syllables, and they will have to learn the rules that apply to these structures to yield stress contours, vowel quality, and so on. Some of this knowledge may be innate, and it might be easier to learn the remaining language-specific items and rules than to acquire all this information about each word separately.

On the other hand, if the *sole* permanent representation of the sound pattern of a word is one that consists of the most abstract description of the sounds of the word, the processes of producing the word or recognizing it will be much more complicated. A speaker would have to compute the actual value of each segment of the word from a very abstract representation of the sound of the word, and a listener would have to do the reverse computation—constructing the abstract representation of the sound of the word to match it to an entry in his or her mental dictionary. It may be that the simplest solution to the problem of learning the sound patterns of words in a language does not result in a representation of the sound pattern of words that makes for the simplest solution to the problem of recognizing and producing the sound patterns of words.

The notion that speakers access a phonological representation that is transformed during the process of planning the articulatory gestures associated with a word receives support from experimental and behavioral observations. The "tip-of-the-tongue (TOT)" phenomenon (Brown & McNeill, 1966) and features of malapropisms (Fay & Cutler, 1977) indicate that a word's onset, the number of syllables in the word, which syllable was stressed, and sometimes the final segment of the word can be accessed separately from other phonological features. Naturally occurring speech errors (Dell, 1984; Fromkin, 1971; Garrett, 1976, 1978, 1980; Levelt, 1989; Shattuck-Hufnagel, 1986) have been said to show that a variety of units of phonological structure—distinctive features, phonemes, syllable components (onsets, rimes, nuclei, codas), and syllables—are all separately activated by the speech production process. Theoretically oriented psychologists have developed models of the word sound production process that incorporate the notion of multiple levels of representation of the sound pattern of a word (see, for instance, Levelt, 1989). These models are broadly compatible with the idea that lexical phonological representations are abstract, although most of them do not postulate highly underspecified segmental values in lexical phonological representations.

Data from reproduction conduction aphasia could bear on the nature of lexical phonological representations, and some models have been articulated on the basis of such data. An early contemporary paper by Lecours and Lhermitte (1969) developed a broad framework for viewing phonemic paraphasias that incorporated a model of lexical phonological representations. In their view, phonemic errors could be seen as additions, deletions, displacements, and replacements of either phonemes or distinctive features of words. Words were considered to consist of sequences of phonemes each of which had a distinctive feature composition; higher order organization of phonemes into syllables and other structures was not considered. The authors hypothesized that substitutions would be more likely to involve phonemes with minimally different distinctive feature composition, and that replacements would be more likely among phonemes that share many distinctive features and that were minimally separated in the word.

Many aspects of this model are likely to be incorrect. The most obvious problem with the model is that the error-generating mechanism can generate any phonological error at all. For instance, as it stands, the model predicts that movements of phonemes to create impossible consonant clusters or vowel sequences are just as likely to occur as movements that create legal sequences. However, actual errors are reasonably highly constrained; for instance, illegal clusters hardly ever occur. These constraints appear to be due to the tempering of phonemic error generation by higher order phonological structures. This implies that these structures are available to the speech production system.

A model of lexical phonological processing that imposes constraints on phonemic paraphasias has been developed by Beland, Caplan, and Nespoulous (1990). These authors based their theory on the observation that phonemic errors respect relationships between three different levels of phonological structure: segments, syllables, and stress contours. In the vast majority of phonemic paraphasias, however complicated, syllabification is appropriate for the phonemic content of an utterance, and stress contour is appropriate for both syllabification and phonemic content. Beland et al. relied on phonological theory to model the intricate interaction between segmental phonology, syllable structure, and word stress contours in phonological errors in a single patient with reproduction conduction aphasia. They argued that the preservation of these relationships would be accounted for if phonemic paraphasias were due to changes in underlying segmental representations that were then subject to the rules of word-level phonology, including syllabification and stress assignment. An abnormal segment would trigger a set of syllabification and stress-assignment rules (not those triggered by the original segment, but those rules that are appropriate for the erroneous segment). Distinctive features would be filled in by word-level phonological rules.

Striking examples of this mechanism were also presented by Schnitzer (1972), in a study of a dyslexic patient. For instance, Schnitzer's patient read the word *reconcile* as /raykan'sil/, providing three changes of vowel quality and a change in the location of main stress. Schnitzer pointed out that all these changes would occur if the patient changed the final long /i/ in *reconcile* to a short /i/ and then applied the syllabification and stress-assignment rules appropriate for the new segment. Beland et al. take their analysis one step further, arguing that particular aspects of the syllabification process are particularly complex, and that makes it likely that segmental errors will occur.

Analyses such as those provided by Beland and her colleagues and by

Schnitzer begin to apply phonological theory to the notion of "planning" the sound pattern of a word. In essence, they claim that the phonological derivation of a word suggested by linguists corresponds to the process of planning the sound pattern of a word. These models are explicit in claiming that planning errors arise because these operations go astray.[5]

An important point is that the errors produced by both Beland et al.'s and Schnitzer's patients arose in tasks in which phonological output representations did not have to be activated by semantics. Beland et al.'s patient made his errors in repetition tasks, and Schitzer's in reading aloud. In addition, Beland et al.'s patient made similar errors in repeating nonwords, as well as words. These features of these patients' performances have been taken by these investigators to imply that phonological output is computed from abstract and underspecified phonological representations in these tasks. There are two ways this could be the case for words: Either the subject must be constrained to use the semantically based repetition route (or its equivalent in reading aloud), or the normal form-based repetition and reading routes must involve the computation of abstract underspecified phonological representations. Beland (personal communication) has suggested that the latter is the case. On this view, word recognition involves matching a presented lexical item against an abstract and underspecified lexical representation, and word production involves computing the surface values of segments in such a representation. In the case of nonwords, no semantically based repetition or reading mechanism exists. Therefore, if the constraints on phonemic errors described by Beland et al. and Schnitzer do in fact arise because of the nature of the conversion of underlying to surface phonological forms, the process of repeating (and possibly reading) nonwords must include the computation of an abstract phonological representation, despite the fact that such a representation is not a lexical entry. The strongest hypothesis that can be articulated is that all phonological processing

---

[5]The general form of the argument from aphasic patients who produce phonemic paraphasias to the nature of lexical phonological representations and their processing is as follows. If lexical phonological representations are abstract and word sound planning consists of something like the phonological derivations described by linguists, then this process would be expected to be difficult for some patients. This process itself might either be subject to error in such patients, or the degree of complexity of this process might affect a patient's ability to plan aspects of word sound structure. If errors arise at the stage of abstract phonological planning or are influenced by the complexity of this stage or processing in an aphasic patient, we can conclude that such processing takes place. It is implausible that such processing would serve only as a compensatory mechanism, which appears only in the case of the failure of the usual system for word sound production. Such a claim would entail that the usual system for word sound production accesses relatively superficial phonological representations and is simpler with respect to the planning involved in word sound production than the compensatory mechanism is. However, compensatory mechanisms have been shown only to be simplifications of normally more complex processing of abstract representations. Therefore, if aphasic errors arise during the planning of abstract phonological representations, such planning is likely to be a component of normal sound production.

normally involves the extraction of such a representation from linguistic input and the computation of surface phonology from such a representation in speech production. For the reasons just discussed, relating to the complexity of the computations entailed by such a process, this model has not found acceptance among either psychologists or researchers in acoustic phonetics or speech production. However, it remains an interesting possibility that such abstract representations are computed in dealing with linguistic forms, even when semantic processing is not involved.[6]

The key observation that allows phonemic paraphasias to be used as one type of evidence regarding the nature of lexical phonological representations is that phonemic paraphasias are subject to many constraints. Lecours and Lhermitte's model would be best characterized as postulating that such constraints serve as a filter on phonological output. In contrast, Beland et al.'s and Schnitzer's models claim that errors in underlying representations or in the derivation of a phonological representation are constrained by normal phonological processes such as syllabification, stress assignment, vowel reduction, and so on. These models maintain that lexical phonological representations are abstract and that word sound production involves computational stages similar (if not identical) to those postulated in phonological derivations. Hopefully, future descriptions of the phonological errors produced by patients with reproduction conduction aphasia will bear convincingly on the issue of how abstract lexical phonological representations are and where constraints on errors come from in the sound planning process.

CONSEQUENCES OF REPRODUCTION CONDUCTION APHASIA

Whatever the details of the deficit, reproduction conduction aphasia involves an impairment in the formulation and planning of the content and order of phonemes in spoken words (and nonwords). There are at least five other areas of language functioning that, according to at least some contemporary theories of language processing, would be expected to be affected by such a disturbance. These are: (a) speech sound discrimination and auditory word recognition (according to certain versions of the motor theory of speech perception); (b) recognition of written words (either because the inability to formulate output phonology should change the reliance upon spelling-to-sound regularities in written word recognition (if a two-route model of reading is adopted), or because the inability to formulate phonological output should affect back propa-

---

[6]A process of computing an abstract phonological representation from both surface phonology and orthography could account for a variety of phenomena, such as the interference exerted by orthographic forms on auditory rhyme judgments (Seidenberg & Tanenhaus, 1979), although other explanations for such effects are also obviously possible.

gation in a distributed network in which orthographic patterns are recognized (if a model such as that proposed by Seidenberg & McClelland [1989] is adopted); (c) short-term memory (if the inability to plan the phonological form of words affects rehearsal mechanisms); (d) certain metalinguistic tasks at the single-word level that involve rehearsal; and (e) discourse and sentence comprehension (through the effects of reproduction conduction aphasia on rehearsal mechanisms in short-term memory). We explore the predictions made by these theories and review the evidence from patients with reproduction conduction aphasia that bears on these predictions for each of these areas in turn.

Speech Sound Discrimination
and Auditory Word Recognition

The motor theory of speech perception consists of the attractive but elusive claim that the process of auditory perception of speech signals yields percepts whose representation is best described in terms of articulatory configurations and gestures (Liberman & Mattingly, 1985; Zue, 1986). Because some patients with congenital, developmental, and acquired disorders of articulation have been shown to have normal phoneme discrimination and identification (within the limits that these abilities have been tested in these patients), any viable version of the motor theory of speech perception cannot require that an individual be capable of normal speech articulation in order to discriminate and identify speech sounds. Something more abstract than actual articulation must be the basis for the capacity to form appropriate percepts, given these findings from pathology. One possibility, therefore, is that the motor theory of speech perception be formulated to claim that the ability to select and order phonemes is the "motor" capacity that is required for normal speech perception. If this version of the motor theory of speech perception were to be formulated, it would generate the hypothesis that patients with reproduction conduction aphasia should have disturbances affecting speech sound perception and discrimination, and possibly auditory word recognition.

To our knowledge, no patients with reproduction conduction aphasia have been thoroughly studied with respect to their ability to discriminate and identify speech sounds or recognize spoken words. Many patients who make some phonemic paraphasias in spontaneous speech have been said to have normal phoneme discrimination (Allport, 1984a, 1984b; Berndt & Mitchum, 1990; Caramazza, Berndt, & Basili, 1983; Friedrich, Glenn, & Marin, 1984; Friedrich, Martin, & Kemper, 1985; Martin & Caramazza, 1982; Shallice & Butterworth, 1977; Warrington, Logue, & Pratt, 1971), but it is not clear whether these patients made intralexical phonemic paraphasias in connected speech or in single-word production tasks. Moreover, in most cases, phoneme discrimination was tested with only nonsynthetic stimuli, often words, over a small number of phonemic contrasts. Critical data regarding the phoneme discrimination and identification capacities of patients with reproduction conduction aphasia are not available. Convincing evidence *against* the version of the motor theory of speech perception that maintains that the selection and sequencing of phonemes is required for speech perception would be to find that patients with reproduction conduction aphasia have intact phoneme discrimination and identification abilities, and auditory word recognition abilities, when they are tested on a sufficiently demanding task such as, for instance, discrimination and identification of the intermediate values of synthetic continua, or the discrimination and identification of natural or synthetic phonemes under conditions of noise. Such experiments have not been carried out in patients with reproduction conduction aphasia.

Written Lexical Access
and Reproduction Conduction Aphasia

All patients who fall into the category of reproduction conduction aphasia in the contemporary literature have had difficulties reading, making phonemic paraphasias in this task, as well as in repetition and confrontation naming. As discussed earlier, this pattern is presumably attributable to a disturbance in output-side phonological planning. The present question is whether these disturbances lead to an abnormality in visual word recognition.

To the extent that printed or written words are recognized as visual percepts, difficulties in oral speech production would not be expected to interfere with their recognition. However, there is good evidence that at least low-frequency words are partially recognized by a process that converts their sublexical spelling units into sound units. This process is thought to involve the conversion of graphemes to phonemes (Coltheart, 1978). The operation of this process is thought to account for the effect of spelling-to-sound regularity on both pronunciation and lexical decision latencies for low-frequency words (Seidenberg, Waters, Barnes, & Tanenhaus, 1984; Waters & Seidenberg, 1985). The finding is that low-frequency irregular words are slower to read aloud than low-frequency regular words (where regularity is defined in terms of grapheme-to-phoneme frequency), but no such difference is found between irregular and regular high-frequency words. Regularity is thought to affect low-frequency words only because high-frequency words are recognized so quickly as visual patterns that there is no time for sublexical phonological values to be activated and to interfere with pronunciation (Seidenberg et al., 1984; Waters & Seidenberg, 1985). Patients who make phonemic paraphasias when processing words on the output side might be expected to have impairments of this aspect of the reading mechanism. One possible prediction that this line of thinking leads to is that such patients would lose the regularity effect for low-frequency words. To date, no patients with reproduction conduction aphasia have been tested for these effects in either written word naming or lexical decision tasks.

Contemporary connectionist models of word recognition do not postulate separate mechanisms for the conversion of whole-word orthography and sublexical orthography to sound but rather combine all spelling-to-sound transfers in the operations of a single distributed net. This net—or, rather, a series of such nets—represents all the relationships between orthographic and phonological units: irregular words, word endings, word beginnings, graphemes, and so forth are all mapped onto their phonological values in the same system. In the best developed of these models (Seidenberg & McClelland, 1989; see Fig. 6.4), the system "learns" the pronunciation of words by adjusting the weights of the connections between units in a series of such nets. Presented with an orthographic input, the system passes on this input to a set of so-called "hidden units," whose strengths are regulated by feedback derived from the difference between the system's pronunciation and the correct form of a word. Activation then spreads from these hidden units to a set of phonological units, where a phonological representation is computed, and to a set of orthographic units, where an orthographic representation is computed. The difference between the phonological representation that the system computes and the actual phonological representation (which is presented to the system for comparison) is the basis for a self-correction process that adjusts the weights of units in the hidden unit net. These adjustments in turn lead to further adjustments in the weights of the Orthographic Unit net. The output of the Phonological Units is the basis for judging the system's ability to name written words; lexical decision is performed on the basis of the representation computed by the Orthographic Units.

What would be the consequences of a systematic distortion of the phonological output computed by the net? It is extremely risky to predict the consequences of lesioning a parallel distributed processing (PDP) system. However, it seems reasonable to suspect that, because the system continually self-corrects in the manner described above, if there were many errors that somehow arose in the Phonological Units (due to some malfunction at that level), these errors would result in changes in the hidden units and thence in the Orthographic Units. This possible effect is illustrated in Fig. 6.4. It is possible that such a process would have consequences for lexical decision and what is taken as "word recognition" in a distributed system with the Seidenberg–McClelland architecture.

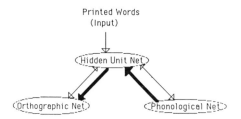

FIG. 6.4. The architecture of the Seidenberg-McClelland PDP reading model. Broad arrows indicate possible effects of a disturbance in word sound production on other parts of the system.

In short, there are several theoretical models of word recognition in which it is possible to imagine that phonological planning disturbances such as those found in reproduction conduction aphasia might give rise to disturbances in written word recognition. These possibilities remain highly speculative even at the theoretical level, and there are no studies of word recognition in reproduction conduction aphasia that bring empirical evidence to bear on this question.

Reproduction Conduction Aphasia and Short-Term Memory

Considering that Shallice and Warrington have gone to great lengths to distinguish between two forms of conduction aphasia—one in which there is a disturbance in the formulation and planning of the constituent sounds of words and a second in which there is a short-term memory (STM) impairment—it is potentially confusing to raise the question of whether reproduction conduction aphasia might lead to a disturbance of short-term memory. However, there are excellent reasons to believe that patients with reproduction conduction aphasia should have a particular form of auditory-verbal short-term memory impairment.

These reasons center around the role of rehearsal processes in auditory-verbal short-term memory. There is much evidence that some form of articulatory rehearsal is required for normal performance on auditory-verbal short-term memory tasks such as span and delayed recall after interference (Brown-Peterson tasks). Baddeley and his colleagues (Baddeley, 1966a, 1966b; Baddeley, Thompson, & Buchanan, 1975; Richardson & Baddeley, 1975) reported an advantage for short words over long words in span tasks. Baddeley, Lewis, and Vallar (1984) as well as Baddeley et al. (1975) found that concurrent articulatory activity abolished this word length effect. Baddeley et al. (1975) also found that span correlated with articulatory rate and argued that "a subject can recall as many words as he can read in 1.6 seconds or can articulate in 1.3 seconds" (p. 581). All these results have suggested to these researchers and others that subvocal rehearsal plays an important role in maintaining items in a short-term memory system and contributes to performance in span, Brown-Peterson, and other STM tasks.

Patients with severe disturbances of articulation (dysarthria) have been shown to have normal memory spans and to retain the effects of word length in span tasks (Baddeley & Wilson, 1985; Bishop & Robson, 1989; Levine, Calvanio, & Popovics, 1982; Nebes, 1975; Vallar & Cappa, 1987). These findings suggest that articulation itself is not required for rehearsal. However, Rochon, Caplan, and Waters (1990) and Waters, Rochon, and Caplan (1991) have demonstrated that, as a group, patients with apraxia of speech have both reduced spans and no word length effect in either visual or auditory span tasks. These results, in conjunction with both the findings in normal subjects and those in patients with dysarthria, are in keeping with the view that rehearsal in short-term memory requires the formulation of the articulatory plans for phonological segments, although not their actual articulation. If this is the case, it is extremely likely that patients who do not activate the correct phonological segments in a word and/or cannot maintain these segments in their correct sequence will also have limited abilities to rehearse verbal material in short-term memory tasks. Accordingly, the expectation is that patients with reproduction conduction aphasia will have impaired performance on span tasks, Brown-Peterson tasks, and possibly other tasks involving auditory-verbal short-term memory.

To date, several patients with reproduction conduction aphasia have been described who have reduced spans. Caplan et al. (1986) reported a patient with reproduction conduction aphasia whose span was three items, as tested on both pointing and probe recognition tasks. However, it is always possible for a reduction in span to be due to a disturbance of a mechanism supporting short-term memory function other than rehearsal. The two most likely candidates for such a disturbed mechanism are the phonological storage system (as has been argued to be impaired in many STM patients; Warrington & Shallice, 1969; Vallar & Baddeley, 1984a, 1984b), and the central executive mechanisms involved in span, as has been demonstrated in patients with Alzheimer's disease (Morris, 1984, 1986, 1987; Morris & Baddeley, 1988). There is no guarantee that the reduction in span in a reproduction conduction aphasia such as the individual reported by Caplan et al. (1986) is due to an impairment of rehearsal rather than a (presumably unrelated) disturbance in these other functional components of the short-term memory system. Evidence indicating that an impairment of rehearsal is a cause of reduction in span would come from the demonstration that the effects associated with rehearsal are absent in such a patient. The simplest prediction is that these patients should perform like normal subjects under conditions of articulatory suppression and like patients with apraxia of speech. This pattern of performance would consist of a mild-to-moderate reduction in span, the absence of word length effects in both auditory and visual span tasks, and the absence of phonological similarity effects in visual span but their maintenance in auditory span. In addition, if the reduction in span is caused only by a disturbance of articulatory-based rehearsal, these patients should continue to show evidence for the operation of the Phonological Store and Central Executive components of the short-term memory system. The integrity of the Phonological Store would be shown by the presence of phonological similarity effects in auditory span tasks,[7] normal recall of terminal items in recall-from-end conditions in supraspan tasks, and little differ-

---

[7]The auditory phonological similarity effect can be reduced or eliminated in cases of severe disruption of articulatory rehearsal (Waters, Rochon, & Caplan, 1991) and therefore is the least reliable of these effects as an indicator of the integrity of the Phonological Store.

ence between decay rates for items within span with filled and unfilled conditions in Brown-Peterson paradigms. Evidence for the integrity of the Central Executive would be the lack of a pathological effect of secondary tasks on span.[8] These observations have yet to be made in patients with reproduction conduction aphasia. At present, it is a reasonable hypothesis that patients with reproduction conduction aphasia will show these patterns, but there is no evidence that this is in fact the case.

Reproduction Conduction Aphasia and Metalinguistic Phonological Processing

If reproduction conduction aphasics are impaired in rehearsal, there are at least some metalinguistic processing tasks involving single words that we would expect them to show disturbances on. Besner and his colleagues (Besner, 1987) demonstrated that visual rhyme judgments are impaired by concurrent articulation in normal subjects, whereas visual homophone judgments are intact (or, at least, less clearly impaired). Waters, Rochon, and Caplan (1991) showed a similar pattern for patients with apraxia of speech. One would expect a similar pattern of performance on the part of reproduction conduction aphasics if their phonological planning disturbance interferes with rehearsal (on the further assumption that one and the same rehearsal mechanisms are relevant to all the tasks aforementioned).

Reproduction Conduction Aphasia and Sentence and Discourse Comprehension

Patients with conduction aphasia were among the first patient groups to be shown to have disturbances of syntactic comprehension (Caramazza & Zurif, 1976; Zurif & Caramazza, 1976). However, these initial patients all probably had repetition conduction aphasia (although many of them were not studied in enough detail to know what their short-term memory functions were like). Thus, we cannot conclude that patients with reproduction conduction aphasia have syntactic comprehension deficits or other comprehension deficits on the basis of these cases. However, these initial studies, and other studies in normal subjects, have led to several suggestions regarding the possible role that STM may play in sentence and discourse comprehension. If these theories are correct, and if reproduction conduction aphasics are impaired in rehearsal abilities to the extent that STM functions are limited, this disturbance would be

---

[8]Morris and his colleague based their analysis of Alzheimer's disease patients as having a Central Executive deficit on the presence of all normal word length and phonological similarity effects in their patients, but not all these effects would be expected to be found in patients with an impairment in articulatory rehearsal.

expected to affect certain comprehension functions at the sentence and discourse level. The nature of the expected disturbance depends on what role STM is thought to play in sentence and discourse comprehension.

One suggestion has been made that STM is involved in maintaining lexical items in a "window" that is then used to enable "mental models or representations" to be constructed (Baddeley, Vallar, & Wilson, 1987; Vallar & Baddeley, 1987). One interpretation of this suggestion is to equate the short-term phonological memory system with the look-ahead buffer postulated in many parsing models (e.g., Frazier and Fodor's "preliminary phrase packager" [Frazier & Fodor, 1978]; the look-ahead buffer in Marcus [1980] or Berwick and Weinberg [1984]). This buffer is involved in preliminary phrasal analysis; if such analysis is limited because of a limitation on the number of items available in the buffer, the construction of more complex structures by later parsing mechanisms will either not be possible at all or will be more costly in terms of resource requirements (see Marcus, 1982, for an illustration of the consequences of reducing the size of the look-ahead buffer). Therefore, if the material in a look-ahead buffer is maintained by rehearsal, we would expect major syntactic complexity effects on comprehension in patients with reproduction conduction aphasia. Caplan et al.'s (1986) patient showed one such effect— difficulty in comprehending sentences with center-embedded relative clauses (e.g., *The horse that the cow kicked chased the pig*). However, other patients with rehearsal disturbances due to other output impairments, such as apraxia of speech, have shown sentence comprehension that is not affected by syntactic complexity (Waters, Caplan, & Hildebrandt, 1991). Altogether, there are four unknowns here: (a) whether there is a look-ahead buffer that is used in sentence comprehension, (b) whether it makes use of a rehearsal mechanism, (c) whether rehearsal impairments exist in patients with reproduction conduction aphasia, and (d) whether the particular type of rehearsal impairment found in reproduction conduction aphasia (if any) affects sentence comprehension.

The second possibility that has been advanced regarding the relationship between a phonological short-term memory system and sentence comprehension is that such a memory system is somehow involved in the operations of the parser itself. Caramazza, Basili, Koller, and Berndt (1981), Caramazza and Berndt (1985), and others maintain versions of this theory. Again, data from Waters, Caplan, and Hildebrandt (1991) indicate that a patient with severely reduced STM capacities and poor rehearsal abilities had good overall syntactic comprehension and showed no effect of syntactic structural complexity on comprehension functions. This is incompatible with a theory that maintains that items are held in phonological form in phrase markers, because performance should be poor if this function is required for all syntactic comprehension. It is also incompatible with a variant of this theory that holds that lexical items are held in phrase markers in phonological form when the demands of syntactic processing increase, because such a state of affairs would lead to complexity effects in syntactic comprehension tasks, not seen here. Again it is possible that the type of rehearsal impairment occasioned by reproduction conduction aphasia (if any) differs from that occasioned by apraxia of speech and other causes, and that the particular rehearsal impairment occasioned by reproduction conduction aphasia (if any) leads to disturbances of the ability to hold items in phonological form in phrase markers. In our view, this is a very unlikely possibility.

A third model of sentence comprehension that has been developed maintains that STM is involved in sentence comprehension when sentences become long. Schwartz and her colleagues (Schwartz, Linebarger, Saffran, & Pate, 1987) have described what they call the "P2" pattern of sentence comprehension deficit, in which sentence length affects comprehension of semantically irreversible sentences in patients who do not appear to have syntactic comprehension problems. Whether the P2 pattern arises in patients with reproduction conduction aphasia is not known.

Several models of discourse comprehension suggest a role for STM, including rehearsal, in this process in an on-line fashion. Kintsch and van Dijk (1978; Van Dijk & Kintsch, 1983) have suggested, for instance, that a listener processes a narrative or text to create its microstructural, macrostructural, and superstructural levels in a sequence. They postulate that a certain number of propositions in a text base must be understood and retained in a memory store in order for higher level discourse structures to be built. Several results indicate that the verbatim form of one or two sentences (or clauses in a complex or compound sentence) can be recalled immediately after a sentence is presented (Jarvella, 1970, 1971; Marslen-Wilson & Tyler, 1976). This suggests that this portion of a discourse may be maintained in phonological form in short-term memory. Murphy (1985) studied the role of sentence form in determining ease of understanding of sentences containing either verb phrase ellipsis or the phrase *do it*. He found that both the length and the form of an antecedent affected reading times for sentences containing both these types of anaphors, as long as the antecedent was in the sentence immediately preceding the anaphor, and that these effects did not occur for more distant antecedents. Although these results do not prove that some co-indexation operations refer back to phonological form, they do suggest that some of these operations do refer back to the surface form of an utterance.

However, although there may be some role for a memory system in discourse comprehension, any model of discourse processing that relies heavily on sequential construction of progressively higher levels of discourse structure is likely to be wrong. The evidence that such models are probably incorrect comes from data documenting the speed of discourse processing. For instance, Tyler and Marslen-Wilson (1977; Marslen-Wilson & Tyler, 1987) reported that logical inferences in discourse processing occur with the same speed as the linguistically based operations that are involved in establishing co-reference and syntactic disambiguation. It thus seems unlikely that rehearsal problems would lead to problems with the on-line comprehension of discourse, although empirical data from reproduction conduction aphasics documenting such disturbances would reopen this question. No such data have been published to date.

Finally, phonological memory systems, including articulatory rehearsal mechanisms, might be involved in processes that arise after sentence meaning is determined on the basis of sentence structure. There are many such processes, including mapping propositional content onto motor actions, mapping propositional content onto semantic memory to verify the truth or plausibility of a proposition, checking the meaning derived from the syntactic processing of a sentence against meanings derived lexicopragmatically, reasoning, and certain aspects of learning (such as updating semantic memory on the basis of propositional content). These different postinterpretive tasks may involve the STM system in different ways. For instance, checking the meaning derived from the syntactic processing of a sentence against meanings derived lexicopragmatically might involve reference to phonological representations to initiate enough of a parse to establish the first thematic roles and other sentential semantic features that are licensed by the parser, thereby also establishing which are erroneously inferred pragmatically. If Perfetti and McCutchen's (1982) suggestion that lexical items are represented by general semantic specifications in propositional representations during first-pass sentence processing is correct, the phonological form of an item may be reviewed if more detailed semantic information is needed about an item in the course of mapping a proposition onto an action or onto information already held in semantic memory. Some performances of patients with STM limitations—including one patient with a rehearsal impairment (Waters et al., 1991a)—suggest that some operations at this latter stage of sentence processing are affected (McCarthy & Warrington, 1987a, 1987b, 1990; see Caplan & Waters, 1990, and Waters, Caplan, & Hildebrandt, 1991, for reviews). However, whether these functions are impaired in patients with reproduction conduction aphasia is unknown, and, in fact, most of these functions have not been tested in patients with STM limitations of any kind. More work is needed to shed light on the exact role of the STM system and rehearsal in these postinterpretive operations.

Another issue regarding the role of rehearsal in sentence and discourse comprehension is whether rehearsal plays more of a role in written sentence and discourse comprehension than in comprehension of spoken language. Models of short-term memory that postulate a role for articulatory mechanisms in both entering visually presented stimuli into a Phonological Store and in rehearsing items in that store suggest that the effect of an impairment in speech sound planning should have more of an effect on memory for written than for auditory materials. This may lead to a disturbance of speech sound planning affecting reading more than auditory comprehension. The data on this issue that come from experiments on normal subjects is superficially contradictory. Several tasks involving reading are affected by articulatory suppression whereas others are not. The ability to make sentence acceptability judgments (Kleiman, 1975), memory for the exact wording of a text (Levy, 1975, 1978), and memory for gist of a passage (Slowiaczek & Clifton, 1980) have all been shown to be affected for written passages by articulatory suppression. However, reading-for-comprehension tasks (Waters, Komoda, & Arbuckle, 1985) and semantic anomaly detection tasks with written stimuli (Waters et al., 1987) have been shown not to be affected by articulatory suppression. Our view is this superficial heterogeneity of results points to a deeper generalization. Tasks that involve metalinguistic judgments and/or verification of the truth of sentence meanings derived from a first-pass comprehension process for written texts are affected by articulatory suppression, whereas tasks emphasizing first-pass comprehension are not (see Caplan & Waters, 1990, and Waters, Caplan, & Hildebrandt, 1991, for discussion). Our view is that rehearsal may be required to accomplish second-pass comprehension tasks with written stimuli, or, at least, that it may be optionally used in these tasks (see Caplan & Waters, 1990, for discussion). This is the same role that we have postulated for STM and rehearsal in processing auditorily presented sentences and discourse. Whether reproduction conduction aphasics have disturbances with written sentence and discourse processing, what these disturbances are (if they exist), and whether they are worse than any difficulties they have with auditorily presented sentences (if *they* exist) remains unknown.

CONCLUSION

It is scarcely necessary to repeat our introductory comment that most of the questions that arise regarding the nature and consequences of reproduction conduction aphasia are unresolved. We do believe, however, that they are of interest and that they are approachable. We can only hope that future research will bring more data to bear on them.

ACKNOWLEDGMENTS

This work was partially supported by grants from the National Institute for Deafness and Communicative Diseases (1 RO1 DC00776-01 and 1 RO1 DC00942-01) and the Medical Research Council of Canada (9761).

REFERENCES

Allport, D. A. (1984a). Auditory–verbal short-term memory and conduction aphasia. In H. Bouma & D. G. Bouwhuis (Ed.), *Attention and performance*. London: Lawrence Erlbaum Associates.

Allport, D. A. (1984b). Speech production and comprehension: One lexicon or two. In W. Prinz & A. F. Sanders (Ed.), *Cognition and motor processes* (pp. 209-228). Berlin, Heidelberg: Springer-Verlag.

Baddeley, A. D. (1966a). The influence of acoustic and semantic similarity on long-term memory for word sequences. *Quarterly Journal of Experimental Psychology, 18,* 302-309.

Baddeley, A. D. (1966b). Short-term memory for word sequences as a function of acoustic, semantic and formal similarity. *Quarterly Journal of Experimental Psychology, 18,* 362-365.

Baddeley, A. D., Lewis, V. J., & Vallar, G. (1984). Exploring the articulatory loop. *Quarterly Journal of Experimental Psychology, 36,* 233-252.

Baddeley, A. D., Thompson, N., & Buchanan, M. (1975). Word length and the structure of short-term memory. *Journal of Verbal Learning and Verbal Behavior, 14,* 575-589.

Baddeley, A. D., Vallar, G., & Wilson, B. (1987). Comprehension and the articulatory loop: Some neuropsychological evidence. In M. Coltheart (Ed.), *Attention and performance* (Vol. 9, pp. 509-530). Hillsdale, NJ: Lawrence Erlbaum Associates.

Baddeley, A. D., & Wilson, B. (1985). Phonological coding and short-term memory in patients without speech. *Journal of Memory and Language, 24,* 490-502.

Barnard, P. (1985). Interacting cognitive subsystems: A psycholinguistic approach to short-term memory. In A. W. Ellis (Ed.), *Progress in the psychology of language* (Vol. 2, pp. 197-258). London: Lawrence Erlbaum Associates.

Beland, R., Caplan, D., & Nespoulous, J.-L. (1990). The role of abstract phonological representations in word production: Evidence from phonemic paraphasias. *Journal of Neurolinguistics, 5,* 125-164.

Berndt, R. S., & Mitchum, C. C. (1990). Auditory and lexical information sources in immediate recall: Evidence from a patient with a deficit to the phonological short-term store. In G. Vallar & T. Shallice (Eds.), *Neuropsychological impairments of short-term memory* (pp. 115-144). Cambridge: Cambridge University Press.

Berwick, R. C., & Weinberg, A. (1984). *The grammatical basis of linguistic performance: Language use and acquisition.* Cambridge, MA: MIT Press.

Besner, D. (1987). Phonology, lexical access in reading, and articulatory suppression: A critical review. *Quarterly Journal of Experimental Psychology, 39,* 467-478.

Bishop, D., & Robson, J. (1989). Unimpaired short-term memory and rhyme judgement in congenitally speechless individuals: Implications for the notion of "articulatory coding." *Quarterly Journal of Experimental Psychology, 41A,* 123-140.

Brown, R., & McNeill, D. (1966). The "tip of the tongue" phenomenon. *Journal of Verbal Learning and Verbal Behavior, 5,* 325-337.

Bub, D., Black, S., Howell, J., & Kertesz, A. (1987). Damage to input and output buffers— What's a lexicality effect doing in a place like that? In E. Keller & M. Gopnick (Eds.), *Motor and sensory processes of language* (pp. 83-110). Hillsdale, NJ: Lawrence Erlbaum Associates.

Bub, D., Cancelliere, A., & Kertesz, A. (1985). Whole-word and analytic translation of spelling-to-sound in a non-semantic reader. In K. E. Patterson, M. Coltheart, & J. C. Marshall (Eds.), *Surface dyslexia* (pp. 15-34). London: Lawrence Erlbaum Associates.

Buckingham, H. (1980). On correlating aphasic errors with slips of the tongue. *Applied Psycholinguistics, 1,* 199-220.

Caplan, D., Vanier, M., & Baker, C. (1986). A case study of reproduction conduction aphasia: I. Word production. *Cognitive Neuropsychology, 3*(1), 99-128.

Caplan, D., & Waters, G. S. (1990). Short-term memory and language comprehension: A critical review of the neuropsychological literature. In G. Vallar & T. Shallice (Eds.), *Neuropsychological impairments of short-term memory* (pp. 337-339). Cambridge: Cambridge University Press.

Caramazza, A., Basili, A., Koller, J. J., & Berndt, R. S. (1981). An investigation of repetition and language processing in a case of conduction aphasia. *Brain and Language, 14,* 234-271.

Caramazza, A., & Berndt, R. S. (1985). A multicomponent view of agrammatic Broca's aphasia. In M. L. Kean (Ed.), *Agrammatism* (pp. 27-64). New York: Academic Press.

Caramazza, A., Berndt, R. S., & Basili, A. G. (1983). The selective impairment of phonological processing: A case study. *Brain and Language, 18,* 128-174.

Caramazza, A., & Zurif, E. (1976). Dissociation of algorithmic and heuristic processes in language comprehension: Evidence from aphasia. *Brain and Language, 3,* 572-582.

Clements, G. N., & Keyser, S. J. (1983). *CV phonology. A generative theory of the syllable.* Cambridge, MA: MIT Press.

Coltheart, M. (1978). Lexical access in simple reading tasks. In B. Underwood (Ed.), *Strategies of information processing* (pp. 151-215). London: Academic Press.

Coltheart, M. (1980). Deep dyslexia: A review of the syndrome. In M. Coltheart, K. Patterson, & J. C. Marshall (Eds.), *Deep dyslexia* (pp. 22-47). London: Routledge & Kegan Paul.

Coltheart, M., Masterson, J., Byng, S., Prior, M., & Riddoch, J. (1983). Surface dyslexia. *Quarterly Journal of Experimental Psychology, 35A,* 469-495.

Dell, G. S. (1984). Representation of serial order in speech: Evidence from the repeated phoneme effect in speech errors. *Journal of Experimental Psychology: Learning, Memory, and Cognition, 10,* 222-233.

Dell, G. S. (1986). A spreading activation theory of retrieval in sentence production. *Psychological Review, 93*(3), 283-321.

Dell, G. S. (1988). The retrieval of phonological forms in production: Tests of predictions from a connectionist model. *Journal of Memory and Language, 27,* 124-142.

Dell, G. S., & Reich, P. A. (1981). Stages in sentence production: An analysis of speech error data. *Journal of Verbal Learning and Verbal Behavior, 20,* 611-629.

Dubois, J., Hecaen, H., Angelergues, R., Maufras de Chatelier, A., & Marcie, P. (1973). Neurolinguistic study of conduction aphasia. *Neuropsychologia, 2,* 9-44. In H. Goodglass & S. Blumstein (Eds. and Trans.), *Psycholinguistics and aphasia* (pp. 283-300). Baltimore: Johns Hopkins University Press. (Original work published 1964)

Fay, D., & Cutler, A. (1977). Malapropisms and the structures of the mental lexicon. *Linguistic Inquiry, 8,* 505-520.

Frazier, L., & Fodor, J. D. (1978). The sausage machine: A new two-stage parsing model. *Cognition, 6,* 291-325.

Friedrich, F. J., Glenn, C. G., & Marin, O. S. M. (1984). Interruption of phonological coding in conduction aphasia. *Brain and Language, 22,* 266-291.

Friedrich, F. J., Martin, R., & Kemper, S. J. (1985). Consequences of a phonological coding deficit on sentence processing. *Cognitive Neuropsychology, 2*(4), 385-412.

Fromkin, V. A. (1971). The non-anomalous nature of anomalous utterances. *Language, 47,* 27-52.

Garrett, M. F. (1976). Syntactic processes in sentence production. In R. J. Wales & E. Walker (Eds.), *New approaches to language mechanisms* (pp. 231-256). Amsterdam: North-Holland.

Garrett, M. F. (1978). Word and sentence perception. In R. Held, H. W. Liebowitz, & H.-L. Toyber (Eds.), *Handbook of sensory physiology. Vol. 8: Perception* (pp. 611-623). Berlin: Springer.

Garrett, M. F. (1980). Levels of processing in sentence production. In B. Butterworth (Ed.), *Language production: Vol 1. Speech and talk* (pp. 177-220). London: Academic Press.

Garrett, M. F. (1982). Production of speech: Observations from normal and pathological language use. In A. W. Ellis (Ed.), *Normality and pathology in cognitive functions* (pp. 19-75). London: Academic Press.

Garrett, M. F. (1990). *Processing vocabularies in language production.* Paper presented at the third annual conference on Human Sentence Processing, New York.

Geschwind, N. (1965). Disconnection syndromes in animals and man. *Brain, 88,* 237-294, 585-644.

Goldsmith, J. (1976). *Autosegmental phonology.* Doctoral dissertation, Department of Linguistics, MIT, Cambridge, MA.

Goodglass, H., Kaplan, E., Weintraub, S., & Ackerman, N. (1976). The "tip of the tongue" phenomenon in aphasia. *Cortex, 12,* 145-153.

Grignon, A. M. (1984). *Phonologie lexicale tri-dimensionnelle du Japonais.* Unpublished doctoral dissertation, Universite de Montreal.

Halle, M., & Mohanan, K. P. (1985). Segmental phonology in modern English. *Linguistic Inquiry, 16,* 57-116.

Halle, M., & Vergnaud, J.-R. (1987). *An essay on stress.* Cambridge, MA: MIT Press.

Jarvella, R. V. (1970). Effects of syntax on running memory span for connected discourse. *Psychonomic Science, 19,* 235–236.

Jarvella, R. V. (1971). Syntactic processing of connected speech. *Journal of Verbal Learning and Verbal Behavior, 10,* 409–416.

Kinsbourne, M. (1972). Behavioral analysis of the repetition deficit in conduction aphasia. *Neurology, 22,* 1126–1132.

Kintsch, W., & Van Dijk, T. A. (1978). Toward a model of text comprehension and production. *Psychological Review, 85*(5), 363–394.

Kiparsky, P. (1978). Issues in phonological theory. In J. Weinstock (Ed.), *The Nordic languages and modern linguistics.* Austin, TX: University of Texas Press.

Kleiman, G. (1975). Speech recording in reading. *Journal of Verbal Learning and Verbal Behavior, 14,* 323–329.

Kohn, S. (1989). The nature of the phonemic string deficit in conduction aphasia. *Aphasiology, 3*(3), 209–239.

Lecours, A. R., & Lhermitte, F. (1969). Phonemic paraphasias: Linguistic structures and tentative hypotheses. *Cortex, 5,* 193–228.

Levelt, W. J. M. (1989). *Speaking: From intention to articulation.* Cambridge, MA: MIT Press.

Levine, D. N., Calvanio, R., & Popovics, A. (1982). Language in the absence of inner speech. *Neuropsychologia, 20,* 391–409.

Levy, B. A. (1975). Vocalization and suppression effects in sentence memory. *Journal of Experimental Child Psychology, 16,* 304–316.

Levy, B. A. (1978). Speech processing during reading. In A. M. Lesgold, J. W. Pellegrino, S. D. Fokkema, & R. Glaser (Eds.), *Cognitive psychology and instruction* (pp. 123–151). New York: Plenum.

Liberman, A. M., & Mattingly, I. G. (1985). The motor theory of speech perception revised. *Cognition, 21,* 1–36.

Liberman, M., & Prince, A. (1977). On stress and linguistic rhythm. *Linguistic Inquiry, 8,* 249–336.

Lichtheim, L. (1885). On aphasia. *Brain, 7,* 433–484.

Marcel, A. J. (1980). Surface dyslexia and beginning reading: A revised hypothesis of the pronunciation of print and its impairments. In M. Coltheart, K. E. Patterson, & J. C. Marshall (Eds.), *Deep dyslexia* (pp. 227–258). London: Routledge.

Marcus, M. P. (1980). *A theory of syntactic recognition for natural language.* Cambridge, MA: MIT Press.

Marcus, M. P. (1982). Consequences of functional deficits in a parsing model: Implications for Broca's aphasia. In M. A. Arbib, D. Caplan, & J. C. Marshall (Eds.), *Neural models of language processes* (pp. 115–134). New York: Academic Press.

Marslen-Wilson, W., & Tyler, L. K. (1976). Memory and levels of processing in a psycholinguistic context. *Journal of Experimental Psychology: Human Learning and Memory, 2*(No. 2), 112–119.

Marslen-Wilson, W., & Tyler, L. K. (1987). Against modularity. In J. L. Garfield (Eds.), *Modularity in knowledge representation and natural-language understanding* (pp. 37–62). Cambridge, MA: MIT Press.

Martin, R. C., & Caramazza, A. (1982). Short-term memory performance in the absence of phonological coding. *Brain and Cognition, 1,* 50–70.

McCarthy, J. (1979). *Formal problems in Semitic phonology and morphology.* Unpublished doctoral dissertation, MIT, Cambridge, MA.

McCarthy, R., & Warrington, E. K. (1987a). Understanding: A function of short-term memory? *Brain, 110,* 1565–1578.

McCarthy, R., & Warrington, E. K. (1987b). The double-dissociation of short-term memory for lists and sentences: Evidence from aphasia. *Brain, 110,* 1545–1563.

McCarthy, R., & Warrington, E. K. (1990). Auditory-verbal span of apprehension: A phenomenon in search of a function? In G. Vallar & T. Shallice (Eds.), *Neuropsychological impairments of short-term memory* (pp. 167–186). Cambridge: Cambridge University Press.

McLeod, P., & Posner, M. I. (1984). Privileged loops from percept to act. In H. Bouma & D. G. Bouwhuis (Eds.), *Attention and performance X: Control of language processes* (pp. 55–66). London, UK: Lawrence Erlbaum Associates.

Miceli, G., Giustolisi, L., & Caramazza, A. (1990). *The interaction of lexical and non-lexical processing mechanisms: Evidence from anomia.* The Cognitive Neuropsychology Laboratory, Baltimore: Johns Hopkins University.

Michel, F., & Andreewsky, E. (1983). Deep dysphasia: An auditory analogue of deep dyslexia in the auditory modality. *Brain and Language, 18,* 212-223.

Miller, D., & Ellis, A. W. (1987). Speech and writing errors in neologistic jargonaphasia: A lexical activation hypothesis. In M. Coltheart, G. Sartori, & R. Job (Eds.), *The cognitive neuropsychology of language.* London: Lawrence Erlbaum Associates.

Mohanan, K. P. (1982). *Lexical phonology.* Unpublished doctoral dissertation, Department of Linguistics, MIT, Cambridge, MA.

Monsell, S. (1984). Components of working memory verbal skills: A "distributed capacities" view. In H. B. & B. Bouwhuis (Eds.), *Attention and performance: Control of language processes.* Hillsdale, NJ: Lawrence Erlbaum Associates.

Morris, R. G. (1984). Dementia and the functioning of the articulatory loop system. *Cognitive Neuropsychology, 1*(2), 143-157.

Morris, R. G. (1986). Short-term forgetting in senile dementia of the Alzheimer's type. *Cognitive Neuropsychology, 3*(1), 77-97.

Morris, R. G. (1987). Articulatory rehearsal in Alzheimer type dementia. *Brain and Language, 30,* 351-362.

Morris, R. G., & Baddeley, A. D. (1988). Primary and working memory functioning in Alzheimer-type dementia. *Journal of Clinical and Experimental Neuropsychology, 10*(2), 279-296.

Morton, J., & Patterson, K. E. (1980). A new attempt at an interpretation, or, an attempt at a new interpretation. In M. Coltheart, K. E. Patterson, & J. C. Marshall (Eds.), *Deep dyslexia* (pp. 91-118). London: Routledge & Kegan Paul.

Murphy, G. L. (1985). Processes of understanding anaphora. *Journal of Memory and Language, 24,* 290-303.

Nebes, R. D. (1975). The nature of internal speech in a patient with apraxia. *Brain and Language, 2,* 489-497.

Pate, D. S., Saffran, E. M., & Martin, N. (1987). Specifying the nature of the production impairment in a conduction aphasic: A case study. *Language and Cognitive Processes, 2*(1), 43-84.

Patterson, K. E., Marshall, J. C., & Coltheart, M. (Eds.). (1985). *Surface dyslexia* (pp. 335-359). London: Lawrence Erlbaum Associates.

Patterson, K., Seidenberg, M. S., & McClelland, J. L. (1989). Connections and disconnections: Acquired dyslexia in a computational model of reading processes. In R. Morris (Ed.), *Parallel distributed processing: Implications for psychology and neurobiology* (pp. 131-181). New York: Oxford University Press.

Perfetti, C., & McCutchen, D. (1982). Speech processes in reading. In N. Lass (Ed.), *Advances in speech and language.* New York: Academic Press.

Pesetsky, D. (1979). *Russian morphology and lexical theory.* Unpublished manuscript, Department of Linguistics, MIT, Cambridge, MA.

Pulleyblank, D. (1986). *Tone in lexical phonology.* Dordrecht: Reidel.

Richardson, J. T. E., & Baddeley, A. D. (1975). The effect of articulatory suppression in free recall. *Journal of Verbal Learning and Verbal Behavior, 14,* 623-629.

Rochon, E., Caplan, D., & Waters, G. (1990). Short-term memory processes in patients with apraxia of speech: Implications for the nature and structure of the auditory verbal short-term memory system. *Journal of Neurolinguistics, 5,* 237-264.

Schnitzer, M. L. (1972). *Generative phonology: Evidence from aphasia.* University Park, PA: Pennsylvania State University.

Schwartz, M. F., Linebarger, M. C., Saffran, E. M., & Pate, D. S. (1987). Syntactic transparency and sentence interpretation in aphasia. *Language and Cognitive Processes, 2,* 85-113.

Seidenberg, M. S., & McClelland, J. L. (1989). A distributed, developmental model of word recognition and naming. *Psychological Review, 96*(No. 4), 523-568.

Seidenberg, M. S., & Tanenhaus, M. K. (1979). Orthographic effects on rhyme monitoring. *Journal of Experimental Psychology: Human Learning and Memory, 5,* 546–554.

Seidenberg, M. S., Waters, G. S., Barnes, M. A., & Tanenhaus, M. K. (1984). When does irregular spelling or pronunciation influence word recognition? *Journal of Verbal Learning and Verbal Behavior, 23,* 383–404.

Selkirk, E. (1984). *Phonology and syntax: The relation between sound and structure.* Cambridge, MA: MIT Press.

Shallice, T., & Butterworth, B. (1977). Short-term memory impairment and spontaneous speech. *Neuropsychologia, 15,* 729–735.

Shallice, T., Mcleod, P., & Lewis, K. (1985). Isolating cognitive modules with the dual-task paradigm: Are speech perception and production different processes? *Quarterly Journal of Experimental Psychology, 37A,* 507–532.

Shallice, T., & Warrington, E. (1977). Auditory–verbal short-term memory and conduction aphasia. *Brain and Language, 4,* 479–491.

Shattuck-Hufnagel, S. (1985). Context similarity constraints on segmental speech errors: An experimental investigation of the role of word position and lexical stress. In J. Lauter (Ed.), *On the planning and production of speech in normal and hearing-impaired individuals: A seminar in honour of S. Richard Silverman* (pp. 43–49). ASHA (Report 15).

Shattuck-Hufnagel, S. (1986). The role of word onset consonants in speech production planning: New evidence from speech error patterns. In E. Keller & M. Gopnik (Eds.), *Motor and sensory processes in language* (pp. 17–51). Hillsdale, NJ: Lawrence Erlbaum Associates.

Slowiaczek, M. L., & Clifton, C. J. (1980). Subvocalization and reading for meaning. *Journal of Verbal Learning and Verbal Behavior, 19,* 573–582.

Stemberger, J. P. (1982). The nature of segments in the lexicon: Evidence from speech errors. *Lingua, 56,* 235–259.

Stemberger, J. P. (1983a). The nature of /r/ and /l/ in English: Evidence from speech errors. *Journal of Phonetics, 11,* 139–147.

Stemberger, J. P. (1983b). *Speech errors and theoretical phonology: A review.* Bloomington: Indiana Linguistics Club.

Stemberger, J. P. (1985). An interactive action model of language production. In A. W. Ellis (Ed.), *Progress in the psychology of language* (Vol. 1, pp. 143–186). Hillsdale, NJ: Lawrence Erlbaum Associates.

Stemberger, J. P., & MacWhinney, B. (1986). Frequency and the lexical storage of regularly inflected forms. *Memory and Cognition, 14,* 17–26.

Stemberger, J. P., & Treiman, R. (1986). The internal structure of word-initial consonant clusters. *Journal of Memory and Language, 25,* 163–180.

Tyler, L. K., & Marslen-Wilson, W. (1977). The on-line effects of semantic context on syntactic processing. *Journal of Verbal Learning and Verbal Behaviour, 16,* 683–692.

Vallar, G., & Baddeley, A. D. (1984a). Fractionation of working memory: Neuropsychological evidence for a phonological short-term store. *Journal of Verbal Learning and Verbal Behavior, 23,* 151–161.

Vallar, G., & Baddeley, A. D. (1984b). Phonological short-term store, phonological processing and sentence comprehension: A neuropsychological case study. *Cognitive Neuropsychology, 1,* 121–141.

Vallar, G., & Baddeley, A. D. (1987). Phonological short-term store and sentence processing. *Cognitive Neuropsychology, 4*(4), 417–438.

Vallar, G., & Cappa, S. F. (1987). Articulation and verbal short-term memory. *Cognitive Neuropsychology, 4*(1), 55–78.

Van Dijk, T. A., & Kintsch, W. (1983). *Strategies of discourse comprehension.* New York: Academic Press.

Warrington, E. K., Logue, V., & Pratt, R. T. C. (1971). The anatomical localisation of selective impairment of auditory verbal short-term memory. *Neuropsychologia, 9,* 377–387.

Warrington, E. K., & Shallice, T. (1969). The selective impairment of auditory verbal short-term memory. *Brain, 92,* 885–896.

Waters, G. S., Caplan, D., & Hildebrandt, N. (1987). Working memory and written sentence comprehension. In M. Coltheart (Ed.), *Attention and performance XII* (pp. 531–555). London: Lawrence Erlbaum Associates.

Waters, G. S., Caplan, D., & Hildebrandt, N. (1991). On the structure of verbal short-term memory and nature and its functional role in sentence comprehension: A case study. *Cognitive Neuropsychology, 2,* 81–126.

Waters, G. S., Komoda, M., & Arbuckle, T. (1985). The effects of concurrent tasks on reading: Implications for phonological recoding. *Journal of Memory and Language, 24,* 27–45.

Waters, G. S., Rochon, E., & Caplan, D. (1991). The role of high-level speech planning in rehearsal: Evidence from patients with apraxia of speech. *Journal of Memory and Language, 31,* 54–73.

Waters, G. S., & Seidenberg, M. S. (1985). Spelling-sound effects in reading: Time course and decision criteria. *Memory and Cognition, 13,* 557–572.

Wernicke, C. (1874). *Der aphasische symptomenkomplex.* Breslau: Cohn & Weigart.

Zue, V. W. (1986). *Models of speech recognition III: The role of analysis by synthesis in phonetic recognition.* In P. Mermelstein (Ed.), *Proceedings of the Montreal satellite symposium on speech recognition* (Twelfth International Congress on Acoustics).

Zurif, E., & Caramazza, A. (1976). Psycholinguistic structures in aphasia: Studies in syntax and semantics. In H. Whitaker & H. Whitaker (Eds.), *Studies in neurolinguistics* (Vol. 1, pp. 261–292). New York: Academic Press.

Chapter 7

Conclusions: Toward a Working Definition of Conduction Aphasia

Susan E. Kohn
Braintree Hospital
Boston University School of Medicine

If one follows the standard clinical description of conduction aphasia as a disturbance in repetition that is paired with relatively preserved spontaneous speech and auditory comprehension (see Goodglass, this volume), a heterogeneous group of patients will result. At this level, the possible underlying deficits responsible for conduction aphasia are so varied as to render this syndrome of little use at both the clinical and experimental level. However, by examining the range of behaviors associated with conduction aphasics, more homogeneous sets of aphasics should emerge.

As indicated by the preceding description of conduction aphasia, impaired repetition is often considered of prime importance for identifying this syndrome. However, it is not clear that this behavior should be the focus when rendering a diagnosis of conduction aphasia. Various chapters in this book argue that the frequent production of phonemic paraphasias is the key (i.e., phonological distortions of identifiable words that are free from phonetic error). That is, the production of phonemic paraphasias in essentially all speech contexts (e.g., spontaneous speech, repetition, oral reading, picture naming) is viewed by many as the most prominent "defining symptom" of conduction aphasia (i.e., necessary for diagnosis; see Introduction). Moreover, characteristics of these paraphasias help distinguish this aphasia from others (Kohn, in press; see following).

Confusion about the role of impaired repetition versus paraphasic speech in conduction aphasia existed from the inception of this syndrome (see Henderson, this volume). More recently, work by Shallice and Warrington (1977) presented a possible solution to this issue by distinguishing "repetition conduction aphasia'' and ''reproduction conduction aphasia.'' They argued that a deficit in auditory-verbal short-term memory was responsible for impaired repetition in some conduction aphasics and that an independent deficit in speech programming was responsible for the paraphasic output in other conduction aphasics. However, why should aphasics with such divergent underlying deficits be considered members of the same general diagnostic category (see Introduction)? Because of the restricted effect of the memory deficit on speech (i.e., only impairing repetition), it is reasonable to exclude patients with isolated repetition deficits from the category of conduction aphasia. Then, in Shallice and Warrington's terminology, we would consider only reproduction conduction aphasics as true conduction aphasics.

This latter decision does not rule out the presence of impaired repetition in conduction aphasia, but merely specifies that output based on other input modalities must also be impaired in conduction aphasia. Moreover, one should not expect repetition to be the most impaired modality. In contrast to picture naming and oral reading, repetition involves input that is already in a phonological form, so that conversion into an articulable form (i.e., from acoustic-phonetic to articulatory-phonetic information) requires fewer transformations (Kohn & Smith, 1991b; Kohn, Smith, & Alexander, in press). This notion is supported by cases of conduction aphasia in which noun production during picture naming, oral reading, and repetition has been systematically compared, and repetition has been least impaired (Kohn, 1989; Kohn & Smith, 1991a).

If patients with pure repetition deficits are removed, the remaining patients with a possible diagnosis of conduction aphasia are those who produce phonemic paraphasias in essentially all modalities. This group of patients is still heterogeneous because of two basic sources of phonemic paraphasias: lexical and postlexical (or, in Caplan, Vanier, & Baker's [1986] terminology, at the level of underlying and superficial phonological representations; see also chapters by Buckingham and by Caplan & Waters). From a diagnostic standpoint, as several chapters have indicated, we are left with a group that consists of recovering Wernicke's aphasics and reproduction conduction aphasics.

Once again, we are faced with an issue that arose in early discussions of conduction aphasia, namely, determining the differences between Wernicke's and conduction aphasia (see Henderson, this volume). This confusion is perpetuated by the common current practice of reclassifying a Wernicke's aphasic as a conduction aphasic following the improvement of auditory comprehension, reduction of paragrammatisms, and evolution of neologisms toward more recognizable forms (i.e., phonemic paraphasias; e.g., Basso, Capitani, & Zanobio, 1982; Naeser & Hayward, 1978; also see chapter by Kohn & Smith). Such instances of reclassification likely contribute to Kertesz's (1979) identification of a bimodal distribution of conduction aphasia (see Buckingham, this volume).

As suggested in the Introduction, one can decide categorically to never relabel an aphasic, thus eliminating acute Wernicke's aphasics from the potential pool of conduction aphasics (see also chapter by Palumbo, Alexander, & Naeser). However, there may be clinical reasons for combining these two classes of patients, such as treating mild disturbances in auditory comprehension (see later).

But in terms of delivering the proper speech rehabilitation and conducting research on the underlying deficits responsible for phonemic paraphasias, one should attempt to distinguish these two basic classes of aphasics. This decision follows from the likelihood that the deficits responsible for phonemic parapha-sias differ in conduction and Wernicke's aphasia (Kohn, in press). More research is needed to determine the features of phonemic paraphasias that best distinguish these two syndromes. This was the goal of a recent case compari-son by Kohn and Smith (1991c). A so-called mild Wernicke's aphasic (who could by some standards be reclassified as a conduction aphasic) and a moder-ate conduction aphasic were compared on their single-word production. They were similar with respect to producing numerous phonemic paraphasias on a variety of tests on which they achieved similar scores. Despite these general similarities, details of their performance revealed differences that pointed to different underlying phonological deficits, as defined by a cognitive model of single-word production: impaired activation of stored phonological represen-tations (i.e., a lexical deficit) in the mild Wernicke's aphasic and impaired pho-nemic planning (i.e., a postlexical deficit) in the conduction aphasic.

Some of the distinguishing results involved statistical analyses that are too detailed to be used at a clinical level (e.g., proportion of target and nontarget phonemes in nonword responses). However, there were behavioral differences that indicate ways of distinguishing these two basic types of phonological out-put disorders during a bedside exam. On tests of single-word production, the lexical disorder was associated with a tendency to embed responses in phrases and produce random extra syllables, phonic verbal paraphasias (i.e., phono-logically related real words), and functor substitutions. By contrast, the post-lexical deficit was associated with word fragments and exaggerated syllabification. Moreover, the patient with the lexical deficit had fluent spon-taneous speech that was not derailed by her phonological distortions, whereas the patient with the postlexical deficit had fluent spontaneous speech that be-came hesitant and dysfluent during instances of phonological distortion (e.g., *conduites d'approche*).

One decision that can be made on the basis of such data is to associate con-duction aphasia only with the behavioral traits associated with a postlexical deficit in phonemic planning. This approach is consistent with the notion of conduction aphasia employed in much work on French-speaking conduction aphasics (e.g., Dubois, Hécaen, Angelergues, Maufras de Chatelier, & Marcie, 1964/1973; Nespoulous, Joanette, Ska, Caplan, & Lecours, 1987). A lexical-phonological deficit would then be associated with some form of Wernicke's aphasia, most likely involving neologistic jargon, at least during the acute phase.

Such a decision emphasizes the importance of identifying the locus of phonological breakdown in fluent aphasics, as opposed to the severity of their deficit(s), so that treatment goals can be set realistically (see Introduction). For example, a conduction aphasic, as defined before, should be presented with treatment that is geared toward improving phonemic planning. This was the goal of a treatment program that successfully used sentence repetition to increase speech fluency in a conduction aphasic (Kohn, Smith, & Arsenault, 1990). By contrast, such a treatment program would be inappropriate for a patient whose phonemic paraphasias are lexical in origin (e.g., a Wernicke's aphasic).

A definition of conduction aphasia based on a primary behavioral deficit can also be used to identify groups of fairly homogeneous subjects for experimental studies. One can then begin to systematically examine the relationship between the secondary behaviors that have been associated with conduction aphasia and their primary phonemic deficit (see Caplan & Waters, this volume). Additionally, one can initiate more detailed case examinations to uncover the likely variations in phonemic deficits that would point to subtypes of conduction aphasia.

As indicated by the Caplan and Water's chapter, some researchers may not want to restrict conduction aphasia to a general deficit in postlexical phonemic planning (or surface phonology). In particular, these authors suggest that (reproduction) conduction aphasia should be fractionated along "route-specific lines." For example, they consider the possibility that a disturbance in phonemic planning could be confined to oral reading, and that such a deficit be a possible subtype of conduction aphasia. However, this suggestion contradicts a decision made earlier in this chapter. It is consistent to exclude all modality-specific sources of phonological output errors from this aphasia diagnosis, given the prior decision to exclude cases with isolated repetition disturbances from the classification of conduction aphasia. With respect to the Caplan and Water's example, then, phonological errors restricted to oral reading should be continued to be viewed as a form of alexia. Nonetheless, this issue deserves further consideration.

Finally, by associating conduction aphasia with behavioral indices of an output disorder involving phonemic planning, we should be able to clarify the lesion responsible for this aphasia. The variability often associated with lesions attributed to conduction aphasia would seem more systematic if one were to (a) distinguish impaired phonemic planning from more abstract phonological output disturbances, with the latter being more indicative of Wernicke's aphasia (Kohn & Smith, 1991b, 1991c); and (b) consider impaired auditory comprehension as a "characteristic symptom" of conduction aphasia (i.e., one that is possible, but not necessary, for diagnosis; see Kohn & Smith, this volume). Following this basic orientation, Palumbo et al. (this volume) found a consistent association of damage to the left supramarginal gyrus in their cases of conduction aphasia. The auditory comprehension deficits seen in some conduction aphasics and lexical-phonological output disturbances are likely due to lesion in the temporal lobe (see Palumbo et al., this volume).

Moreover, it is important to note that by associating conduction aphasia with the dysfunctioning of a stage of phonological processing, we cannot view this syndrome as due solely to the restricted flow of information to a language center (i.e., a disconnection syndrome), but should include damage to the implicated language center as well. Again, there is historical precedent for this approach, in the early writings of Freud (see Henderson, this volume).

With more careful attention to aphasic symptoms and models of cognitive processing, conduction aphasia (including clear subtypes) can be defined in a way that is both theoretically and clinically valid.

ACKNOWLEDGMENT

This work was supported, in part, by NIH Grant DC00447.

REFERENCES

Basso, A., Capitani, E., & Zanobio, M. E. (1982). Pattern of recovery of oral and written expression and comprehension of aphasic patients. *Behavioral Brain Research, 6,* 115–128.

Caplan, D., Vanier, M., & Baker, C. (1986). A case study of reproduction conduction aphasia I: Word production. *Cognitive Neuropsychology, 3,* 99–128.

Dubois, J., Hécaen, H., Angelergues, R., Maufras de Chatelier, A., & Marcie, P. (1973). Etude neurolinguistique de l'aphasie de conduction [Neurolinguistic study of conduction aphasia]. In H. Goodglass & S. E. Blumstein (Eds. and Trans.), *Psycholinguistics and aphasia* (pp. 283–300). Baltimore: Johns Hopkins University Press. (Original work published 1964)

Kertesz, A. (1979). *Aphasia and associated disorders: Taxonomy, localization, and recovery.* New York: Grune & Stratton.

Kohn, S. E. (1989). The nature of the phonemic string deficit in conduction aphasia. *Aphasiology, 3,* 209–239.

Kohn, S. E. (in press). Segmental disorders in aphasia. In G. Blanken, J. Dittmann, H. Grimm, J. C. Marshall, & C.-W. Wallesch (Eds.), *Linguistic disorders and pathologies. An international handbook.* Berlin: Walter de Gruyter.

Kohn, S. E., & Smith, K. L. (1991a). The relationship between oral spelling and phonological breakdown in a conduction aphasic. *Cortex, 27,* 631–639.

Kohn, S. E., & Smith, K. L. (1991b). *Evolution of impaired access to the phonological lexicon.* Unpublished manuscript, Braintree Hospital, Braintree, MA.

Kohn, S. E., & Smith, K. L. (1991c). *Distinguishing two phonological deficits: Activation of stored phonological representations vs. construction of phonemic representations.* Unpublished manuscript, Braintree Hospital, Braintree, MA.

Kohn, S. E., Smith, K. L., & Alexander, M. P. (in press). A longitudinal comparison of the oral reading and repetition of nouns in acute fluent aphasics. *Aphasiology.*

Kohn, S. E., Smith, K. L., & Arsenault, J. K. (1990). The remediation of conduction aphasia via sentence repetition: A case study. *British Journal of Disorders of Communication, 25,* 45–60.

Naeser, M. A., & Hayward, R. W. (1978). Resolving stroke and aphasia: A case study with computerized tomography. *Archives of Neurology, 36,* 233–235.

Nespoulous, J.-L., Joanette, Y., Ska, B., Caplan, D., & Lecours, A. R. (1987). Production deficits in Broca's and conduction aphasia: Repetition vs. reading. In E. Keller & M. Gopnik (Eds.), *Motor and sensory processes in language* (pp. 53–79). Hillsdale, NJ: Lawrence Erlbaum Associates.

Shallice, T., & Warrington, E. (1977). Auditory-verbal short-term memory impairment and conduction aphasia. *Brain and Language, 4,* 479–491.

Author Index

Page numbers in *italics* denote complete bibliographical information.

A

Ackerman, N., 123, *145*
Alajouanine, T., 44, *48*
Albert, M. L., 13, 45, *18, 49*
Alexander, M. P., 7, 13, 73, 152, *18, 74,*
  152, *155*
Allard, L., 110, *113*
Allport, D. A., 134, *143, 144*
Andreewsky, E., 47, 121, *49, 147*
Angelergues, R., 18, 46, 48, 94, 95, 108, 109,
  124, 153, *19, 48, 114, 145, 155*
Appelbaum, M., 110, *113*
Arbuckle, T., 143, *149*
Ardila, A., 105, 107, *113*
Aronson, A. E., 83, *115, 116*
Arsenault, J. K., 16, 154, *20, 154, 155*
Auerback, S., 72, *75*

B

Baddeley, A. D., 137, 138, 140, *144, 147,*
  148
Badecker, W., 2, 4, 11, 14, 17, *18, 19*
Baker, C., 80, 84, 86, 87, 94, 95, 96, 103,
  124, 125, 126, 138, 140, 152, *114,*
  144, 155

Barnard, P., 119, *144*
Barnes, M. A., 135, *148*
Basili, A., 109, 134, 140, *114, 144*
Basso, A., 2, 4, 152, *18, 20, 155*
Bastian, H. C., 24, 26, 29, 30, 31, *37*
Bates, E., 110, *113*
Baum, S. R., 96, *113*
Beland, R., 79, 86, 87, 88, 93, 94, 103,
  107, 112, 131, *113, 144*
Benson, D. F., 6, 8, 13, 36, 52, 53, 71, 72,
  73, *18, 19, 37, 74, 75*
Berndt, R. S., 51, 109, 134, 140, *74, 114,*
  144
Berwick, R. C., 140, *144*
Besner, D., 139, *144*
Bishop, D., 137, *144*
Black, S., 124, 126, *144*
Blumstein, S. E., 79, 80, 96, *113*
Bogen, G. M., 111, *113*
Bogen, J. E., 111, *113*
Bouchard, R., 8, 36, 52, 53, 71, 72, 73, *19,*
  37, 74
Broca, P., 24, 25, *37*
Brown, J. W., 3, 5, 14, 16, 18, *19*
Brown, R., 123, 130, *144*
Brownell, H. H., 2, 7, 12, *21*
Bryans, B., 105, *115*

Subject Index